THE
EVERYTHING®
NATURALLY SUGAR-FREE
COOKBOOK

Dear Reader,

Thank you for joining us as we pursue a healthier and more energetic lifestyle! Whether you are new to sugar-free baking or have been at it for years, we invite you to explore the art of naturally sweet baking and join us in taking the sugar-free challenge. We have seen the benefits of omitting refined sugar and artificial sweeteners in our own lives and hope that you will do the same as you create healthier alternatives in your own kitchen.

As sisters who live scattered across the country from each other, we find that good food truly brings us together. We have discovered we don't need to sacrifice great-tasting food or our families' favorite recipes in our pursuit of health because natural sweeteners help us create the foods we love. We are passionate about the effects healthy foods have on our bodies and we love creating and sharing recipes on our website *www .naturalsweetrecipes.com*.

There is no greater gift we can give ourselves or our loved ones than to take care of our own health. It might seem daunting at first to eliminate refined sugar from your diet, but we are here to show you not only how to do it but also how delicious it can be! We can't wait to help you get started!

Annie, Holly, and Chelsea Forsyth

Welcome to the EVERYTHING® Series!

These handy, accessible books give you all you need to tackle a difficult project, gain a new hobby, comprehend a fascinating topic, prepare for an exam, or even brush up on something you learned back in school but have since forgotten.

You can choose to read an Everything® book from cover to cover or just pick out the information you want from our four useful boxes: e-questions, e-facts, e-alerts, and e-ssentials.

We give you everything you need to know on the subject, but throw in a lot of fun stuff along the way, too.

We now have more than 400 Everything® books in print, spanning such wide-ranging categories as weddings, pregnancy, cooking, music instruction, foreign language, crafts, pets, New Age, and so much more. When you're done reading them all, you can finally say you know Everything®!

QUESTION

Answers to common questions

FACT

Important snippets of information

ALERT

Urgent warnings

ESSENTIAL

Quick handy tips

PUBLISHER Karen Cooper

MANAGING EDITOR, EVERYTHING® SERIES Lisa Laing

COPY CHIEF Casey Ebert

ASSISTANT PRODUCTION EDITOR Alex Guarco

ACQUISITIONS EDITOR Lisa Laing

SENIOR DEVELOPMENT EDITOR Brett Palana-Shanahan

EVERYTHING® SERIES COVER DESIGNER Erin Alexander

Visit the entire Everything® series at *www.everything.com*

THE EVERYTHING®
NATURALLY SUGAR-FREE COOKBOOK

Annie, Holly, and Chelsea Forsyth of
www.naturalsweetrecipes.com

Avon, Massachusetts

To our Queen Mum, Leslie Forsyth,
who inspires us in and out of the kitchen.

An Everything® Series Book.
Everything® and everything.com® are registered trademarks of F+W Media, Inc.

Published by
Adams Media, a division of F+W Media, Inc.
57 Littlefield Street, Avon, MA 02322. U.S.A.
www.adamsmedia.com

ISBN 10: 1-4405-8348-X
ISBN 13: 978-1-4405-8348-3
eISBN 10: 1-4405-8349-8
eISBN 13: 978-1-4405-8349-0

Printed in the United States of America.

10 9 8 7 6 5 4 3 2 1

Always follow safety and commonsense cooking protocol while using kitchen utensils,
operating ovens and stoves, and handling uncooked food. If children are assisting in the
preparation of any recipe, they should always be supervised by an adult.

Cover and interior photographs by Annie, Holly, and Chelsea Forsyth
of *www.naturalsweetrecipes.com.*
Nutritional statistics by Nicole Cormier, RD.

This book is available at quantity discounts for bulk purchases.
For information, please call 1-800-289-0963.

Contents

Introduction

THE NATURALLY SWEET RECIPES found in this book feature whole ingredients and natural sweeteners. These foods contain vitamins, minerals, and
enzymes that sustain and support life. These nutrients are what set the founda-
tion for optimal health and help you attain the quality of life you deserve. However, most foods Americans eat every day do not contribute to optimal health.
It is typically packaged, processed, and full of the food industry's favorite pre-
servative: sugar. Sugar is found on just about every ingredient list on foods in
grocery stores today. Spice blends, yogurts, dried fruits, bread, and even meats
contain sugar. It is difficult to find convenience food without refined sugar.

Enjoying convenience foods such as a favorite soft drink or dessert on a regular basis may seem harmless, but when it's done consistently, sugar begins taking its toll. Health threats and diseases linked to diets high in processed foods
and sugar are ever increasing. According to researchers at the University of Cal-
ifornia, San Francisco School of Medicine, Americans consume roughly 130
pounds of added sugar per person per year. Excess sugar consumption is linked
to diabetes and heart disease caused by chronic inflammation of the body.

The Everything® Naturally Sugar-Free Cookbook will help you create satisfying meals and mouthwatering baked goods without refined sugar and artificial
sweeteners. The recipes in this book are all-natural alternatives that are beneficial instead of detrimental to health and well-being. Reducing or even eliminating refined sugar and artificial sweeteners doesn't have to be painful or boring.
It's possible to create delectable foods and treats that will please the eye and
the taste buds without sacrificing long-term health.

Going sugar-free might seem impossible, but the recipes in this book can
inspire a desire to start. Take the sugar-free challenge by substituting one dessert
a week with a naturally sweetened dessert or make one day a sugar-free day—
for example, Naturally Sweetened Wednesday. Ditch the freezer waffle or artificially sweetened cereal and make a nutritious smoothie for breakfast instead.
Another popular approach to this challenge is to completely abstain from sugar
for a specific number of days or weeks. It doesn't matter where you start, but

making little healthy changes is the key. You will enjoy weight loss, improved mental clarity, improved dental health, and a stronger immune system, to name a few benefits. These rewards will encourage you to continue incorporating natural sweeteners in all your cooking and baking on a regular basis.

The following pages are full of recipes that traditionally call for white sugar—such as candies, cakes, cookies, and ice cream—but are created here using healthy sweeteners instead. You might also be surprised by how much refined sugar is in non-dessert foods. Items such as salad dressings and sauces for common entrées are often packed with sugar to make them delicious, and this book includes alternatives for those as well. Since the goal is to make naturally sweetened recipes available to everyone, also included are recipes geared toward allergies and special diets.

There is something in this book for every taste and skill level. Be adventurous and experiment with new ingredients and we know you'll be smitten with the results.

Acknowledgments

TO OUR READERS AND FRIENDS who follow Natural Sweet Recipes, you are some of the most creative and supportive people we know. Thank you for your friendship and feedback. You inspire us daily!

This book would not have been possible without the loving support of our family. Travis Tidball and Chris Badurek, we are so thankful for your patience and support. Your constant encouragements always keep us going! We love you more than we can say. To our mother, who never stops learning and sharing her wisdom with us, thank you for all the recipe testing. We are so lucky to be your daughters. To our dad, who always keeps us laughing, we sure really love you! Thanks for thinking our recipes are "totally righteous." To Ben, who didn't get his name on the cover just because he turned out a boy, we love you so much! Thank you for your support in everything we do. To Liz Forsyth, the newest addition to our crazy family, thank you for your input and contribution to these pages! A very special thank-you to the little sweethearts in our lives whose tender love and excitement always encourage us. Whitney, Natalie, and Olivia, you are our favorite taste-testers!

CHAPTER 1

Going Sugar-Free

In order to inspire positive health changes through the reduction of refined sugars, it's crucial to understand why change is necessary. Understanding what sugar is, where it comes from, and why it's harmful will allow consumers to make choices based on facts and not be swayed by tradition or current food fads. Knowledge of the body's reaction to sugar will create more mindful eating as consumers begin to read labels and recognize hidden processed and artificial sugars in foods. "Every addition to true knowledge is an addition to human power." —Horace Mann

Sugar's Dirty Little Secret

The secret is out; sugar is everywhere! And it's not the benign substance many manufacturers would have you believe. What was quite harmless a few hundred years ago has become, through the modern refining process, an unnatural substance that causes negative effects on the body. As the sugar cane plant makes its way through the refining process to become the white granules known as sugar, it becomes void of any nutrition and wreaks havoc on all systems of the body.

From Living Plant to Lifeless Food

The process of manufacturing sugar involves a series of chemical-laden steps. Sugar cane plants are often grown with the help of heavy fertilizers. Once the plant is harvested, it is crushed to release the juice and juice is then evaporated, boiled, and stored. While in storage it can become contaminated and take on an unpleasant taste. The refining process takes care of this by killing off any bacteria present and making the granulated sugar sweet and sparkling white. Any nutrients left from the original plant are killed during processing and the resulting product becomes lifeless.

Why is lifeless food harmful to the body? In addition to the heavy chemicals sugar is exposed to during the refining process, consumption of unnatural food by living bodies causes serious problems. Sugar and other lifeless foods strip the body of vital nutrients, such as B vitamins, without giving the body anything back. Why are B vitamins so critical to humans? B vitamins are important for the absorption of calcium and allow the nervous system to function properly. B vitamin deficiencies affect mood and energy levels. Naturally sweet foods, such as fruits and whole grains, are inherently rich in B vitamins that help to metabolize the sugars that naturally occur within them. On the other hand, lifeless food such as refined sugar takes from the body and gives nothing in return.

Besides being a lifeless food, sugar lowers the power of the immune system by slowing down the bacteria-fighting cells in the body. This suppression of the immune system happens for several hours after sugar is consumed. And typically, by the time the immune system has had a chance to recover, it is already being bombarded with more sugar.

The Metabolism of Sugar

The human body is not equipped to quickly metabolize processed sugar. The liver attempts to manage the consumed sugar by depositing some of the glucose from the sugar into the bloodstream, or stores it for later use. If the liver is already completely full of glucose it stores the extra as triglycerides, or fat. Fructose, another component of sugar, also has to be managed by the liver and is stored as glycogen. The liver can only hold about 100 grams of glycogen before it has to convert the rest to fat. Once the liver is filled with glucose and glycogen it becomes overtaxed and a whole host of problems can surface. When the liver is constantly overloaded with sugar, it becomes susceptible to liver disease. Also common for people with diets high in sugar, is insulin resistance, which can cause diabetes. Insulin resistance creates a highly toxic atmosphere throughout the entire body, allowing cancer cells to flourish.

The "Sugar High"

To make matters even worse, sugar is addictive. It causes physical reactions in the brain that result in manufactured feelings of happiness or relaxation. Dopamine receptors are located all over the brain and release feelings of pleasure whenever sugar is eaten, similar to the effect of heroin or cocaine, although on a smaller scale. This is where the term "sugar high" comes from. The mind and body begin to crave the dopamine high created by the sugar and the brain sends out powerful messages to the body reminding it to continuously feed this addiction.

Eric Stice, a neuroscientist at the Oregon Research Institute (*www .ori.org*), conducted MRI scans to illustrate what happens in the brains of overweight people when they consume soda, ice cream, and other sugary foods. He found that the brain actually builds up a resistance to the dopamine effect. In other words the more sugar they consumed, the more they needed to create the same level of pleasure. The body becomes addicted and desensitized at the same time. It craves more but is never satisfied. This overconsumption of sugar leads to the overconsumption of all foods and promotes habits perfect for obesity.

Trends and Statistics

On average, Americans consume approximately 130 pounds of sugar per person per year, or roughly 3 pounds per week. Children and teenagers on average consume even more, about 1 cup of sugar per day. Soda and other sweetened drinks are possibly the worst culprits because people become addicted to the high amount of sugar as well as to the caffeine that some drinks contain. A 12-ounce soda contains 10 teaspoons of sugar, and an average American drinks 53 gallons of soda per year. These high rates of sugar consumption are up 45 percent from sugar consumption thirty years ago.

Sugar As Reward

Societal trends also perpetuate the overconsumption of sugar. Sugar is often treated as a reward. Children are praised with candy and adults are treated with gourmet cupcakes at the office. If you're having dinner at a restaurant, you might drink soda, lemonade, or sugar-laden cocktails, and have dessert as well. You could easily consume more sugar in one evening than you should have in an entire month! A traditional child's birthday party is loaded with sugar. It seems that a party isn't complete without a cake served with ice cream, a piñata stuffed to capacity with candy, and the ubiquitous favor bags with more candy and sweet treats.

It's a sugar-obsessed world, and it's fun to indulge. Not only is sugar physically addicting, but sugary treats are associated with celebrations and holidays. Candy, cookies, and cake are used to say "Good job," "I love you," "Happy anniversary," and "Thank you." While there is nothing wrong with this on a small scale, it's important to be aware of how, in excess, these rewards and celebrations perpetuate the sugar-craze.

Sugar's Effect on Health

In 2013 Credit Suisse's Research Institute reported that as a nation the United States spends $1 trillion annually on health-care issues directly related to the consumption of excess sugar. This figure represents 30–40 percent of the total health-care costs in the United States. Robert Lustig, a pediatric endocrinologist from University of California–San Francisco, published articles stating that sugar is a big player in the current decline of health in America and that 75 percent of disease is brought on by a person's lifestyle. Lustig believes that because of this health decline, today's generation of American children could end up being the first to have a shorter life expectancy than their parents. This is the sad outcome of our overconsumption of sugar; it's literally killing us.

The Meaning of Sugar-Free

The term "sugar-free" is often used to describe foods, such as cookies, gum, and drinks, that have chemical and artificial sweeteners in place of sugar. Artificial sweeteners approved by the U.S. Food and Drug Administration include saccharin, acesulfame potassium, aspartame, neotame, and sucralose. These artificial sweeteners are found in products like Sweet'N Low, Equal, and Splenda. These products are indeed free of refined white sugar and are often calorie-free, but simply being "sugar-free" does not mean they are healthy. Diets heavy in foods with artificial sweeteners are as unhealthy as diets high in refined white sugar.

Research shows that similarly to sugar, artificial sweeteners desensitize the body's reaction to sweet food, leaving the body unsatisfied. This results in consuming food in excess to satisfy hunger. Artificial sweeteners are much sweeter than regular sugar, causing a person's proverbial "sweet tooth" to be continuously overstimulated. Over time, that overstimulation changes tastes and preferences. Naturally sweet foods such as fruit don't taste as good as they once did, and non-sweet, simple foods such as vegetables can become truly unappetizing.

Studies also show that artificial sweeteners are just as addictive as white sugar. A 2007 study at University of Bordeaux in France found that rats overwhelmingly preferred saccharine to cocaine, suggesting the addictive quality of the substance. Researchers provided rats with a choice of saccharin-sweetened water and intravenous cocaine. The rats could press a lever and receive either a shot of cocaine or a sip of saccharin-sweetened water as often as they wanted. The animals chose the high from artificial sugar water 94 percent of the time. Researchers in the study believe their findings reveal that the concentrated sweetness of artificial sugars creates a more intense pleasurable sensation and addiction than cocaine does.

Benefits of Going Sugar-Free

The results of eliminating sugar and artificial sweeteners can be astonishing, and the long- and short-term benefits can be wide-ranging. Physical benefits go beyond just weight loss. By allowing more room in the diet for healthy foods, vital nutrients can promote increased energy, a stronger immune system, improved complexion, better digestion, steadier blood sugar levels, and improved sleep. In addition, long-term health risks of developing heart disease, diabetes, obesity, and diseases associated with these conditions can be reduced, if not eliminated.

Eliminating or even reducing processed sugar and artificial sweeteners from your diet has the added benefit of promoting improved mental health. You may experience clearer thinking, decreased irritability, fewer mood swings, and an increase in self-control. Less mental energy directed toward fighting cravings or addictions promotes better overall health.

A Guide to Natural Sweeteners

Naturally sweetened recipes such as those found in this book are free of refined white sugar *and* artificial sweeteners. Natural, whole-food sweeteners including honey, coconut sugar, pure maple syrup, and molasses are used instead.

ALERT

Please be mindful that although these natural sweeteners promote health and are full of vitamins and minerals, they should be used in moderation and with knowledge of how each sweetener affects the body.

Following is an overview of the natural sweeteners used in this book.

Coconut Sugar

Coconut sugar, often called coconut palm sugar, is made from the flowers of the coconut tree. Coconut sugar does not have the same tropical flavor usually associated with coconuts. Coconut sugar closely resembles brown sugar in appearance and has a distinctly sweet scent. It caramelizes like sugar, so it works particularly well in baking. Coconut sugar replaces sugar cup-for-cup in recipes and mimics the taste and appearance of brown sugar. It's naturally full of vitamins and minerals like amino acids, potassium, magnesium, iron, and zinc. Coconut sugar is a whole food and does not drastically impact blood sugar levels. It's a safe diabetic sugar substitute, with a low glycemic index of 35.

Date Sugar

Date sugar is dehydrated, ground-up dates. Dates are a healthy fruit, high in vitamins, fiber, and minerals, and they provide delicious natural sweetness to a recipe. Dehydrating and grinding the dates to sugar does not compromise the health benefits of whole dates and the dry product is a convenient natural sweetener. Because date sugar is dehydrated, it can drain baked goods of moisture, so most recipes with date sugar need a lot of liquid. Date sugar is a pure fruit, so it has a relatively high glycemic index and is not a good choice for diabetics.

ALERT

When using date sugar in recipes, experiment to see how much liquid is needed to maintain moistness and enjoy date sugar treats within a day of making of them.

Raw Honey

Raw honey is unfiltered, unprocessed, and straight from the beehive. It's an alkaline food and contains the vitamins, enzymes, minerals, and water needed to sustain life. Raw honey contains B vitamins, vitamin C, amino acids, and minerals such as magnesium, calcium, zinc, potassium, and phosphate.

When a recipe calls for honey, any kind of honey will do. However, to get all of the antibacterial, anti-inflammatory, and antiallergic health benefits, raw honey is recommended.

Raw honey can aid in neutralizing toxins in the body, has cancer-fighting properties, can soothe coughs and sore throats, and can help reduce fevers. It is often used topically to help heal skin rashes, acne, or eczema. When raw honey is mixed with ginger or cinnamon it can help calm upset stomachs, constipation, and nausea.

Honey should not be fed to children under one year of age due to the possible presence of botulism bacteria, which can cause serious food poisoning. Older babies and adults have more developed digestive systems and are not affected by the bacteria.

Processed honey, which is any honey that does not specifically say it's raw, is void of most of the health benefits mentioned. Processing occurs to create a product that is clear and lighter in color than it's natural state, which most consumers prefer. It also keeps it from crystallizing as quickly as raw honey does. Antibiotics, added sweeteners such as high-fructose corn syrup, and water are often present in processed honey.

All honey, whether raw or processed, begins to crystallize over time. Crystallization does not mean the honey has gone bad and does not harm the nutritional benefits of honey at all. To soften crystallized honey, simply place the jar of honey in warm water for a few minutes.

All honey is processed similarly to refined sugar in the body, so honey is not a low-glycemic food, ranking a 50 on the glycemic index scale. It should be used with care by those who suffer from diabetes.

Powdered Honey

Powdered honey is dehydrated honey. It can be called honey powder, granulated honey, or dried honey. There are many different brands of powdered honey available, and quality can vary greatly. Differences in products include whether or not the honey is organic, whether it is pure honey or contains fillers, and how finely it is powdered. Some products have thicker, bigger "grains" while others are extremely fine and look like a golden baking soda.

Honey powder is a great natural sweetener with some but not all of the health benefits of raw honey. It contains many vitamins and minerals and has a lower glycemic index than white sugar. Powdered honey has a subtle floral flavor and provides a great texture to baked goods, keeping the final product moist and tender.

ALERT

Desserts made with honey powder can turn golden brown quickly when baking. Covering a dish halfway through cooking time is a good idea if the dessert has browned on top but hasn't finished baking.

Maple Syrup

Pure maple syrup is produced by boiling the sap of the maple tree. It contains amino acids, magnesium, zinc, and other vitamins and minerals. It has become popular in the health food industry because it is a natural source of antioxidants, similar to broccoli and blueberries. Antioxidants have been proven to fight cancer cells and to decrease the effects of aging. Maple syrup is a natural source of energy and nutrition when eaten raw. It's a healthy sweetener, but should be consumed sparingly for those with diabetes, as it ranks 54 on the glycemic index.

FACT

In Canada maple syrup cannot be labeled as such if it is not made 100 percent from maple tree sap. In the United States, however, it can be made *almost* entirely from maple tree sap to be labeled "maple." So read labels carefully and purchase only maple syrup labeled 100 percent maple syrup.

Maple syrup comes in different grades, from extra light to dark. In the United States, there are two grades of maple syrup, Grade A and Grade B. Grade A typically has a milder flavor and pale color. Grade B has a very sharp maple flavor and is darker in appearance. Both grades of maple syrup work equally well for cooking and baking.

Maple Sugar

Like maple syrup, maple sugar also comes from the sap of the maple tree. The maple tree sap is boiled until no water remains, creating a solid maple sugar product. Solid maple sugar is sold as a bar or ground into a granulated powder and sold by the bag. Maple sugar is almost twice as sweet as refined sugar, and has a distinct maple flavor. Maple sugar holds up well in baked items and caramelizes well.

Different brands of maple sugar have different size maple sugar granules. If one brand is too coarse, you can process the sugar in a blender to create a finer powder.

Molasses

There are a few different sources of molasses, but the two most common in the United States come from the sugar cane plant and the sorghum plant. Molasses is a great alternative to sugar because of its slightly sweet taste, its high mineral and vitamin content, and its accessibility. There are a few varieties of molasses that can come from the sugar cane plant, with blackstrap molasses ranking as the most nutritious option. Blackstrap molasses contains high levels of iron, calcium, potassium, copper, and magnesium, which are all important nutrients for the body. Sorghum molasses also has significant nutritional benefits and is a natural source of sweetness. Sorghum molasses (also commonly called sorghum syrup) is an unprocessed product that contains many important minerals and B vitamins. Whichever type of molasses is used, organic, unsulphured molasses is recommended. Blackstrap molasses ranks 55 on the glycemic index, with sorghum ranking at 50.

Stevia

Stevia is a sweet herb native to South America and has been used for centuries. It's almost 300 times sweeter than sugar and is most commonly used in a liquid or powder form. It makes a great sweetener for teas and drinks.

Stevia is a healthy food, but there are many products on the market today that contain stevia with additional unhealthy fillers such as chemicals, animal byproducts, and sugar. Stevia is a plant that is so sweet that it is impossible to make a product in which stevia replaces sugar cup-for-cup.

For instance, one would never use one cup of stevia to replace one cup of sugar in a recipe because pure stevia is too concentrated. If a stevia product claims it is equal to sugar in use, it contains unhealthy fillers to create the extra bulk. Look for plain stevia, either in liquid or powder form, with just one or two ingredients listed on the label.

Stevia is one of the few sweeteners acceptable for the candida diet. Those suffering from any kind of yeast or fungal infection can enjoy stevia while undergoing treatment. A major benefit of stevia is that it is a zero-calorie, zero-carb sweetener. It has little effect on glucose levels and is completely safe for those with diabetes.

Xylitol

Xylitol is a natural sugar alcohol found in the fiber of plants and fruit. It is commonly extracted from certain types of tree bark, cornhusks, and mushrooms. It is a sugar substitute with almost a third of the calorie content of sugar. Xylitol has a flavor and consistency similar to sugar and therefore is ideal for a variety of recipes. However, it does not caramelize like sugar when baked, so this sweetener works especially well in ice creams, drinks, or frostings.

People are often familiar with xylitol because of its association with sugar-free gum and candy. Although other unhealthy ingredients are sometimes associated with sugar-free products like those, xylitol is a whole food, is nontoxic, and is very safe for consumption. It is important to note that because xylitol is a sugar alcohol, high consumption can upset the stomach or cause bloating. Introduce this sweetener into your diet slowly and monitor your body's reaction to it closely so it is not eaten in excess.

Xylitol, like stevia, is acceptable for the candida diet. Not only is it acceptable, but it is the only sweetener that actually fights candida and helps kill yeast growth and infections. Xylitol doesn't raise blood sugar levels and can even promote dental health. Xylitol has been proven to help fight plaque and rebuild tooth enamel. Xylitol is unsafe for pets, and pregnant women should only use xylitol after consulting with their doctor.

CHAPTER 2

Breakfast

Almond Flour Chocolate Chip Pancakes

Packed with protein and just enough sweetness, these pancakes will sustain you far better than the traditional version.

INGREDIENTS | SERVES 2

2 large eggs, lightly beaten

⅔ cup unsweetened almond milk

1½ teaspoons vanilla extract

1 tablespoon maple syrup

¼ teaspoon sea salt

1 teaspoon baking powder

1⅓ cups almond meal

⅓ cup rice flour

¼ cup sugar-free chocolate chips

Turn Gently

Almond flour and rice flour are more fragile than regular flour because of their lack of gluten. Flip these pancakes carefully to avoid breakage.

1. In a medium mixing bowl, whisk the eggs with the almond milk and vanilla.

2. Add the maple syrup, salt, baking powder, almond meal, and flour and whisk until just combined. Stir in the chocolate chips. Be careful not to overmix the batter.

3. Heat a nonstick griddle to medium heat or 250°F. Pour ¼ cup of the batter into the skillet for each pancake. The pancakes will start to bubble when they need to be flipped. Gently flip pancakes and cook until golden. Serve with your favorite pancake toppings.

PER SERVING Calories: 818 | Fat: 51g | Protein: 28g | Sodium: 651.5mg | Fiber: 11g | Carbohydrates: 69g | Sugar: 27.5g

Apple Cinnamon Waffles

These soft and fluffy waffles are more cinnamon than apple and are sure to delight. Top these thick waffles with applesauce for more apple flavor!

INGREDIENTS | SERVES 4

2 large eggs

1½ cups almond milk

¼ cup grapeseed oil

3 tablespoons applesauce

2 tablespoons coconut sugar

¼ teaspoon sea salt

4 teaspoons baking powder

1½ teaspoons vanilla extract

1 tablespoon cinnamon

1¾ cups white whole-wheat flour

1 tablespoon ground flaxseed

Waffle Toppings

Try applesauce, nut butters, and coconut oil on top of your next batch of waffles instead of traditional butter and sugary syrups.

1. In a large mixing bowl, whisk all ingredients together until combined.

2. Bake in a hot waffle iron per waffle maker instructions and top with your favorite waffle toppings.

PER SERVING Calories: 627 | Fat: 19g | Protein: 17g | Sodium: 721mg | Fiber: 5g | Carbohydrates: 95g | Sugar: 12g

Baked Tomato, Basil, and Feta Frittata

This frittata is the perfect excuse to use up fresh basil and ripe tomatoes from the garden. Besides being hearty and full of flavor, this breakfast will also make the house smell wonderful!

INGREDIENTS | SERVES 2

5 large eggs
⅓ cup unsweetened almond milk
½ teaspoon garlic powder
¼ cup chopped fresh basil
⅛ teaspoon lemon pepper
¼ teaspoon sea salt
¼ teaspoon ground black pepper
⅓ cup diced tomato
¼ cup feta cheese

1. Preheat oven to 400°F. Grease a 9" × 9" baking dish and set aside.

2. In a large mixing bowl, whisk together the eggs, almond milk, garlic powder, basil, lemon pepper, salt, and pepper. Gently stir in tomato and cheese. Pour egg mixture into the prepared baking dish.

3. Bake for 18–22 minutes. The frittata should be puffy and springy in the middle when finished.

PER SERVING Calories: 238 | Fat: 16.5g | Protein: 19g | Sodium: 681mg | Fiber: 0.578g | Carbohydrates: 4g | Sugar: 2.5g

Always Versatile

Eggs can handle a great many spices. It is almost always safe to use whatever fresh or dried spices you have on hand to liven up an egg dish.

Easy Mini German Apple Pancakes

This healthy version of a German pancake still contains plenty of protein-rich eggs, while adding delicious apple flavoring. Orange zest subtly enhances this dish with a surprising hint of citrus.

INGREDIENTS | SERVES 6

6 large eggs
1 cup coconut milk
1 teaspoon vanilla extract
½ teaspoon cinnamon
½ teaspoon sea salt
½ teaspoon fresh orange zest
⅔ cup chopped apple
⅔ cup white spelt flour
⅓ cup powdered xylitol

1. Preheat oven to 400°F. Line a muffin tin with 12 liners and spray liners with cooking spray.

2. Beat eggs, milk, vanilla, cinnamon, salt, and orange zest together until well mixed.

3. Mix apples and flour into the mixture until just combined.

4. Pour batter evenly between the 12 prepared muffin cups. Bake for 10–12 minutes or until set.

5. Sprinkle with powdered xylitol while still hot and serve.

PER SERVING Calories: 231 | Fat: 13g | Protein: 8.5g | Sodium: 272mg | Fiber: 0.642g | Carbohydrates: 25g | Sugar: 2g

Baked Cinnamon Apple Oatmeal

Serve this warm baked cereal with fresh or dried fruit for extra sweetness. This recipe could easily become a dessert if served with sugar-free frozen yogurt on top!

INGREDIENTS | SERVES 2

1 cup rolled oats

3 tablespoons coconut sugar

1 teaspoon cinnamon

½ teaspoon baking powder

¼ teaspoon sea salt

⅔ cup unsweetened almond milk

3 tablespoons coconut oil, melted

⅓ cup applesauce

½ teaspoon vanilla extract

¼ cup diced apple

1. Preheat oven to 350°F. Grease two 8-ounce ramekins with cooking spray.

2. In a medium bowl, combine oats, coconut sugar, cinnamon, baking powder, and salt until blended. Mix in almond milk, coconut oil, applesauce, and vanilla extract. Gently stir in diced apples.

3. Pour mixture into ramekins and bake for 13–15 minutes.

PER SERVING Calories: 483 | Fat: 24.5g | Protein: 8g | Sodium: 467mg | Fiber: 6g | Carbohydrates: 60g | Sugar: 29g

Chia Apple Spice Pudding

This pudding is great warmed for breakfast or as an afternoon pick-me-up straight out of the fridge. Try drizzling the coconut cream from the Green Lemon Crepes recipe in this chapter over the top of this pudding for an even more delicious treat.

INGREDIENTS | SERVES 2

¼ cup chia seeds

¾ cup unsweetened applesauce

2 tablespoons unsweetened almond milk

½ teaspoon vanilla extract

½ teaspoon cinnamon

⅛ teaspoon nutmeg

In a container with a lid, mix all the ingredients together and refrigerate for at least 2 hours or overnight. Enjoy chilled or warmed slightly in the microwave.

PER SERVING Calories: 144 | Fat: 8g | Protein: 4g | Sodium: 14mg | Fiber: 5g | Carbohydrates: 17g | Sugar: 10g

Banana Pancakes

Packed with protein and a full serving of fruit, these pancakes are a great start to the morning. Whole-wheat flour makes these both hearty and fluffy.

INGREDIENTS | SERVES 8

3 cups white whole-wheat flour

½ cup coconut sugar

4 teaspoons baking powder

2 teaspoons sea salt

¾ cup full-fat plain yogurt

2¼ cups whole milk

4 large eggs

2 teaspoons vanilla extract

2 teaspoons grated lemon zest

3 medium ripe bananas, peeled and diced

Peanut Butter Sauce (see recipe in Chapter 12)

Nut Butter Options

If time is short, a generous slather of peanut butter with a drizzle of honey over the top can substitute for Peanut Butter Sauce for a similar sweet effect!

1. Heat a nonstick griddle over medium-high heat.

2. Combine flour, coconut sugar, baking powder, and salt in a large bowl.

3. In a separate bowl, mix together yogurt, milk, eggs, vanilla, and zest. Mix together wet and dry ingredients until combined.

4. Pour about ¼ cup of batter per pancake onto the hot griddle and sprinkle diced bananas on top. When pancakes get tiny bubbles throughout, flip to cook the other side.

5. Serve with warm Peanut Butter Sauce.

PER SERVING Calories: 340 | Fat: 6g | Protein: 13g | Sodium: 915mg | Fiber: 7g | Carbohydrates: 62g | Sugar: 24g

Blueberry Blintzes

Lemon ricotta cheese is wrapped inside delicate crepes and smothered with thick blueberry compote for a delicious early morning or late-night treat.

INGREDIENTS | SERVES 6

2 tablespoons water

1 tablespoon cornstarch

3 cups frozen blueberries

2 tablespoons maple syrup

¼ teaspoon cinnamon

1½ cups ricotta cheese

2 tablespoons plain low-fat yogurt

¼ teaspoon lemon zest

Classic French Crepes (see recipe in this chapter)

Better Blueberries

Blueberry pie filling is usually packed with sugar, high-fructose corn syrup, and preservatives. Homemade filling, made with ingredients you know and trust, is perfect served over pancakes and waffles, and, of course, in your favorite summer pie.

1. In a small saucepan, whisk together water and cornstarch until cornstarch is dissolved. Add blueberries, maple syrup, and cinnamon and begin cooking over medium heat for 10 minutes, stirring often. Set aside and keep warm.

2. Preheat oven to 350°F. Spray a 9" × 13" baking dish with cooking spray.

3. In a small bowl, mix ricotta, yogurt, and lemon zest. Place 2 tablespoons ricotta mixture in the middle of each prepared crepe and fold into a pocket. Set crepe pockets in a single layer into the prepared dish. Cover with foil and heat crepe pockets for 20 minutes until they are warmed through. Serve with warm blueberry sauce over top.

PER SERVING Calories: 172.5 | Fat: 9g | Protein: 7g | Sodium: 56mg | Fiber: 2g | Carbohydrates: 17g | Sugar: 11g

"Buttermilk" Chocolate Chip Pancakes

This recipe uses a special buttermilk and egg substitution, making these pancakes vegan. These pancakes are light, fluffy, and have chocolate chips scattered in every bite, making them simply divine.

INGREDIENTS | SERVES 4

1½ tablespoons ground flaxseed

1⅔ cups unsweetened almond milk, divided

2 teaspoons apple cider vinegar

1½ cups spelt flour

3 tablespoons coconut oil, melted

2 tablespoons maple syrup

2 teaspoons baking powder

¼ teaspoon baking soda

½ teaspoon sea salt

1 teaspoon vanilla extract

⅔ cup sugar-free vegan chocolate chips or chopped chocolate

1. In a small bowl, combine ground flaxseed with 2 tablespoons of almond milk and set aside.

2. In a separate small bowl, combine the remaining almond milk with apple cider vinegar and set aside.

3. In a large mixing bowl combine all remaining ingredients except the chocolate chips and mix to combine. Stir in both the flaxseed and the almond milk mixture. Stir in chocolate chips until just incorporated, being careful not to overmix.

4. Heat a nonstick griddle over medium heat. Pour ¼ cup batter onto the griddle for each pancake. When pancakes get tiny bubbles throughout, flip to cook the other side.

PER SERVING Calories: 629 | Fat: 26g | Protein: 15g | Sodium: 26mg | Fiber: 6g | Carbohydrates: 84g | Sugar: 36g

Cinnamon Chia Seed Pudding

This chia pudding is a quick meal rich with cinnamon and vanilla flavoring. With only a few minutes of preparation the night before, this delicious pudding is ready to go in the morning.

INGREDIENTS | SERVES 2

½ cup chia seeds
1½ cups unsweetened almond milk
½ teaspoon vanilla extract
8 drops liquid stevia
2 teaspoons cinnamon

1. Mix chia seeds, almond milk, vanilla, stevia, and cinnamon together in a lidded container and refrigerate overnight.

2. Remove the pudding from the fridge and enjoy!

PER SERVING Calories: 293 | Fat: 18g | Protein: 12g | Sodium: 102mg | Fiber: 9g | Carbohydrates: 24g | Sugar: 9g

Chia Power

Chia seeds are filled with antioxidants, fiber, and omega-3 fatty acids! They can also help regulate insulin levels and help lower bad cholesterol while raising HDL, or "good," cholesterol levels.

Crustless Quiche Bites

Savory eggs in cute little bite-size portions are the perfect way to squeeze lots of veggies into your family without complaint!

INGREDIENTS | SERVES 8 (24 BITES)

6 large eggs
⅓ cup coconut milk
3 tablespoons finely diced bell pepper
3 tablespoons finely chopped broccoli
2 tablespoons finely chopped onion
3 tablespoons finely chopped tomato
⅓ cup finely chopped spinach
½ teaspoon sea salt
½ teaspoon ground black pepper
¼ teaspoon lemon pepper
⅛ teaspoon nutmeg
1 teaspoon garlic powder
1 tablespoon finely chopped fresh basil

1. Preheat oven to 350°F. Spray two mini muffin tins with cooking spray and set aside.

2. In a medium mixing bowl, whisk together eggs and coconut milk. Add all the other ingredients and mix well.

3. Pour mixture into prepared pans and bake for 10–12 minutes or until set.

PER SERVING Calories: 63 | Fat: 4g | Protein: 5g | Sodium: 201mg | Fiber: .3g | Carbohydrates: 2g | Sugar: 1g

Classic French Crepes

These crepes are extremely versatile! They can be filled with fruit, applesauce, or chocolate for a sweet indulgence in the morning. Try eggs, chicken salad, or deli meats for a savory meal later in the day.

INGREDIENTS | SERVES 4

1 large egg
1 cup whole milk
1 tablespoon coconut oil
½ teaspoon vanilla extract
½ teaspoon sea salt
1 cup white spelt flour

1. In a medium bowl, whisk egg and milk together well. Add remaining ingredients and whisk until smooth.

2. Heat a nonstick crepe pan or frying pan over medium heat. Spray with cooking spray and pour ⅛ cup batter into the center of the pan and quickly pick up the pan to rotate it, creating a thin layer of batter on your pan. If batter is too thick, more milk can be added.

3. Crepe is ready to be flipped when tiny bubbles form on the top and the edges begin to brown and lift. Carefully flip the crepe with a spatula and cook the second side. Remove from heat. Repeat with remaining batter.

PER SERVING Calories: 200.5 | Fat: 7g | Protein: 7g | Sodium: 339mg | Fiber: 0.844g | Carbohydrates: 27g | Sugar: 3g

French Toast

Serve this hot toast with your favorite nut butter and applesauce, butter and maple syrup, or a sunny-side-up egg.

INGREDIENTS | SERVES 4

⅛ cup almond milk
3 large eggs
1 teaspoon cinnamon
½ teaspoon vanilla extract
½ tablespoon molasses
⅛ teaspoon sea salt
8 slices whole-wheat bread

1. Heat a nonstick griddle over medium heat.

2. In a medium mixing bowl, whisk together all ingredients except bread.

3. Dredge each slice of bread into the egg mixture, coating both sides.

4. Place on the hot griddle and cook each side for about 2 minutes, or until egg mixture is cooked.

PER SERVING Calories: 201 | Fat: 5.5g | Protein: 9g | Sodium: 472mg | Fiber: 1.5g | Carbohydrates: 29g | Sugar: 4g

Hidden Protein

A trick to sneak more protein into a child's school lunch is to make a tasty almond butter and honey sandwich on leftover French toast bread. He won't know he is eating eggs too!

Easy Honey Granola

Making granola only requires a little mixing and the occasional stir in the oven as it bakes. Not only is homemade granola healthier and free of preservatives and refined sugar, it's also much cheaper. Enjoy this sweet granola as a cereal with milk, with fruit and yogurt, or as an ice cream topping.

INGREDIENTS | MAKES 10 CUPS

5 cups rolled oats

1 cup slivered almonds

1 cup walnut pieces

1 cup pecan pieces

1 cup unsweetened shredded coconut

¾ cup honey

2 tablespoons cinnamon

1 teaspoon sea salt

¾ cup melted coconut oil

1. Heat the oven to 200°F. Spray a large baking dish or jelly-roll pan with oil.

2. Mix all ingredients well and pour into the prepared pan.

3. Bake for 1 hour, stirring granola every 20 minutes. For extra-crunchy granola, after 1 hour of baking add another ¼ cup of oil and bake for another 20 minutes.

PER SERVING (½ cup) Calories: 286 | Fat: 19g | Protein: 5g | Sodium: 120.5mg | Fiber: 3g | Carbohydrates: 26g | Sugar: 11g

A Little Nutty

Nuts are full of good fats, protein, phytonutrients, and vitamins, and some—such as almonds, walnuts, and Brazil nuts—can even elevate your mood by increasing serotonin levels. Studies show that people are at lower risk for heart disease when they regularly consume nuts of any kind.

Granola and Fruit Parfaits

Kids and adults alike will love these parfaits because of their naturally sweet ingredients. You can vary the fruit combination to include your family's favorites.

INGREDIENTS | SERVES 2

1½ cups plain low-fat Greek yogurt

3 tablespoons xylitol

⅓ cup sliced strawberries

⅓ cup sliced banana

⅓ cup sliced raspberries

1 cup Easy Honey Granola (see recipe in this chapter)

Toppings

Pretend the yogurt is ice cream and create a delicious sundae. Try toppings such as raspberries and chocolate chips with a swirl of honey, or peanut butter with banana and maple syrup.

1. In a small dish, combine the yogurt and xylitol until creamy and smooth.

2. In 2 parfait dishes or tall glasses, alternate layers of yogurt, fruit, and granola until all ingredients have been used. Enjoy immediately.

PER SERVING Calories: 490 | Fat: 19.5g | Protein: 23g | Sodium: 200mg | Fiber: 6g | Carbohydrates: 46g | Sugar: 23g

Green Lemon Crepes

*Adding a bit of spinach to these crepes boosts the vitamin content
while creating a fun color. No one will taste the difference!*

INGREDIENTS | SERVES 4

½ cup almond milk

2 tablespoons finely chopped spinach

1½ tablespoons lemon juice

2 tablespoons melted coconut oil

1½ tablespoons honey

1 large egg

½ teaspoon lemon zest

¼ teaspoon sea salt

¼ teaspoon vanilla extract

⅓ cup white spelt flour

"Filling" Perfect

Try mixing 1 cup full-fat coconut cream,
1 tablespoon maple syrup, and 1 teaspoon
vanilla extract for an amazing filling for
these crepes. This perfect filling also complements a cup of hot chocolate or a slice
of cake.

1. In a blender, blend almond milk, spinach, and lemon juice until smooth. Add remaining ingredients to the blender and mix until smooth. The batter will be runny.

2. Heat a nonstick pan or griddle to medium heat.

3. Pour ⅛ cup batter into the center of the pan and rotate it in a circle to create a thin layer.

4. Flip crepe when bubbles appear throughout. Repeat with remaining batter.

PER SERVING Calories: 159 | Fat: 9g | Protein: 4g | Sodium: 183mg | Fiber: 0.5g | Carbohydrates: 17g | Sugar: 8g

Peaches and Dream Cereal

Delicious peaches and aromatic spices combine for a hot cereal that cooks while you sleep. Just a few minutes of preparation the night before will eliminate the stressful rush in the morning to eat something nutritious! Serve this cereal with milk or top it with whipped cream for a luscious dessert.

INGREDIENTS | SERVES 6

1 cup pearled barley

1 teaspoon sea salt

½ teaspoon cinnamon

¼ teaspoon allspice

5 cups water

3 cups finely diced peaches, fresh or frozen

½ cup raisins

¼ cup honey

1. Spray the inside of a 4- to 6-quart slow cooker with cooking spray.

2. In a mixing bowl, combine all ingredients and mix well. Pour into prepared slow cooker.

3. Cook on low for 8–10 hours or overnight.

PER SERVING Calories: 110 | Fat: 0.258g | Protein: 1g | Sodium: 401mg | Fiber: 2g | Carbohydrates: 29g | Sugar: 25g

Barley Benefits

Barley is packed with vitamins, minerals, and fiber that aid the body in a number of ways. It can help lower cholesterol and is good for intestinal health. Barley's soluble fiber also feeds good bacteria in the digestive tract, promoting good digestion.

Old-Fashioned Lemon Scones

These fresh citrus scones are delicious with sugar-free jam, creamed honey, butter, or all three!

INGREDIENTS | SERVES 6

1¼ cups white whole-wheat flour
½ cup rolled oats
2 teaspoons baking powder
¼ teaspoon sea salt
⅓ cup cold butter
3 tablespoons honey
2 tablespoons lemon juice
2 teaspoons grated lemon peel
2 large eggs, divided
¼ cup half-and-half

Pastry Blending

Using a pastry blender or two knives to cut the butter or other solid fat into the dry ingredients of your dough is critical for flaky, moist pastries.

1. Preheat oven to 400°F.

2. Mix flour, oats, baking powder, and salt in a large bowl. Using a pastry blender or two knives, cut the butter into the mixture until the butter looks like pea-size crumbs.

3. Stir in honey, lemon juice, lemon peel, 1 egg, and half-and-half until the dough pulls away from the sides of the bowl.

4. Turn the dough onto a lightly floured surface and knead 10 times. Roll dough into a rectangle about ½" thick. Cut the dough into 4" squares and then cut into triangles.

5. Place triangles about 2" apart on a parchment-lined baking sheet. Beat remaining egg in a small bowl. Use a pastry brush to brush top and sides of the scones with beaten egg.

6. Bake 10–12 minutes until golden brown.

PER SERVING Calories: 272 | Fat: 14g | Protein: 7g | Sodium: 293mg | Fiber: 4g | Carbohydrates: 33g | Sugar: 9g

No-Bake Granola Nut Bars

These easily prepared bars provide quick protein and can be packed in a purse or briefcase for later. They are similar in taste to healthy store-bought protein bars but are much cheaper!

INGREDIENTS | SERVES 8

1¼ cups rolled oats

½ cup puffed Kamut or quinoa

¼ cup whole-wheat flour

¼ cup chopped walnuts

2 tablespoons natural almond butter

¼ cup ground flaxseed

1 teaspoon cinnamon

⅛ teaspoon nutmeg

1 teaspoon vanilla extract

2 tablespoons unsweetened applesauce

¼ cup honey

1 teaspoon molasses

1. In a medium mixing bowl, combine oats, puffed Kamut or quinoa, whole-wheat flour, and walnuts. Add remaining ingredients and mix well.

2. Press into an 8" × 8" baking dish.

3. Freeze for 30 minutes or until firm.

4. Cut into bars and store in airtight container in the refrigerator until ready to eat or pack.

PER SERVING Calories: 204 | Fat: 7g | Protein: 6g | Sodium: 596mg | Fiber: 2g | Carbohydrates: 32g | Sugar: 8g

Puffed Cereals

Puffed cereals are great ways to get additional healthy grains into your diet. Branch out from traditional puffed rice cereal the next time you are in the cereal aisle of the health food store.

Whole-Wheat Peanut Butter Banana Blintzes

These hearty crepes re-create nostalgic peanut butter and jelly flavor with peanut butter filling and sweet strawberry sauce. If you prefer to skip the strawberry sauce, a nice drizzle of sugar-free chocolate syrup is a wonderful accompaniment.

INGREDIENTS | SERVES 6

1 large egg

1 cup almond milk

1½ tablespoons melted coconut oil, divided

¾ teaspoon vanilla extract

1 teaspoon sea salt

5 drops liquid stevia

¾ cup whole-wheat flour

⅔ cup natural peanut butter

2 medium bananas, peeled and sliced

Strawberry Sauce (see recipe in Chapter 6)

1. In a blender, pulse the egg, almond milk, 1 tablespoon coconut oil, vanilla, salt, and stevia until smooth. Add the flour and pulse until smooth.

2. Heat a nonstick skillet or griddle over medium heat.

3. Pour ⅛ cup batter into the center of the pan and rotate quickly to create a thin circle crepe. Allow crepe to cook until bubbles form and edges lift from pan. Gently flip to cook the other side. Repeat with remaining batter.

4. Fill crepes with peanut butter and sliced bananas and roll into a log. Drizzle sauce over the top.

PER SERVING Calories: 320 | Fat: 20g | Protein: 12g | Sodium: 558mg | Fiber: 5g | Carbohydrates: 28g | Sugar: 9g

Pumpkin Chocolate Chip Waffles

*These deliciously spiced waffles, complete with a sinful amount of chocolate,
taste divine and still pack a healthful punch of vitamin A.*

INGREDIENTS | SERVES 6

1¼ cups white whole-wheat flour

3 tablespoons coconut sugar

2 teaspoons baking powder

1½ teaspoons cinnamon

½ teaspoon nutmeg

⅛ teaspoon cloves

½ teaspoon sea salt

1 large egg

½ cup canned pumpkin

1 teaspoon vanilla extract

2 tablespoons melted butter

1 cup unsweetened almond milk

⅓ cup sugar-free chocolate chips

1. Heat waffle iron.

2. In a medium bowl, combine flour, coconut sugar, baking powder, cinnamon, nutmeg, cloves, and salt.

3. In a separate bowl, mix together egg, pumpkin, vanilla, butter, and almond milk. Add to flour mixture and mix well. Gently stir in chocolate chips.

4. Pour about ½ cup batter into preheated waffle iron. Cook waffles according to manufacturer's instructions. Serve warm.

PER SERVING Calories: 106 | Fat: 5.5g | Protein: 3g | Sodium: 395mg | Fiber: 1g | Carbohydrates: 12g | Sugar: 9g

Spices of the Gods

Cinnamon is a powerful spice used to treat sore throats, coughs, and bacterial infections. Studies show that it may help lower blood sugar levels and cholesterol in the body. Nutmeg is a powerful detoxifier, brain stimulator, and pain reliever.

Raspberry Lemon Poppy Seed Pancakes

The robust flavors and bright colors of these pancakes make them perfect for a special brunch or a surprise breakfast in bed.

INGREDIENTS | SERVES 4

1 cup whole-wheat flour

1½ teaspoons baking powder

¼ teaspoon baking soda

½ teaspoon sea salt

1 cup unsweetened almond milk

3 tablespoons coconut oil, melted

4 tablespoons honey

1 teaspoon vanilla extract

3 tablespoons unsweetened applesauce

Juice and zest of 3 large lemons

1 teaspoon poppy seeds

¾ cup fresh raspberries

1. Heat a nonstick griddle over medium heat.

2. In a large mixing bowl, combine flour, baking powder, baking soda, and salt.

3. Add almond milk, oil, honey, vanilla, applesauce, lemon juice and zest, and poppy seeds. Be careful not to overmix.

4. Gently fold in the raspberries.

5. Pour about ¼ cup of batter for each pancake onto the griddle. Cook on both sides until golden brown.

PER SERVING Calories: 323 | Fat: 12g | Protein: 7g | Sodium: 591mg | Fiber: 7g | Carbohydrates: 51g | Sugar: 23g

Sour Cream Doughnuts

These dense, muffin-like doughnuts are hearty with a fun shape for dipping into a favorite warm drink. If you don't have a doughnut maker, you can easily turn these into waffles using a waffle iron.

INGREDIENTS | SERVES 8

2¼ cups whole-wheat flour
1½ teaspoons baking powder
1 teaspoon sea salt
¾ teaspoon nutmeg
¾ cup coconut sugar, divided
2 tablespoons oil
2 large eggs
⅔ cup sour cream
¾ cup milk
⅛ teaspoon cinnamon
¼ cup melted butter

Cream Supreme

Using sour cream and full-fat yogurt in baking creates dense, moist and delicious baked goods. The fat content from these dairy products adds richness and enhances flavor and texture.

1. Heat the doughnut maker.

2. In a large bowl, mix flour, baking powder, salt, nutmeg, and ½ cup coconut sugar together well.

3. Add in the oil, eggs, sour cream, and milk and mix until smooth. Pour into doughnut maker and bake according to doughnut maker's instructions.

4. Place remaining coconut sugar in a high-powered blender or food processor and pulse on high until sugar becomes a fine powder.

5. Mix coconut sugar with cinnamon in a shallow bowl.

6. Dip warm doughnuts in melted butter, then in the powdered coconut sugar mixture. These are best served warm.

PER SERVING Calories: 344 | Fat: 16g | Protein: 7g | Sodium: 437mg | Fiber: 4g | Carbohydrates: 47g | Sugar: 22g

Easy Cinnamon Rolls

These rolls are a healthy take on an all-time favorite guilty pleasure. Unlike traditional cinnamon rolls, they are yeast-free and require no rise time. Top with a cream cheese or vanilla glaze frosting for the ultimate treat.

INGREDIENTS | SERVES 8

½ teaspoon vinegar

1¼ cups unsweetened almond milk

3 cups plus 2 tablespoons white spelt flour, divided

⅔ cup coconut sugar, divided

1¼ teaspoons baking powder

½ teaspoon baking soda

½ teaspoon sea salt

1 tablespoon plus ½ teaspoon cinnamon, divided

⅓ cup butter, melted

3 tablespoons butter, softened

1 foot unflavored dental floss

Classic Cream Cheese Frosting (see recipe in Chapter 12)

Buttermilk Substitutes

Buttermilk is a popular ingredient for pancakes and other baked goods. In a pinch, adding vinegar or lemon juice to dairy or almond milk and allowing it to sit for 5 minutes will give you a great buttermilk substitute. The acidity from the vinegar or lemon juice creates the bitter, sour buttermilk taste.

1. In a small bowl, mix vinegar with the almond milk and set aside.

2. Preheat oven to 425°F. Spray an 8" × 8" baking dish with oil.

3. In a large mixing bowl, combine 3 cups flour, 3 tablespoons coconut sugar, baking powder, baking soda, salt, and ½ teaspoon cinnamon. Add melted butter and almond milk mixture.

4. Mix and knead until the dough comes together into a smooth ball. If the dough is a little sticky, add 1 tablespoon more flour.

5. On a floured work surface, roll dough into a 12" × 8" rectangle.

6. Spread the softened butter onto the rolled-out dough. Sprinkle with ½ cup coconut sugar and 1 tablespoon cinnamon. Starting at the long side, roll up the dough into a log shape. Using dental floss, cut the log into 2" slices by sliding the floss under the log, parallel with the end of the log, crossing the ends of the floss over the top of the log and pulling to cut it. (Dental floss cuts easily through the dough without ripping or smashing the dough.)

7. Place the slices, swirl side up, in prepared dish and bake for 12–15 minutes. Frost rolls with frosting and serve.

PER SERVING Calories: 377 | Fat: 13g | Protein: 6g | Sodium: 251mg | Fiber: 2g | Carbohydrates: 58g | Sugar: 18g

Gingerbread Granola

Turn ordinary granola into a truly gourmet breakfast with flavors reminiscent of a gingerbread cookie! Ginger, molasses, and pumpkin seeds make this a warm spiced dish that is perfect for fall.

INGREDIENTS | MAKES 8 CUPS

4 cups rolled oats
½ cup chopped almonds
½ cup chopped walnuts
½ cup raw sunflower seeds
½ cup raw pumpkin seeds
½ cup unsweetened shredded coconut
¼ cup ground flaxseed
½ teaspoon sea salt
1 tablespoon cinnamon
1 tablespoon ginger
½ cup coconut oil, melted
½ cup pure maple syrup
¼ cup molasses
½ teaspoon vanilla extract
½ cup raisins

1. Preheat oven to 250°F. Line a large jellyroll pan with parchment paper.

2. In a large bowl, mix together oats, almonds, walnuts, sunflower seeds, pumpkin seeds, coconut, flaxseed, salt, cinnamon, and ginger.

3. In a small bowl, whisk together oil, maple syrup, molasses, and vanilla.

4. Pour the oil mixture over the oat mixture and mix well.

5. Spread the granola onto the jellyroll pan and bake for 2 hours, stirring every 30 minutes.

6. Remove from oven and cool. Add raisins and store in the refrigerator in an airtight container.

PER SERVING (½ cup) Calories: 304 | Fat: 18g | Protein: 7g | Sodium: 80mg | Fiber: 5g | Carbohydrates: 32g | Sugar: 12g

Pumpkin Chia Pudding Parfaits

Begin the morning with a boost of energy from this protein-packed breakfast. This recipe makes a thick pudding with warm pumpkin pie flavors and velvety coconut cream. Sprinkle the top with chocolate shavings if you like.

INGREDIENTS | SERVES 3

½ cup chia seeds

¼ cup unsweetened almond milk

¼ cup xylitol

2 cups pumpkin purée

1 teaspoon cinnamon

2 teaspoons vanilla extract, divided

2 teaspoons pumpkin pie spice

⅛ teaspoon sea salt

1 (13.5-ounce) can full-fat coconut milk, chilled

3 tablespoons agave inulin

3 drops liquid stevia

1. In a bowl with a lid, combine chia seeds, almond milk, and xylitol. Mix together and cover. Refrigerate overnight.

2. In the morning, add pumpkin, cinnamon, 1 teaspoon vanilla, pumpkin pie spice, and salt to chia seeds. Mix well.

3. In a separate bowl, whip cold coconut milk using hand beaters. Add agave, stevia, and remaining vanilla.

4. In a parfait dish or tall glass, layer chia pudding and coconut cream alternating until you reach the top.

PER SERVING Calories: 440 | Fat: 34g | Protein: 8g | Sodium: 130mg | Fiber: 12g | Carbohydrates: 39g | Sugar: 3g

Protein, Protein, Protein

Chia seeds are a great source of protein and fiber. They contain antioxidants and healthy omega 3 fatty acids. Adding chia seeds to breakfast in the morning can help maintain consistent energy levels throughout the day. They can be added to absolutely anything because they do not have a distinctive taste.

Vanilla Chia "Chai" Pudding

Enjoy the delicate floral flavors of a traditional chai tea in this sweet breakfast pudding. Enjoy cold from the fridge or gently warmed over the stove.

INGREDIENTS | SERVES 2

½ cup chia seeds

1 teaspoon allspice

⅛ teaspoon cardamom

1 teaspoon cinnamon

¼ teaspoon cloves

1 tablespoon honey

1¼ cups unsweetened almond milk

2 teaspoons vanilla extract

⅛ teaspoon sea salt

½ cup Dairy-Free Whipped Cream (see recipe in Chapter 12)

In a large container with a cover, mix chia seeds, allspice, cardamom, cinnamon, cloves, honey, almond milk, vanilla, and salt. Cover and refrigerate overnight. Serve with Dairy-Free Whipped Cream.

PER SERVING Calories: 493 | Fat: 36g | Protein: 13g | Sodium: 257mg | Fiber: 9g | Carbohydrates: 32g | Sugar: 16g

CHAPTER 3

Breads

Almond Orange Poppy Seed Bread

The lovely orange and almond flavors of this dessert bread complement each other beautifully. The sweet glaze moistens the cake while also adding sweet citrus flavor.

INGREDIENTS | SERVES 8

1⅓ cups white whole-wheat flour

1 teaspoon sea salt

¾ teaspoon baking powder

1½ tablespoons poppy seeds

¾ cup butter, melted

1½ teaspoons vanilla extract, divided

2 teaspoons almond extract, divided

2 large eggs

1 cup powdered honey

⅓ cup sour cream

⅓ cup water

2 teaspoons orange zest

3 tablespoons orange juice

¼ cup xylitol

1. Preheat the oven to 350°F. Spray a 9" × 5" loaf pan with cooking spray.

2. In a large mixing bowl, combine flour, salt, baking powder, poppy seeds, butter, 1 teaspoon vanilla, 1 teaspoon almond extract, and eggs. Stir in powdered honey, sour cream, water, and zest. Mix until just combined. Pour into prepared pan.

3. Bake for 35 minutes or until the top starts to turn golden brown.

4. While the bread bakes, whisk together the finishing glaze. Mix the orange juice, the remaining vanilla and almond extracts, and the xylitol. Pour this glaze over the top of the loaf when it comes out of the oven.

5. Allow bread to cool before slicing.

PER SERVING Calories: 563 | Fat: 24g | Protein: 11g | Sodium: 374.6mg | Fiber: 8g | Carbohydrates: 84g | Sugar: 36.6g

Almond Poppy Seed Muffins

These lovely, moist, golden yellow muffins with pretty deep blue flecks are easy, healthy, and delicious! Slather with butter and honey for a satisfying treat.

INGREDIENTS | SERVES 18

2 cups white whole-wheat flour

1 teaspoon baking powder

¾ teaspoon sea salt

1 tablespoon poppy seeds

1 cup honey

½ cup grapeseed oil

2 large eggs

½ teaspoon vanilla extract

2 teaspoons almond extract

The Poppy Packs a Punch

In addition to adding flavor and crunch to baked goods, poppy seeds are a great source of essential minerals, are rich in omega-3 fatty acids, and can help with inflammation and pain in the body.

1. Heat oven to 350°F. Place 18 muffin liners in two muffin pans and spray liners with cooking spray.

2. Combine all ingredients in a medium mixing bowl and mix until just combined.

3. Spoon batter into the muffin liners, filling about ¾ of the way full.

4. Bake for 20 minutes or until a toothpick poked into the center of a muffin comes out clean.

PER SERVING Calories: 167 | Fat: 7g | Protein: 2.7g | Sodium: 134.7mg | Fiber: 1.8g | Carbohydrates: 25.5g | Sugar: 15.6g

Blueberry Streusel Muffins

Sweet muffins with delicious bursts of tart blueberry are great out of the oven or packed for a picnic the next day. The sweet streusel makes these muffins extra special and extra sweet!

INGREDIENTS | SERVES 12

⅓ cup plain low-fat yogurt

½ cup plus 2 tablespoons maple sugar, divided

1 large egg

½ teaspoon vanilla extract

⅓ cup unsweetened almond milk

¼ teaspoon lemon zest

1 teaspoon baking powder

½ teaspoon sea salt

1 cup plus 1 tablespoon white spelt flour, divided

½ cup fresh blueberries

¼ teaspoon cinnamon

2 tablespoons unsalted butter, diced

What Is Spelt?

Spelt is a whole-grain food that is much easier for the body to digest than wheat. It is wonderfully high in fiber and minerals and has a slightly nutty taste. Spelt flour can be substituted for wheat in many recipes.

1. Preheat oven to 375°F and place 12 muffin liners in a muffin pan.

2. In a medium bowl, mix together yogurt, ½ cup maple sugar, egg, vanilla, almond milk, and lemon zest. When combined, mix in the baking powder, salt, and 1 cup flour.

3. Gently fold in the blueberries.

4. In a separate bowl, create the crumb topping by mixing 2 tablespoons maple sugar, 1 tablespoon flour, cinnamon, and diced butter.

5. Pour batter into prepared muffin tin and spoon the crumb topping over the top.

6. Bake for 18 minutes or until tops become golden brown.

PER SERVING Calories: 102 | Fat: 2.7g | Protein: 2.3g | Sodium: 154.3mg | Fiber: 0.52g | Carbohydrates: 17.3g | Sugar: 7.82g

Easy Chocolate Chip Banana Bread

Bananas are sure to become a pantry staple after you make this deliciously healthy dessert bread. Coconut milk adds a rich flavor and keeps the bread moist.

INGREDIENTS | SERVES 8

3 medium ripe bananas
⅓ cup full-fat coconut milk
½ cup honey
1 teaspoon vanilla extract
½ teaspoon sea salt
1 teaspoon baking soda
1⅔ cups white spelt flour
½ cup sugar-free dark chocolate chips

Honey Properties

Honey gives goodies a darker, more golden color than traditional refined sugar. It is helpful to cover cakes made with honey with foil halfway through their baking time to ensure the top does not brown too much. Check for doneness with a toothpick before removing the cake from the oven.

1. Preheat oven to 350°F and spray a 9" × 5" loaf pan with cooking spray.

2. In a medium bowl, mash bananas with a fork. Add coconut milk, honey, vanilla, salt, and baking soda and mix well. Add flour and chocolate chips and mix until just combined.

3. Pour batter into the loaf pan and bake for 40 minutes. Watch closely and cover the top with foil for the last 10 minutes of baking if the top looks brown.

PER SERVING Calories: 411 | Fat: 4.6g | Protein: 8g | Sodium: 313mg | Fiber: 3.9g | Carbohydrates: 85.2g | Sugar: 31g

Cinnamon Pull-Apart Rolls

*With a sweet cinnamon exterior and a soft chewy interior, these rolls
are a bit messy to eat and a whole lot of fun to share.*

INGREDIENTS | SERVES 8

1½ teaspoons active dry yeast
¼ cup warm water heated to 110°F
⅓ cup plus 3 tablespoons powdered honey, divided
¾ cup unsweetened almond milk
½ cup (8 tablespoons) butter, divided
1 large egg
½ teaspoon sea salt
2¾ cups white whole-wheat flour
2 tablespoons cinnamon

1. Preheat oven to 400°F. Spray a 9" × 9" baking dish with cooking spray.

2. Combine yeast and the warm water with 1 tablespoon of powdered honey and set aside.

3. Scald the almond milk on the stove by heating it over medium heat just until bubbles begin popping up around the edges of the pan. Remove from heat. Add 3 tablespoons of butter to the scalded milk and stir until melted. Let cool.

4. In a large mixing bowl, beat egg, 2 tablespoons powdered honey, and salt. Stir in milk mixture and yeast mixture. Mix until well combined. Add flour and knead the dough on a floured surface for 5 minutes.

5. Return dough to the bowl and cover the top with a towel. Place bowl in a warm place for 30 minutes as the dough rises.

6. Melt the remaining 5 tablespoons of butter and place into a small bowl. In another small bowl, combine ⅓ cup powdered honey with the cinnamon.

7. Pinch out 1½" balls of dough and form each one into a smooth topped ball. Dip each in butter and then into the honey mixture. Place in the prepared dish, touching each other, in rows.

8. Bake rolls for 20 minutes or until the tops are golden.

PER SERVING Calories: 194 | Fat: 13g | Protein: 2g
| Sodium: 171mg | Fiber: 1.1g | Carbohydrates: 21g | Sugar: 19g

Cranberry Orange Scones

Sweet citrus-flavored scones make the perfect pick-me-up with a cup of tea in the afternoon or served at a special luncheon or party.

INGREDIENTS | SERVES 8

1¼ cups white whole-wheat flour

½ cup rolled oats

2½ teaspoons baking powder

½ teaspoon sea salt

⅓ cup cold butter

3 tablespoons honey

2 tablespoons orange juice

3 teaspoons grated orange zest

2 large eggs, divided

2–3 tablespoons chopped dried cranberries

¼ cup full-fat coconut milk

1 teaspoon water

Zesting Tips

Be sure to wash your citrus well before zesting. A microplane will achieve the smallest slivers of zest, creating the most flavor in the recipe. A zester or a grater can also be used, however. Remove only the colored rind, as the white pith is bitter; rotate the fruit often as you zest to avoid the pith.

1. Preheat the oven to 400°F. Line a baking sheet with parchment paper.

2. Combine flour, oats, baking powder, and salt. Using two knives or a pastry cutter, chop the butter into the flour mixture until butter pieces are pea-size.

3. Stir in honey, orange juice, zest, 1 egg, and cranberries. Stir in the coconut milk until the dough pulls away from the sides of the bowl.

4. On a floured surface, knead the dough with your hands 10 times. Roll out the dough until it is a rectangle about ½" thick.

5. Cut the dough into 4 (3") squares and then cut each square diagonally creating 8 triangles. Place triangles 2" apart on the prepared baking sheet.

6. In a small bowl, beat the remaining egg with water and brush egg wash over the top and sides of each scone.

7. Bake for 10 minutes or until golden brown.

PER SERVING Calories: 290 | Fat: 10g | Protein: 8g | Sodium: 813mg | Fiber: 6g | Carbohydrates: 45g | Sugar: 9g

Easy Brownie Muffins

Satisfy a chocolate craving while providing the body with healthy fats, probiotics, and minerals.

INGREDIENTS | SERVES 10

½ cup plain low-fat yogurt

1 cup honey

1 tablespoon molasses

1 large egg

2 tablespoons coconut oil

1 teaspoon vanilla extract

½ cup unsweetened almond milk

1½ teaspoons baking powder

½ teaspoon sea salt

½ cup cocoa

⅔ cup sugar-free chocolate chips

1½ cups spelt flour

1. Preheat the oven to 350°F. Place 10 cupcake liners in a muffin pan and spray liners with cooking spray.

2. In a medium bowl, combine yogurt, honey, molasses, egg, and coconut oil and stir well. Add remaining ingredients and mix to combine.

3. Pour batter into muffin pan and bake for 15–18 minutes.

PER SERVING Calories: 310 | Fat: 8g | Protein: 5g | Sodium: 217mg | Fiber: 3g | Carbohydrates: 58g | Sugar: 24g

Sugar-Free Chocolate Chips

Be sure to purchase chocolate chips without harmful artificial sweeteners. Maltitol is a common sweetener used in several brands of chocolate chips, such as Hershey's Sugar Free Chocolate Chips, and seems to be safe in moderate amounts. Even better choices are grain-sweetened dark chocolate baking chips or stevia-sweetened chocolate chips, found in health food stores and online.

Homemade Sandwich Buns

Perfect for hamburgers, chicken salad, or even peanut butter and jelly,
this versatile bread can easily replace any sandwich bread.

INGREDIENTS | SERVES 10

1 package active dry yeast
3 tablespoons honey
1 cup warm water, heated to 110°F
3 tablespoons unsweetened almond milk
1 large egg
2 teaspoons sea salt
¼ teaspoon minced garlic
4½ cups white whole-wheat flour

Bread Blues

It is often hard to find commercially made bread that is sugar-free. In fact, high-fructose corn syrup and lots of other unsavory ingredients used as preservatives are commonplace in the bread aisle. Breads that do not contain sugar are often extremely expensive. With just a little preparation, Homemade Sandwich Buns can save money and the headache of finding healthy bread at the grocery store.

1. Dissolve yeast and honey in warm water in a large mixing bowl. Wait 5 minutes for it to bubble.

2. Stir in almond milk, egg, salt, and garlic to the yeast mixture. Add flour and knead for 5 minutes on a floured countertop. Place dough in a covered bowl and allow to rise for 1 hour in a warm place.

3. Pinch out 1½" balls of dough. Roll each ball flat with a rolling pin or a tortilla press. Lay the rounds on a baking sheet lined with parchment paper 2" apart. Allow the buns to rise again for another 30 minutes.

4. Preheat oven to 350°F. Bake for 10 minutes until lightly golden.

PER SERVING Calories: 214g | Fat: 2g | Protein: 8g | Sodium: 480g | Fiber: 7g | Carbohydrates: 45g | Sugar: 6g

Honey Wheat Bread

This basic bread recipe creates wonderful sandwiches! It's also perfect paired with a bowl of soup or a seasonal salad.

INGREDIENTS | SERVES 8

2 cups warm water, heated to 110°F

2 tablespoons yeast

4 tablespoons honey, divided

5 cups white whole-wheat flour, divided

¼ cup coconut sugar

1½ teaspoons sea salt

1 tablespoon ground flaxseed

⅔ cup 2% milk

¼ cup coconut oil

Ground Flaxseed Facts

The oils in ground flaxseed go rancid quickly, so for optimal health benefits, don't purchase ground flaxseed. Purchase raw whole flaxseeds and grind them as you need them in a recipe. Grinding can be done in a food processor or high-powered blender.

1. In a medium bowl, combine water, yeast, and 1 tablespoon of honey. Let sit for 5 minutes until it bubbles.

2. In the bowl of an electric mixer, combine 4 cups of flour with coconut sugar, salt, and ground flaxseed.

3. With mixer running at low speed, add yeast mixture to the flour mixture. Then add milk, remaining 3 tablespoons of honey, and coconut oil. Add in the remaining flour and mix on medium speed for 5 minutes.

4. Remove mixing bowl from the electric mixer and cover with a towel to rise for 1 hour.

5. Preheat oven to 375°F. Spray a 9" × 5" loaf pan with cooking spray.

6. Roll out and form dough into a loaf shape and place into prepared pan.

7. Bake for 15 minutes. Reduce oven heat to 350°F and bake another 15 minutes. The top should be golden brown.

PER SERVING Calories: 397 | Fat: 9g | Protein: 12g | Sodium: 458mg | Fiber: 10g | Carbohydrates: 71g | Sugar: 16g

Maple Oat Bread

Filled with lots of healthy grains and mineral-packed maple syrup, this bread is a great breakfast treat or soup accompaniment.

INGREDIENTS | SERVES 8

¾ cup warm water, heated to 110°F

2¼ teaspoons instant yeast

2 cups white whole-wheat flour

½ cup rolled oats

⅓ cup plus 2 tablespoons maple syrup, divided

1 teaspoon vanilla extract

¼ cup butter, softened

½ teaspoon sea salt

½ teaspoon cinnamon

Maple Syrup Makes the Grade

Maple syrup is graded for its color. Grade B has a slightly stronger and richer flavor than A. Both are good quality natural sweeteners and will give excellent flavor to any treat.

1. In a small bowl, combine water with yeast. Allow it to sit for 5 minutes until it bubbles.

2. In the bowl of an electric mixer, mix flour, oats, ⅓ cup maple syrup, vanilla, butter, salt, and cinnamon. Add the yeast mixture and run the machine on medium low for 5 minutes while the dough kneads.

3. Remove the bowl from the mixer and cover with a towel. Place bowl in a warm place to rise for 1 hour.

4. Remove the dough from the mixing bowl. Spray a 9" × 5" loaf pan with cooking spray and place dough inside. Allow dough to rise for another hour. Preheat oven to 350°F. Lightly grease a loaf pan.

5. Transfer dough to loaf pan, forming a loaf. Drizzle loaf with remaining 2 tablespoons maple syrup and bake for 25 minutes or until a knife inserted into the center of the loaf comes out clean.

PER SERVING Calories: 225 | Fat: 7g | Protein: 5g | Sodium: 152mg | Fiber: 4.5g | Carbohydrates: 38g | Sugar: 11g

Maple Vanilla Muffins

Real vanilla beans add incredibly warm floral notes to these moist muffins.
They are so deliciously sweet, they can almost pass as cupcakes.

INGREDIENTS | SERVES 12

¼ cup unsweetened applesauce
1 tablespoon ground flaxseed
1½ cups wheat flour
1½ teaspoons baking powder
½ teaspoon sea salt
¼ teaspoon cinnamon
⅔ cup maple syrup
½ cup unsweetened almond milk
¼ cup butter, melted
1 teaspoon vanilla extract
Seeds of 1 vanilla bean

Vanilla Bean Pods

Don't throw away the pods of a vanilla bean after using the seeds. The pod can be placed in a container of milk in the refrigerator for flavoring and added to any of your favorite hot drinks. And after being soaked in milk, the pod can be rinsed, dried, and ground to flavor baked dishes.

1. Preheat oven to 375°F. Line 1 muffin pan with liners and lightly spray liners with cooking spray.

2. In a small bowl, combine applesauce and flaxseed.

3. In a mixing bowl, whisk together the flour, baking powder, salt, and cinnamon. Make a well in the center of these dry ingredients and pour in maple syrup, almond milk, butter, vanilla extract, vanilla bean seeds, and the applesauce mixture. Mix everything until just combined.

4. Pour batter into prepared muffin liners.

5. Bake muffins for 12 minutes or until toothpick comes out clean.

PER SERVING Calories: 150 | Fat: 4g | Protein: 2g | Sodium: 166mg | Fiber: 1g | Carbohydrates: 26g | Sugar: 12g

Mini Skinny Lemon Poppy Seed Muffins

When muffins this good come in small portions, eating 3 or 4 isn't a problem for the waistline and is still extremely satisfying.

INGREDIENTS | SERVES 8

½ cup plain low-fat Greek yogurt

¼ cup coconut oil, melted

1 large egg

1 tablespoon unsweetened almond milk

½ teaspoon vanilla extract

½ cup honey

Juice and zest of 1 large lemon

¼ teaspoon baking powder

½ teaspoon baking soda

1 tablespoon poppy seeds

¼ teaspoon sea salt

1 cup spelt flour

1. Preheat oven to 400°F. Line two mini muffin tins with 24 cupcake liners and spray liners with cooking spray.

2. In a medium mixing bowl, mix together yogurt, oil, egg, almond milk, vanilla, honey, lemon juice, and lemon zest until well combined.

3. In a small bowl, combine baking powder, baking soda, poppy seeds, salt, and flour.

4. Add the flour mixture to the mixing bowl, just mixing until the ingredients barely come together.

5. Spoon the mixture into the muffin liners and bake for 10 minutes or until a toothpick poked into the center of a muffin comes out clean.

PER SERVING Calories: 208 | Fat: 8g | Protein: 3.5g | Sodium: 190mg | Fiber: 1g | Carbohydrates: 31g | Sugar: 18g

Mini Cinnamon Sugar Muffins

A delicious combination of several natural sweeteners is used in these muffins. Coconut sugar creates a brown-sugar-like topping appearance and the xylitol gives a white-sugar-like experience to the senses.

INGREDIENTS | SERVES 12

½ cup powdered honey
1 cup butter, divided
½ teaspoon nutmeg
1¼ teaspoons cinnamon, divided
½ cup unsweetened almond milk
1 teaspoon baking powder
1 cup white whole-wheat flour
¼ teaspoon vanilla extract
¼ cup coconut sugar
1 tablespoon xylitol

1. Preheat oven to 350°F. Line two mini muffin tins with cupcake liners and spray liners with cooking spray.

2. In a medium mixing bowl, combine powdered honey, ½ cup butter, nutmeg, ¼ teaspoon cinnamon, almond milk, baking powder, flour, and vanilla.

3. Pour batter into prepared muffin tins and bake for 18 minutes or until a toothpick poked into the center comes out clean.

4. While muffins are baking, melt the remaining butter and mix it with the coconut sugar, xylitol, and remaining cinnamon.

5. When muffins are done, pour the melted butter mixture over the tops and allow to cool slightly before eating.

PER SERVING Calories: 238 | Fat: 16g | Protein: 2g | Sodium: 50mg | Fiber: 2g | Carbohydrates: 25g | Sugar: 16g

One-Hour Dinner Rolls

Here's a tasty and quick recipe for dinner rolls that will have people believing you spent hours in the kitchen.

INGREDIENTS | SERVES 12

½ cup warm water heated to 110°F

¼ cup plus 1 tablespoon powdered honey, divided

1 tablespoon yeast

1¼ cups whole milk

5 tablespoons butter, softened

2 large eggs

1 teaspoon sea salt

4½ cups white whole-wheat flour

2 tablespoons butter, melted

Activating Yeast

A simple kitchen thermometer is the best way to ensure water is warm enough to activate the yeast in a recipe but not so hot that it kills the yeast, leaving it inactive. Using water that is either too cold or too hot will hinder the yeast from making bread rise. Fresh yeast and a bit of honey added to 110°F water will cause bubbles and foaming in the mixture after 5 minutes. This foaming lets you know the yeast has been activated properly for baking.

1. In a small bowl, combine water, 1 tablespoon powdered honey, and yeast. Allow to sit for 5 minutes until it bubbles.

2. Scald milk in the microwave for 2 minutes. Melt softened butter into the milk and let cool.

3. In a large mixing bowl, beat together eggs, ¼ cup powdered honey, salt, and the milk and butter mixture.

4. Add yeast mixture to the batter. While continuing to mix, add flour. Knead dough for 5 minutes. If the dough is too sticky, add just a bit more flour, but do not exceed 5 cups.

5. Place dough back in the bowl and cover with a towel. Set the bowl in a warm place for 30 minutes for the dough to rise.

6. Preheat oven to 400°F. Spray 2 muffin pans with cooking spray.

7. Pinch 1" balls from the dough and roll until smooth. Place three of these 1" balls into the bottom of each muffin cup.

8. Bake for 10 minutes or until golden brown on top. Brush with melted butter and serve.

PER SERVING Calories: 288 | Fat: 10g | Protein: 9g | Sodium: 237mg | Fiber: 6g | Carbohydrates: 43g | Sugar: 10g

Pumpkin Spice Muffins

Warm, moist, and comforting, these muffins are wonderful served with Dairy-Free Cinnamon Honey Butter (see recipe in Chapter 6) or paired with an afternoon cup of tea.

INGREDIENTS | SERVES 12

1 cup canned pumpkin
⅓ cup grapeseed oil
2 large eggs
1 cup powdered honey
½ cup maple sugar
1 teaspoon molasses
1 teaspoon vanilla extract
½ teaspoon baking soda
¾ teaspoon baking powder
½ teaspoon sea salt
½ tablespoon pumpkin pie spice
2 teaspoons cinnamon
⅛ teaspoon nutmeg
1½ cups spelt flour

1. Preheat oven to 350°F. Line a muffin pan with muffin liners and spray liners with cooking spray.

2. In a large mixing bowl, add all ingredients and whisk until combined.

3. Pour batter into prepared muffin liners, filling ¾ of the way full.

4. Bake for 20 minutes or until a toothpick poked into the center of a muffin comes out clean.

PER SERVING Calories: 391 | Fat: 7.5g | Protein: 7g | Sodium: 197mg | Fiber: 2.4g | Carbohydrates: 75g | Sugar: 30g

Raspberry Muffins

Tart raspberries combined with a delicious hint of citrus make these muffins incredibly delicate and flavorful.

INGREDIENTS | SERVES 24

4 cups white whole-wheat flour

1⅓ cups powdered honey

4 teaspoons baking powder

1 teaspoon sea salt

½ cup butter, softened

½ cup grapeseed oil

1½ cups full-fat coconut milk

2 large eggs

½ teaspoon vanilla extract

2 cups frozen raspberries

2 tablespoons xylitol

Powdered Honey

Powdered honey is a great dry sweetener for baking. Powdered honey bakes similarly to regular liquid honey in that it browns quickly. Watch these muffins carefully toward the end of baking and cover with foil if they are browning too quickly.

1. Preheat oven to 400°F. Line 2 muffin pans with cupcake liners and spray liners with cooking spray.

2. In a medium bowl, combine flour, powdered honey, baking powder, and salt. Stir in butter and oil.

3. In a second bowl, mix coconut milk, eggs, and vanilla. Add the coconut milk mixture to flour mixture and mix until just barely combined.

4. Fill each muffin cup ¼ of the way full. Place 2 or 3 raspberries on top of the batter and add more batter over the raspberries. Each muffin cup should be filled ¾ of the way to the top. Sprinkle xylitol on top.

5. Bake muffins for 15 minutes or until a toothpick poked into the center of a muffin comes out clean.

PER SERVING Calories: 237 | Fat: 9g | Protein: 4g | Sodium: 195mg | Fiber: 3.5g | Carbohydrates: 38g | Sugar: 20g

Vegan Banana Nut Bread

The perfect combination of sweet and nutty, this egg- and dairy-free bread is a delicious alternative to regular banana bread, whether you are vegan or not.

INGREDIENTS | SERVES 8

2 large ripe bananas
¾ cup date sugar
¼ cup unsweetened applesauce
⅓ cup unsweetened almond milk
1 tablespoon lemon juice
¼ cup melted coconut oil
½ teaspoon sea salt
1 tablespoon vanilla extract
1¼ cups white rice flour
¼ teaspoon xanthan gum
1 teaspoon baking soda
½ teaspoon baking powder
1 tablespoon ground flaxseed
1 tablespoon cinnamon
½ cup chopped walnuts

1. Preheat oven to 350°F. Spray a 9" × 5" loaf pan with cooking spray.

2. In a large bowl, mash bananas with date sugar until smooth. Add applesauce, almond milk, lemon juice, oil, salt, and vanilla.

3. In a small bowl, mix flour, xanthan gum, baking soda, baking powder, flaxseed, and cinnamon.

4. Add the flour mixture to the banana mixture and whisk together until well combined. Add walnuts. Pour batter into prepared pan.

5. Bake for 30 minutes or until a toothpick poked into the center comes out clean.

PER SERVING Calories: 322 | Fat: 13g | Protein: 4g | Sodium: 343mg | Fiber: 3g | Carbohydrates: 50g | Sugar: 25g

Healthy Zucchini Bread

*Ribbons of green vegetables aren't the only reason this bread is a winner.
It's full of heart-healthy oils, whole grains, and even some fruit!*

INGREDIENTS | SERVES 12

3 cups spelt flour

1 teaspoon sea salt

1 teaspoon baking soda

1 teaspoon baking powder

2½ teaspoons ground cinnamon

3 large eggs

½ cup grapeseed oil

½ cup unsweetened applesauce

2 cups coconut sugar

1 tablespoon vanilla extract

2 cups grated zucchini

1. Preheat oven to 325°F. Spray two 9" × 5" loaf pans with cooking spray.

2. In a medium mixing bowl, whisk together flour, salt, baking soda, baking powder, and cinnamon.

3. In a large bowl, beat together eggs, oil, applesauce, coconut sugar, and vanilla. Stir in flour mixture. Fold in grated zucchini.

4. Pour batter into pans and bake for 40–45 minutes or until a knife poked into the center comes out clean.

PER SERVING Calories: 354 | Fat: 11g | Protein: 5g | Sodium: 362mg | Fiber: 2g | Carbohydrates: 60g | Sugar: 35g

Natural Baking Mix

A healthy alternative to store-bought baking mixes, this homemade version stores easily in the freezer for up to 2 months. Make delicious waffles, pancakes, and biscuits in minutes!

INGREDIENTS | MAKES 6 CUPS

5 cups white whole-wheat flour

¼ cup baking powder

2 tablespoons powdered honey

½ teaspoon sea salt

1 cup cold butter

1. In a large mixing bowl, combine the flour, baking powder, powdered honey, and salt. With two knives, cut butter into the flour mixture until the butter is broken up into small pieces, but not completely mixed in.

2. Store this mixture in the freezer in a gallon-size zip-top plastic bag or freezer-safe glass jar and use in recipes that call for baking mixes.

PER SERVING (¼ cup) Calories: 636 | Fat: 32g | Protein: 14g | Sodium: 1,181mg | Fiber: 12g | Carbohydrates: 80g | Sugar: 6g

Baking Mix 101

Store-bought baking mixes are typically filled with hydrogenated oils and refined sugar. This baking mix yields great-tasting results with ingredients that are nourishing for the body.

Soft Pretzels

Buttery, salty, and extra soft, these pretzels are sure to hit the spot. Yeast and honey and a baking soda glaze are the secret ingredients for super delicious pretzels at home. Pretzels are best when freshly buttered and salted, warm from the oven.

INGREDIENTS | SERVES 10

2¼ teaspoons active dry yeast

2 teaspoons honey

1½ cups warm water, divided

2½ cups white whole-wheat flour

¼ teaspoon sea salt

1 tablespoon baking soda

¼ cup melted butter

1 tablespoon coarse salt

Homemade Is Better!

Soft chewy pretzels from the mall always look and smell great, but a traditional salted mall pretzel contains 10 grams of sugar. By making your own, you control the amount and quality of the salt and sugar you are eating.

1. In a small bowl, combine yeast, honey, and 1 cup warm water heated to 110°F. Mix gently and set aside for 5 minutes.

2. In the bowl of a stand mixer, combine flour and sea salt. Stir in yeast mixture and mix at medium speed for 5 minutes. Remove the bowl from the mixer and cover with a towel; place in a warm spot and let rise for 30 minutes.

3. Preheat oven to 500°F. Line a baking sheet with parchment paper.

4. When the dough has risen for 30 minutes, turn it out onto a lightly floured surface, and shape into a loaf. Using a knife, cut the dough into 10 equal parts. Roll each part into a rope, about ¾" thick. Loop and fold each piece of dough into a pretzel shape. Place on the baking sheet and let stand for 5 minutes.

5. In a small bowl, combine ½ cup warm water and baking soda. Dip each pretzel in the baking soda water and return to baking sheet.

6. Bake for 8–10 minutes until tops are golden brown. Remove from the oven and brush with melted butter and sprinkle with coarse salt.

PER SERVING Calories: 150 | Fat: 5g | Protein: 5g | Sodium: 1,060mg | Fiber: 4g | Carbohydrates: 23g | Sugar: 1g

CHAPTER 4

Appetizers

Apricot-Stuffed Dates

*Sweet, bite-size dates perfectly accompany an assortment of cheeses,
fruits, and crackers for an elegant party platter.*

INGREDIENTS | SERVES 8

16 Medjool dates
⅓ cup dried apricots
⅓ cup walnuts
1½ teaspoons vanilla extract
½ teaspoon cinnamon
1 teaspoon honey

1. Gently slice dates lengthwise. Remove the pits and set dates aside.

2. In a food processor, combine apricots, walnuts, vanilla, cinnamon, and honey. Process the mixture until it becomes a rough paste.

3. Spoon the apricot mixture into the pitted dates.

PER SERVING Calories: 97 | Fat: 3g | Protein: 1g | Sodium: 1mg | Fiber: 2g | Carbohydrates: 17g | Sugar: 14g

Apple Pecan Salad

Sweet and crunchy toppings make this a salad no one will pass up.

INGREDIENTS | SERVES 4

4 cups fresh baby spinach
1 medium Fuji apple, peeled, cored, and cut into cubes
½ cup chopped pecans, toasted
½ cup crumbled blue cheese
¼ cup fresh sprouts
Raspberry Vinaigrette (see recipe in Chapter 6)
¼ teaspoon sea salt

1. Place the spinach, apple, pecans, blue cheese, and sprouts in a salad bowl.

2. Gently toss the salad with dressing, sprinkle with salt and serve.

PER SERVING Calories: 216 | Fat: 18g | Protein: 6g | Sodium: 473mg | Fiber: 3g | Carbohydrates: 9g | Sugar: 6g

Green Blood Orange Salad

This beautiful salad has unbeatable color, taste, and texture!

INGREDIENTS | SERVES 2 SIDE SALADS

6 ounces mixed dark green lettuce
2 small blood oranges
¼ cup chopped walnuts
6 Medjool dates, pitted and chopped
¼ cup chopped celery
3 tablespoons olive oil
1 tablespoon fresh lemon juice
⅛ teaspoon sea salt
⅛ teaspoon ground black pepper

1. Wash and dry the lettuce and place in a salad bowl.

2. Cut the ends off the oranges and gently cut off the rind from top to bottom in slices. Place the oranges on their sides and gently cut ¼" slices, creating circles.

3. Layer walnuts, dates, and celery over the lettuce in the salad bowl. Arrange oranges in a circle on top of the bed of lettuce.

4. Drizzle salad with olive oil, lemon juice, and sprinkle with salt and pepper.

PER SERVING Calories: 418 | Fat: 30g | Protein: 5g | Sodium: 177mg | Fiber: 7g | Carbohydrates: 38g | Sugar: 30g

Cabbage, Beet, and Celery Slaw

This incredibly colorful salad is rich in nutrients and antioxidants and pretty enough to brighten up any meal.

INGREDIENTS | SERVES 6

1½ cups finely grated purple cabbage
1½ cups finely grated beets
1½ cups finely chopped celery
¼ cup chopped walnuts
⅛ cup chopped yellow onion
⅛ cup red wine vinegar
½ cup olive oil
½ teaspoon sea salt
⅛ teaspoon powdered stevia
1 teaspoon poppy seeds

1. In a medium salad bowl, combine cabbage, beets, celery, and walnuts.

2. In a blender, process onion, vinegar, oil, salt, and stevia for 1 minute.

3. Pour dressing over the salad and sprinkle with poppy seeds.

PER SERVING Calories: 220 | Fat: 22g | Protein: 2g | Sodium: 251mg | Fiber: 2g | Carbohydrates: 6g | Sugar: 4g

Sweet Roasted Carrots

This side dish with its gorgeous color and aroma elevates a simple meal into an elegant and sophisticated one.

INGREDIENTS | SERVES 4

8 medium carrots, peeled

3 tablespoons olive oil

¼ cup plus 1 tablespoon coconut sugar, divided

1 tablespoon molasses

½ teaspoon kosher salt

2 tablespoons finely chopped pecans

1 teaspoon dried thyme

1. Preheat oven to 400°F. Line a baking sheet with parchment paper.

2. Place carrots on the baking tray and cover them with the olive oil, ¼ cup coconut sugar, molasses, and salt.

3. Bake carrots for 40 minutes. After 20 minutes, roll carrots around in the pan so they are in as much of the oil and sugar as possible.

4. During the last 10 minutes of baking, add remaining coconut sugar, pecans, and thyme.

5. Serve carrots hot.

PER SERVING Calories: 244 | Fat: 13g | Protein: 2g | Sodium: 381mg | Fiber: 4g | Carbohydrates: 33g | Sugar: 26g

Maple Roasted Brussels Sprouts

Caramelizing Brussels sprouts with maple syrup gives them a tenderness and sweetness that almost makes them taste like candy!

INGREDIENTS | SERVES 6

1 pound Brussels sprouts
3 tablespoons coconut oil
1 tablespoon apple cider vinegar
3 tablespoons maple syrup
1 tablespoon coconut sugar
1 teaspoon sea salt
½ teaspoon ground black pepper

Eating Brussels

Two great reasons to include Brussels sprouts in the diet: they have the highest cancer-fighting properties of any cruciferous vegetable, and they are high in vitamins C and A and folate.

1. Preheat the oven to 400°F. Line a baking sheet with parchment paper.

2. Wash and dry the Brussels sprouts. Cut off the white ends and quarter each Brussels sprout.

3. In a bowl, combine Brussels sprouts, oil, vinegar, maple syrup, coconut sugar, salt, and pepper. Stir until ingredients are evenly distributed throughout.

4. Place Brussels sprouts on lined baking sheet and roast in the oven for 20 minutes, stirring after 10 minutes. Brussels sprouts should be caramelized and soft.

PER SERVING Calories: 127 | Fat: 7g | Protein: 2.5g | Sodium: 412mg | Fiber: 3g | Carbohydrates: 15g | Sugar: 9g

Cucumber Hummus Bites

These easy appetizers come together quickly and look lovely on a platter lined with kale leaves. Add extra veggies on top for a healthy, light lunch.

INGREDIENTS | SERVES 8

¼ cup hummus

1 large cucumber, sliced into ½" disks

3 large mushrooms, diced

8 fresh basil leaves, sliced into thin ribbons

1 medium tomato, diced

1. Spread hummus on one side of each cucumber slice. On half of the cucumber slices, arrange mushrooms. On the other half, arrange basil and tomatoes.

2. Serve immediately.

PER SERVING Calories: 23 | Fat: 1g | Protein: 1g | Sodium: 31mg | Fiber: 1g | Carbohydrates: 3g | Sugar: 1g

Honey Roasted Almonds

These nuts are amazing in a salad, over homemade ice cream, with Greek yogurt, or just by the handful. They store well in airtight containers for an on-the-go snack.

INGREDIENTS | SERVES 4

1 cup raw almonds

¼ cup honey

2 tablespoons coconut oil

⅛ teaspoon sea salt

2 teaspoons cinnamon

Extra Energy

These honey-sweetened almonds are the perfect energy boost! Honey and cinnamon help eliminate unhealthy cravings, and protein and healthy fats keep you running all day long.

1. Preheat broiler. Line a baking sheet with parchment paper.

2. In a small bowl, mix all ingredients together. Spread the mixture onto the baking sheet. It will stick and clump a bit, but that's okay.

3. Broil for 3 minutes, then stir the nuts around a bit and broil another 3 minutes until the almonds are bubbly and lightly browned. Cool for 5 minutes before serving.

PER SERVING Calories: 263 | Fat: 18g | Protein: 5g | Sodium: 75mg | Fiber: 3.5g | Carbohydrates: 23g | Sugar: 18g

Orange Kale Salad

This bright, fresh salad is unbeatable in nutrition and taste. Sweet strawberry and orange cut the bitter taste of kale and add delicious texture.

INGREDIENTS | SERVES 2

1 bunch kale
½ cup chopped strawberries
½ cup chopped orange slices
¼ cup chopped cucumber
⅛ cup slivered almonds, toasted
Orange Vinaigrette (see recipe in Chapter 6)

Save It for Later

Kale leaves are tougher than the average lettuce. Typically once a salad is dressed, it's best to consume it right away. This is not the case with kale. It will hold up very well if prepared in the morning and taken to work for lunch. Just make sure it's refrigerated.

1. Pull the kale leaves from the stems and discard stems. Wash and dry the leaves.

2. In a salad bowl, add the kale, strawberries, oranges, cucumber, and almonds.

3. Drizzle salad dressing over the top and toss to evenly distribute the dressing.

PER SERVING Calories: 142 | Fat: 10g | Protein: 2g | Sodium: 134mg | Fiber: 3g | Carbohydrates: 12g | Sugar: 9g

Watermelon Salsa

A sweet fruity salsa laced with lime is the perfect addition to a barbecue or summer potluck. This unique salsa is surprisingly delicious served with fish or chicken!

INGREDIENTS | SERVES 6

Zest of 1 medium lime
1 teaspoon fresh lime juice
1 tablespoon xylitol
2 cups chopped seedless watermelon
1 large kiwi, peeled and diced
⅓ large cucumber, peeled and chopped
3 tablespoons diced orange bell pepper
2 tablespoons chopped fresh mint

Juice It!

Combine the ingredients in this salsa except for the bell pepper in a blender. Blend until everything is liquefied. Add water to dilute if desired. This combination creates an extremely refreshing summertime drink.

1. In a small bowl, mix zest, lime juice, and xylitol.

2. In a serving bowl, combine watermelon, kiwi, cucumber, bell pepper, and mint. Drizzle with lime mixture and serve.

PER SERVING Calories: 36 | Fat: 0.165g | Protein: 0.5g | Sodium: 2mg | Fiber: 1g | Carbohydrates: 8g | Sugar: 3g

Salmon Cream Cheese Bites

This appetizer can be made quickly and will disappear at a party almost as fast!

INGREDIENTS | SERVES 8

½ cup cream cheese, softened
¼ cup goat cheese crumbles
¼ teaspoon garlic powder
2 sprigs fresh dill
1 (8-ounce) package hearty crackers, such as Milton's
4 ounces smoked salmon

1. In a small bowl, mix cream cheese, goat cheese, and garlic powder.

2. Wash and dry the dill and separate the leaves from the stems. Mix the dill leaves into the cream cheese mixture.

3. On the crackers, spread the cream cheese and top with smoked salmon. Garnish with more dill if desired.

PER SERVING Calories: 81 | Fat: 7g | Protein: 4g | Sodium: 215mg | Fiber: 1g | Carbohydrates: 1g | Sugar: 0.5g

Pear Gorgonzola Salad

This lovely side salad is made with simple, fresh ingredients.

INGREDIENTS | SERVES 4

4 cups dark green salad mix

½ cup chopped walnuts, toasted

2 large pears, peeled, cored, and sliced

½ cup crumbled gorgonzola cheese

1 tablespoon apple cider vinegar

2 tablespoons lime juice

2 tablespoons honey

4 tablespoons olive oil

½ teaspoon sea salt

¼ teaspoon ground black pepper

1. In a salad bowl, layer green salad mix, walnuts, pears, and cheese.

2. In a small bowl, whisk together vinegar, lime juice, honey, oil, salt, and pepper.

3. Drizzle dressing over the salad and serve immediately.

PER SERVING Calories: 337 | Fat: 23g | Protein: 4g | Sodium: 332mg | Fiber: 5g | Carbohydrates: 33g | Sugar: 20g

Fresh Pears

Bartlett, Anjou, or Bosc pears work wonderfully in this simple salad. Besides being juicy and sweet, they provide good sources of vitamin C, E, B_2, and fiber.

Strawberry Kale Salad

Sweet and packed full of vitamins, this salad is a great start to any meal. Add 4 ounces of Ahi tuna and an extra 2 tablespoons of almonds and it becomes an easy, delightful meal.

INGREDIENTS | SERVES 4

1 bunch of kale
3 tablespoons olive oil
3 tablespoons fresh lemon juice
3 tablespoons raw honey
½ cup sliced strawberries
2 tablespoons slivered almonds

Kale Massage

Citrus juices break down the tough fibers of the kale leaves. When the leaves are massaged with citrus dressings, the leaves become much sweeter and easier to chew.

1. Pull the kale leaves from the tough stems and discard stems. Wash and dry the leaves.

2. In a medium bowl, whisk oil and lemon juice together. Add kale leaves and work the dressing into the leaves with your hands. Massage the leaves for 1 minute.

3. Drizzle honey, strawberries, and almonds over the salad and toss to combine.

4. Serve salad immediately.

PER SERVING Calories: 196 | Fat: 12g | Protein: 3g | Sodium: 32mg | Fiber: 2g | Carbohydrates: 22g | Sugar: 14g

Watermelon Salad with Feta and Mint

This salad provides rejuvenation to the body and is a great way to cool down in the summer. Watermelon is high in arginine, which helps the heart and the circulatory system, and lycopene, a powerful antioxidant. The slightly salty feta rounds out the sweetness perfectly.

INGREDIENTS | SERVES 6

1 small seedless watermelon, chilled
¼ cup fresh mint leaves, washed and dried
2 tablespoons extra-virgin olive oil
3 tablespoons fresh lemon juice
1 teaspoon sea salt
¼ teaspoon freshly ground black pepper
1 teaspoon apple cider vinegar
½ cup crumbled feta cheese

1. Wash watermelon and cut off rind. Cut the watermelon into 1" cubes. Chiffonade mint leaves.

2. In a large bowl, whisk oil, lemon juice, salt, pepper, and vinegar. Add watermelon, feta, and mint to the bowl. Toss gently to combine all ingredients.

3. Serve immediately.

PER SERVING Calories: 77 | Fat: 7g | Protein: 2g | Sodium: 500mg | Fiber: 1g | Carbohydrates: 1.6g | Sugar: 0.6g

Sweet Deviled Eggs

Slightly sweet and a tad tangy, these deviled eggs are anything but typical. They come together easily using a spoon to fill them, or you can make them look professionally made by using a pastry bag with a frosting tip instead.

INGREDIENTS | YIELDS 14

7 large eggs
3½ tablespoons mayonnaise
2 teaspoons mustard
2 tablespoons honey
1 teaspoon lemon juice
¾ teaspoon sea salt
½ teaspoon ground black pepper
¼ teaspoon paprika

1. In a large pot, lay eggs in a single layer and cover with cold water. Water should cover the eggs by 1". Heat the water until it reaches a rolling boil. When the water is boiling, remove pot from the heat and cover with a lid. Set the timer for 12 minutes.

2. After 12 minutes, run eggs under cold water to stop the cooking process. Allow to cool completely.

3. Peel eggs and cut in half lengthwise. Carefully remove the yolks from the whites and place yolks in a small mixing bowl. Add mayonnaise, mustard, honey, lemon juice, salt, and pepper. Mash with a fork until creamy.

4. Spoon or pipe the yolk mixture back into the hollowed-out egg whites. Sprinkle with paprika and serve or refrigerate.

PER SERVING Calories: 70 | Fat: 5g | Protein: 3g | Sodium: 189mg | Fiber: 1g | Carbohydrates: 3g | Sugar: 3g

Tomato and Goat Cheese Pastries

Warm herbed cheese and tomato make a divine appetizer when nestled in flaky pastry. These make an excellent brunch and party food.

INGREDIENTS | YIELDS 2

1 sheet frozen puff pastry, thawed

2 tablespoons grated Parmesan cheese

¼ teaspoon garlic

2 teaspoons chopped fresh thyme, divided

1 teaspoon grated lemon zest

¼ cup herbed goat cheese

2 large tomato slices

⅛ teaspoon sea salt

⅛ teaspoon ground black pepper

1 tablespoon extra-virgin olive oil

1. Preheat oven to 425°F. Line a baking sheet with parchment paper.

2. Very lightly flour a work surface and gently unfold the pastry and gently flatten out. Cut 2 large circles out of the pastry dough. Next, gently make a smaller circle indentation inside the two cut circles, cutting them far enough apart to get 2 large equal circles. Be careful not to go all the way through! Prick inside circle with a fork so the inside circle remains flat and the outside rim will puff up.

3. In a small bowl, combine Parmesan cheese, garlic, 1 teaspoon thyme, and lemon zest. Mix together and divide up between the two pastries, spreading the mixture in the inside circle of the tarts. Crumble up the goat cheese and add on top of the mixture. Top with tomato slices.

4. Sprinkle with salt and pepper and drizzle with olive oil. Garnish with remaining thyme. Bake for 15 minutes, until golden brown. Serve hot or cold.

PER SERVING Calories: 121 | Fat: 7g | Protein: 7g | Sodium: 487mg | Fiber: 2g | Carbohydrates: 8g | Sugar: 5g

CHAPTER 5

Main Dishes

Almond Vegetable Stir-Fry

This Asian-inspired dish with lots of flavor and crunchy vegetables is a great topping for rice or noodles. You'll want to have friends—and chopsticks—on hand when you whip up this sweet and spicy dish.

INGREDIENTS | SERVES 4

2 teaspoons cornstarch

⅓ cup coconut sugar

⅓ cup water

3 tablespoons soy sauce

2 teaspoons sesame oil

1 teaspoon powdered ginger

⅔ cup slivered almonds

4 tablespoons grapeseed oil

3 cups Thai or Asian frozen vegetable mix

½ teaspoon sea salt

½ teaspoon ground black pepper

¼ teaspoon lemon pepper

2 teaspoons minced garlic

2 cups cooked rice

Soy Sauce Tips

Not all soy sauce is created equal when it comes to health benefits and nutritional properties. Choose one that is labeled as naturally fermented, raw, and unpasteurized. They are the healthiest choices and contain no MSG or added sugar.

1. In a small bowl, combine cornstarch, coconut sugar, water, soy sauce, sesame oil, and ginger until smooth and set aside.

2. In a small skillet over medium heat, toast slivered almonds.

3. In a large skillet, heat oil over medium heat. Add vegetable mix, salt, black pepper, lemon pepper, and garlic. Cook the vegetables, stirring often, until they are cooked through and begin to brown, about 8 minutes.

4. Add the prepared sauce and reduce heat to low. Cook for about 2 minutes until the sauce is heated through and thickened.

5. Serve over rice. Sprinkle with slivered almonds.

PER SERVING Calories: 439 | Fat: 24g | Protein: 6.5g | Sodium: 975mg | Fiber: 2.5g | Carbohydrates: 51g | Sugar: 19g

Baby Meat Loaves

Baking a meat loaf in mini-size cups cuts down on baking time, creates more surface area to cover with tasty sauce, and makes serving a snap.

INGREDIENTS | SERVES 8

1 cup tomato sauce

3 tablespoons maple syrup

1½ tablespoons apple cider vinegar

1 tablespoon olive oil

3 large carrots, peeled and diced

1 small red onion, peeled and diced

3 cloves garlic, diced

1 cup sour cream

1 cup bread crumbs

1 large egg

¼ cup milk

¼ chopped fresh parsley

2 tablespoons Dijon mustard

2½ teaspoons salt

1½ teaspoons dried thyme

1 teaspoon ground black pepper

1 pound organic ground beef

Go for Organic

Organic, grass-fed meats contain omega-3 fatty acids, essential for heart health and conjugated linoleic acid (CLA), which is a powerful antioxidant. Non-organic meats do not have these benefits, and are exposed to synthetic fertilizers, pesticides, and radiation. This exposure is detrimental to animals and humans.

1. Heat oven to 350°F. Prepare a large cookie tray by lining it with parchment paper.

2. In a small dish, combine tomato sauce, maple syrup, and vinegar and set aside.

3. In a medium saucepan, heat oil and sauté carrots, onion, and garlic until onions are translucent, about 5–7 minutes.

4. Take the onion mixture off the heat and stir in ¼ cup of the prepared sauce; set aside to cool.

5. In a large mixing bowl, add all the remaining ingredients, including the onion mixture, and mix well.

6. Use a ½ cup measuring cup to scoop out the meat mixture and arrange in rows on the parchment-lined baking sheet.

7. Spoon the sauce over the baby meat loaves and bake for 35–40 minutes.

PER SERVING Calories: 284 | Fat: 15g | Protein: 16g | Sodium: 1,133mg | Fiber: 2g | Carbohydrates: 22g | Sugar: 10g

Slow Cooker Sweet Pork

This pork is perfect with all the traditional taco fixings, in a sandwich with melted cheese, or over a salad with homemade ranch dressing.

INGREDIENTS | SERVES 12

2 pounds pork tenderloin

2 (12-ounce) cans Zevia Cola

¼ cup coconut sugar

½ teaspoon garlic powder

½ teaspoon sea salt

¼ cup water

1 (4.5-ounce) can sliced green chilies, drained

1 (15-ounce) bottle all-natural enchilada sauce

½ cup honey

Slow Cooker 411

Slow cooking is a great way to achieve tender meats, thanks to the low temperature and long cook times. It is also an easy way to kill vitamins in vegetables. In recipes that call for vegetables, consider cooking them separately or adding them at the very end to retain as much of their nutritional value as possible.

1. Combine pork, 1 can soda, and coconut sugar in a large covered container. Marinate in the refrigerator overnight.

2. Remove pork from the marinade and place in a 4- to 6-quart slow cooker. Discard the marinade.

3. In a medium mixing bowl, stir together remaining can of soda, garlic powder, salt, water, green chilies, enchilada sauce, and honey.

4. Pour sauce over the pork in the slow cooker and bake for 7–8 hours on low.

5. After pork has cooked, shred the meat with two forks and stir the sauce to cover the shredded pork pieces. Let stand uncovered for 10 minutes while the pork soaks up the sauce. Serve hot.

PER SERVING Calories: 176 | Fat: 2g | Protein: 16g | Sodium: 373mg | Fiber: 0g | Carbohydrates: 24g | Sugar: 22g

Chinese Lemon Chicken

In Chinese restaurants, this dish is typically sugar-laden. But you can easily make it at home and control the added sugar. Fresh and tangy, this chicken is delicious over brown rice and smothered with sauce.

INGREDIENTS | SERVES 4

4 large (6-ounce) boneless, skinless chicken breasts

2 tablespoons soy sauce

¾ cup water

¼ cup apple cider vinegar

½ cup honey

⅓ cup plus 2 tablespoons cornstarch, divided

6 tablespoons lemon juice

½ teaspoon sea salt

¼ cup grapeseed oil

1. In a large bowl, marinate chicken in soy sauce for 10 minutes.

2. Meanwhile, in a medium saucepan, add water, vinegar, honey, 2 tablespoons cornstarch, lemon juice, and salt. Cook, stirring, over medium heat until thickened, about 10 minutes.

3. Remove chicken from marinade and cut into bite-size pieces. In a gallon-size plastic bag, add ⅓ cup cornstarch and chicken pieces and shake until chicken is well coated.

4. Heat oil over medium heat in a large skillet. Fry chicken pieces until crispy, about 12 minutes. Remove from oil and place on paper towels.

5. Serve with lemon sauce over top.

PER SERVING Calories: 509 | Fat: 18g | Protein: 36g | Sodium: 949mg | Fiber: 0g | Carbohydrates: 50.5g | Sugar: 35.5g

Maple Glazed Salmon

A simple preparation yields divine results for this heart-healthy fish.
Serve it with rice pilaf or over a bed of fresh leafy greens.

INGREDIENTS | SERVES 4

1 tablespoon grapeseed oil
⅓ cup maple syrup
1 teaspoon apple cider vinegar
2 tablespoons soy sauce
¼ teaspoon garlic
½ teaspoon sea salt
½ teaspoon ground black pepper
4 (6-ounce) salmon steaks
¼ cup bread crumbs

1. Preheat oven to 450°F. Spray a baking dish, just large enough to hold the 4 salmon steaks, with cooking spray.

2. In a small bowl, whisk together oil, maple syrup, vinegar, soy sauce, garlic, salt, and pepper.

3. Place the salmon steaks in the baking dish and pour sauce over the top. Flip the steaks over a few times so the sauce soaks into both sides of the fish.

4. Sprinkle the bread crumbs over the fish, patting them to make them stick to the tops and sides of the fish.

5. Bake for 15 minutes, checking after 10 minutes to see if the fish is cooking too fast. Fish is done when it flakes with a fork.

PER SERVING Calories: 371 | Fat: 14g | Protein: 35g | Sodium: 870mg | Fiber: 0g | Carbohydrates: 24g | Sugar: 16.5g

Healthy Nachos

Game-night food has never been this fresh, nutritious, or satisfying! Use nondairy toppings such as almond cheese or sour cream to complete these nachos in a truly healthy fashion.

INGREDIENTS | SERVES 6

2 chipotle-flavored black bean burgers (such as Gardein), cooked
½ cup cooked black beans
⅓ cup diced orange, yellow, or red bell pepper
¼ cup finely chopped onion
½ teaspoon garlic powder
½ teaspoon lemon zest
½ teaspoon sea salt
½ teaspoon ground black pepper
4 cups tortilla chips
1 cup shredded Cheddar cheese
1 large tomato, diced
1 cup shredded mixed green lettuces
1 large avocado, peeled, pitted, and cut into cubes

1. Preheat broiler. Line a large baking sheet with parchment paper and set aside.

2. In a medium mixing bowl, mash the bean burgers with a fork. Add black beans, bell peppers, onions, garlic powder, lemon zest, salt, and pepper and stir to combine.

3. Lay the chips on the parchment-lined baking tray. Spoon bean burger mixture over the top of the chips, followed by cheese.

4. Broil for 2–3 minutes until the cheese has melted and chips become extra crispy. Watch closely so they don't burn.

5. Remove nachos from the oven and top with tomato, lettuce, and avocado. Serve immediately.

PER SERVING Calories: 380 | Fat: 21g | Protein: 11g | Sodium: 970mg | Fiber: 6g | Carbohydrates: 39g | Sugar: 2.5g

Lentil Lemon Cakes

*Lemon and garlic enhance these protein-rich dinner cakes. Serve them over
a bed of lettuce with avocado, lemon juice, yogurt, and fresh dill.*

INGREDIENTS | YIELDS 8 CAKES

1 cup lentils, soaked for at least 12 hours

3 large eggs, beaten

2 tablespoons nutritional yeast

3 tablespoons chopped onion

3 cloves garlic, minced

½ teaspoon sea salt

¼ cup chopped spinach or kale

1 teaspoon lemon zest

1⅓ cups almond meal

2 tablespoons olive oil

1. In a medium mixing bowl, mix together all the ingredients except the oil until well combined.

2. Heat the olive oil in a large skillet over medium heat.

3. Divide the lentil mix into 8 equal parts and roll each part into a ball before gently flattening it into a round disk, about ½" thick.

4. Cook each lentil cake for 3–4 minutes on each side, or until golden. Serve hot.

PER SERVING Calories: 445 | Fat: 31g | Protein: 21g
| Sodium: 338mg | Fiber: 13g | Carbohydrates: 27g | Sugar: 3g

Burger, Anyone?

Divide the lentil mixture into 4 portions instead of 8 to make delicious veggie burgers. Garnish burgers with lettuce, tomato, avocado, and your favorite tzatziki sauce.

Mexican Quinoa

Quinoa recipes are delicious warm for dinner or cold the next day for lunch. Excellent as a side dish, this quinoa is packed with enough protein and nutrients to serve as a fulfilling main dish as well. Serve it over a bed of lettuce and/or tortilla chips.

INGREDIENTS | SERVES 4

3 tablespoons olive oil, divided

1 cup quinoa

1 garlic clove, minced

2 cups water

Juice and zest of 1 large lime

¼ teaspoon cumin

½ teaspoon sea salt

½ teaspoon lemon pepper

1 (15-ounce) can black beans, drained and rinsed

1 large avocado, peeled, pitted, and cut into cubes

1 large Roma tomato, diced

¼ cup cooked corn

¼ cup chopped onion

¼ cup chopped spinach

2 tablespoons chopped cilantro

1. In a medium saucepan, combine 1 tablespoon olive oil, quinoa, garlic, and water. Stir, cover and simmer on medium heat for 15 minutes or until all the water is absorbed.

2. In a small bowl, make the dressing by combining lime juice, zest, 2 tablespoons olive oil, cumin, salt, and lemon pepper.

3. In a large bowl, combine cooked quinoa, beans, avocado, tomato, corn, onion, spinach, and cilantro.

4. Toss with the dressing and serve warm.

PER SERVING Calories: 439 | Fat: 21g | Protein: 13g | Sodium: 619mg | Fiber: 13g | Carbohydrates: 53g | Sugar: 4g

Orange Quinoa Mint Salad

This salad is bright and beautiful, displaying almost every color of the rainbow. It also is packed with healthy proteins.

INGREDIENTS | SERVES 6

2 cups water

1 cup quinoa

1 teaspoon grated orange zest

1 cup grated cucumber

½ cup grated carrot

¼ cup grated red onion

½ cup diced red bell pepper

2 large oranges, peeled and cut into pieces

1 tablespoon chopped fresh mint

3 tablespoons balsamic vinaigrette salad dressing

½ cup pomegranate juice

1 tablespoon honey

1 tablespoon Dijon mustard

½ teaspoon sea salt

¼ teaspoon ground black pepper

¼ cup small whole mint leaves

1. Bring 2 cups of water to boil in a medium saucepan. Add the quinoa, reduce heat to low, and cover. Cook quinoa for 10–15 minutes. Water should be absorbed but quinoa should have a slight crunch still.

2. Transfer quinoa to a colander and rinse with cold water to stop the cooking process. Transfer to a salad bowl. Add the zest, cucumber, carrot, onion, bell pepper, oranges, and mint to the quinoa.

3. In a small bowl, mix balsamic vinaigrette, pomegranate juice, honey, Dijon mustard, salt, and black pepper.

4. Pour dressing over the salad and garnish with mint leaves. Salad can be stored in the refrigerator for up to 3 days.

PER SERVING Calories: 206 | Fat: 6g | Protein: 5g | Sodium: 242mg | Fiber: 5g | Carbohydrates: 34g | Sugar: 12g

Super Quinoa

Quinoa has long been touted as a super-food by the health-conscious, and rightfully so. It is a complete protein on its own, is high in vitamins and minerals, and is a good source of fiber. It can easily be served as a substitute for rice, which is great because it cooks faster and is more nutritious!

Chicken Lettuce Wraps

These Asian-inspired wraps are impressive in presentation and fun to eat with your hands. Serve with a side of rice or stir-fry vegetables.

INGREDIENTS | SERVES 2

⅓ cup coconut sugar

½ cup warm water

2 tablespoons soy sauce

1½ tablespoons rice wine vinegar

2 tablespoons natural ketchup

2 tablespoons fresh lemon juice

¼ teaspoon sesame oil

1 tablespoon hot mustard

2 teaspoons red chili paste

3 tablespoons grapeseed oil

3 tablespoons chopped onion

1 teaspoon minced garlic

2 (5-ounce) boneless, skinless chicken breasts, cooked and shredded

1 cup diced water chestnuts

4 butter lettuce leaves

¼ teaspoon sea salt

¼ teaspoon ground black pepper

1. In a small bowl, dissolve the coconut sugar in the warm water. Add 2 tablespoons soy sauce, vinegar, ketchup, lemon juice, sesame oil, mustard, and chili paste and stir well. Set sauce aside.

2. In a medium skillet, heat grapeseed oil over medium heat. Add onions and garlic and cook until onions are translucent, about 5–7 minutes. Reduce heat to low and add the shredded chicken, water chestnuts, and 3 tablespoons of the sauce. Cook, stirring, for 5 minutes.

3. Heat the remainder of the sauce in a small saucepan over medium heat for 5 minutes.

4. Spoon 2 tablespoons of the chicken mixture into the center of each lettuce leaf. Sprinkle with salt and pepper. Serve remaining sauce on the side for dipping.

PER SERVING Calories: 586 | Fat: 25g | Protein: 33g | Sodium: 1,342mg | Fiber: 3g | Carbohydrates: 59g | Sugar: 43g

Side Salad

An alternative serving suggestion for these lettuce wraps is to turn them into a salad by chopping the lettuce, spooning the chicken mixture over the top, and drizzling the salad with the sauce.

Pumpkin Pecan Pasta

Warm, savory, and full of flavor, this pasta brings traditional holiday spices to a dish anyone can enjoy year round. Meat lovers can add 2 cups of cooked chicken sausage.

INGREDIENTS | SERVES 6

3 tablespoons olive oil

½ medium onion, peeled and finely chopped

3 cloves garlic

¼ teaspoon cinnamon

½ teaspoon nutmeg

2 bay leaves

1 tablespoon sage

1½ cups apple cider

1 teaspoon apple cider vinegar

½ cup water

1 cup pumpkin

½ teaspoon sea salt

½ teaspoon ground black pepper

½ cup heavy cream

1 pound rice penne pasta

½ cup chopped pecans, toasted

Dairy-Free Option

Substitute the heavy cream called for in this recipe with full-fat coconut cream. The coconut flavor adds a sweet flavor and is just as creamy.

1. In a large skillet, heat the olive oil over medium heat. Add onion and garlic and cook until onions are translucent, about 5 minutes. Add the cinnamon and nutmeg and give a gentle stir while the heat releases their flavors. Remove from heat.

2. To the same skillet, add the bay leaves, sage, apple cider, vinegar, water, and pumpkin. Stir well and return to medium heat. Allow the sauce to cook for about 10 minutes while the liquid reduces, stirring occasionally. Remove sauce from heat and add salt, pepper, and cream.

3. Meanwhile, bring a large pot with 5 quarts of water to boil. Add pasta and cook as package instructs.

4. Toss the cooked penne with the sauce and sprinkle with pecans.

PER SERVING Calories: 535 | Fat: 22g | Protein: 5g | Sodium: 346mg | Fiber: 5g | Carbohydrates: 81g | Sugar: 7g

Vegan Black Bean Burritos

This basic burrito recipe is simple, fast, and fresh. Experiment with toppings such as cheese, sautéed vegetables, or salsa.

INGREDIENTS | SERVES 4

2 cups water

1 cup brown rice

2 (15-ounce) cans black beans, rinsed and drained

1½ teaspoons cumin

½ teaspoon garlic salt

1 tablespoon lime juice

½ cup chopped cilantro

½ teaspoon sea salt

¼ teaspoon ground black pepper

4 (8") flour tortillas

2 medium tomatoes, diced

1 medium avocado, peeled, pitted, and diced

2 cups lettuce or mixed greens

1 tablespoon grapeseed oil

Limes

Limes are an important part of many cultures' cooking. In addition to enhancing flavors immensely, they aid in digestion by activating your salivary glands almost as soon as the lime enters your mouth. Try adding lime to your water and to your cooking to help digest your meals.

1. In a medium saucepan, bring water to a boil. Add rice and stir gently. Cover the pot, reduce heat to simmer, and cook for 30 minutes or until rice has absorbed all the water.

2. Meanwhile, in another medium saucepan, heat beans, cumin, and garlic salt over medium heat until warm, about 8 minutes.

3. When rice is finished cooking, add lime juice, cilantro, salt, and pepper.

4. Assemble the burritos by filling a tortilla with rice, beans, tomatoes, avocado, and lettuce. Fold two opposite sides of the tortilla ¼ of the way toward the center of the burrito. Roll the tortilla up from the bottom to the top, forming a rectangular wrap.

5. Heat oil in a large skillet or grill pan over medium-high heat. Cook burrito about 3 minutes per side before serving.

PER SERVING Calories: 397 | Fat: 6g | Protein: 15.5g | Sodium: 1,228mg | Fiber: 14g | Carbohydrates: 70g | Sugar: 6g

Vegetarian Cobb Salad

A quick weeknight meal or a fancy side dish—this salad is very versatile. Serve on a large platter for an eye-catching presentation full of bright colors. This salad can easily be made for meat lovers by adding bacon crumbles and shredded chicken.

INGREDIENTS | SERVES 4

4 cups mixed salad greens

1 medium tomato, diced

3 large eggs, hard cooked, peeled, and crumbled

½ medium cucumber, sliced and quartered

⅓ cup diced purple onion

1 large avocado, peeled, pitted, and thinly sliced or cubed

⅓ cup chopped yellow or red bell pepper

⅓ cup wheat or gluten-free croutons

¼ cup shredded Cheddar cheese

Honey Mustard Dressing (see recipe in Chapter 6)

1. In a large salad bowl, place all the ingredients for salad.

2. Dress the salad with the dressing and toss, or serve the dressing on the side.

PER SERVING Calories: 172 | Fat: 7g | Protein: 11g | Sodium: 135mg | Fiber: 1g | Carbohydrates: 19g | Sugar: 2g

Pretty Presentation

Instead of the usual tossed salad, try arranging toppings in rows on a bed of lettuce according to shape or color and drizzle dressing over the prepared salad.

Vegetable Ranch Pizza

This pizza offers satisfaction without the grease and guilt a regular pizza leaves behind! It is packed with vegetables and easily customizable to your liking.

INGREDIENTS | SERVES 4

1 tablespoon cornmeal
1 pizza dough
½ cup sugar-free ranch dressing
¼ cup diced broccoli
¼ cup diced tomato
¼ cup chopped spinach
¼ cup diced bell peppers
¼ cup chopped fresh basil
⅛ cup thinly sliced red onion
1½ cups shredded mozzarella cheese

Pizza Night

You don't have to feel bad about eating pizza if you make it with a whole-grain crust and healthy toppings! Pile the pizza high with vegetables, and for a nondairy option, try almond cheese in mozzarella flavor instead of regular mozzarella cheese.

1. Preheat oven to 400°F.

2. Sprinkle cornmeal over a pizza stone or large baking sheet. Roll out pizza dough and place on the stone or baking sheet. Bake pizza crust for 10 minutes. Remove from the oven.

3. Spread the crust generously with ranch dressing and sprinkle all the vegetables over the dressing. Top with mozzarella cheese.

4. Bake pizza for another 20 minutes or until middle of the pizza is cooked through.

PER SERVING Calories: 284 | Fat: 21g | Protein: 19g | Sodium: 353mg | Fiber: 1g | Carbohydrates: 6g | Sugar: 2g

Spicy Shrimp

This tender and flavorful shrimp dish is the perfect filling for tacos or topping for a salad made with black beans, cheese, and avocado. Hot sauce can be added to increase the heat of this dish.

INGREDIENTS | SERVES 6

½ cup sugar-free marinara sauce

3 teaspoons chili powder, divided

1½ tablespoons grapeseed oil, divided

1 pound uncooked shrimp, peeled and deveined

¼ cup white whole-wheat flour

½ teaspoon sea salt

Any Shrimp Will Do

Feel free to use any type of fresh or frozen shrimp for this recipe. Just watch carefully while cooking, as smaller shrimp will cook faster than larger ones. For a delicious lobster flavor, try wild Argentinian red shrimp.

1. In a large skillet, add marinara sauce, 1½ teaspoons chili powder, and ½ tablespoon oil and stir to combine. Add shrimp to the sauce and cook over medium heat for 5 minutes, flipping halfway through.

2. In a small bowl, combine flour, remaining 1½ teaspoons chili powder, and salt.

3. Heat remaining 1 tablespoon oil over medium-high heat in a separate large skillet.

4. Remove shrimp from the sauce and dredge in flour mixture. With tongs, place each shrimp in the pan of hot oil for 30 seconds per side to create a crispy coating. Test shrimp for doneness and remove from heat. Serve hot.

PER SERVING Calories: 148 | Fat: 5.5g | Protein: 16g | Sodium: 405mg | Fiber: 1.5g | Carbohydrates: 8g | Sugar: 2g

CHAPTER 6

Sauces, Dressings, and Spreads

Basil-Rich Marinara Sauce

This flavorful sauce is a wonderful pizza topper, is delicious over pasta, and is perfect as a dip for breadsticks.

INGREDIENTS | MAKES 3¼ CUPS

2 tablespoons olive oil

½ small onion, peeled and chopped

3 cloves garlic, minced

1 (14.5-ounce) can crushed tomatoes

1 (8-ounce) can tomato sauce

2 tablespoons Italian seasoning mix

2 drops liquid stevia

1 teaspoon sea salt

½ teaspoon ground black pepper

1 tablespoon fresh basil

1 tablespoon dried basil

1 tablespoon chopped fresh parsley

1. Heat oil in a large skillet over medium heat. Sauté onions and garlic until translucent, about 5–8 minutes.

2. Add tomatoes, tomato sauce, Italian seasoning, stevia, salt, and pepper and stir well. Reduce heat to low and simmer for 20 minutes. Add basil and parsley and simmer another 2 minutes. Serve warm.

PER SERVING (½ cup) Calories: 44 | Fat: 4g | Protein: 0g | Sodium: 208mg | Fiber: 0g | Carbohydrates: 2g | Sugar: 0g

Leftover Sauces

As is typical of sauces and dressings, the flavors of this sauce are even more delicious the next day. Refrigerate to use within a week, or freeze for up to 3 months.

Avocado Basil Spread

Creamier than a typical pesto sauce, this spread is rich in flavor and can be used as a dip, as a hamburger condiment, or even mixed into an egg salad sandwich.

INGREDIENTS | MAKES ½ CUP

1 large avocado, pitted and peeled
1 tablespoon lemon juice
½ cup finely chopped fresh basil
½ teaspoon minced garlic
½ teaspoon sea salt
¼ teaspoon ground black pepper

In a small bowl, mash the avocado with a fork. Add remaining ingredients and serve.

PER SERVING (2 tablespoons) Calories: 82 | Fat: 7g | Protein: 1g | Sodium: 299 mg | Fiber: 3.5g | Carbohydrates: 5g | Sugar: .5g

Pasta Sauce

Add an extra 1 tablespoon lemon juice and ¼ cup oil for a delicious pasta sauce that is heavenly served with fresh chopped tomatoes on any of your favorite pasta. Corn or quinoa pastas are great gluten-free choices.

Creamy Chocolate Pudding

Avocado serves as the base of this pudding, creating a thick, smooth texture without any avocado aftertaste. Serve this quick raw treat with whipped cream, berries, or sugar-free chocolate chips if desired.

INGREDIENTS | SERVES 2

1 large avocado, peeled and pitted
½ cup cocoa powder
¼ cup unsweetened almond milk
⅓ cup maple syrup
1½ teaspoons vanilla extract
⅛ teaspoon sea salt

1. In a blender, combine avocado, cocoa, and almond milk and pulse until smooth.

2. Add maple syrup, vanilla, and salt and pulse until creamy.

PER SERVING Calories: 358 | Fat: 18g | Protein: 7g | Sodium: 190mg | Fiber: 14g | Carbohydrates: 59g | Sugar: 35g

Chocolate Peanut Butter Pudding

Here's a truly decadent dessert that is fit for any five-star dining establishment. Treat guests to this pudding served in a dainty dish with a wafer cookie alongside.

INGREDIENTS | SERVES 3

1 large avocado, peeled and pitted
⅓ cup creamy peanut butter
⅓ cup maple syrup
½ cup cocoa powder
¼ cup unsweetened almond milk
1 teaspoon vanilla extract
⅛ teaspoon sea salt

1. In a blender, combine avocado, peanut butter, maple syrup, and cocoa and mix well.

2. Add almond milk, vanilla, and salt and pulse to combine.

3. Refrigerate for 30 minutes before serving. Store leftovers in the refrigerator.

PER SERVING Calories: 417 | Fat: 26g | Protein: 12g | Sodium: 251mg | Fiber: 11g | Carbohydrates: 45g | Sugar: 26g

Milk or Dark?

The intensity of the chocolate flavor in this recipe can be adjusted according to preference. For a strong dark chocolate flavor, leave recipe as is. For a sweeter milk chocolate flavor, add an extra 1 teaspoon maple syrup and 4 drops liquid stevia.

Chocolate Chip Cookie Dough Dip

Layer this thick, creamy dip between graham crackers, enjoy it over ice cream—or simply eat it with a spoon right out of the bowl!

INGREDIENTS | MAKES 2 CUPS

3 tablespoons coconut sugar

½ cup butter, softened

¼ cup powdered honey

2 teaspoons molasses

2 teaspoons unsweetened almond milk

½ teaspoon vanilla extract

¼ teaspoon sea salt

1¼ cups white spelt flour

⅓ cup sugar-free chocolate chips

1. Place coconut sugar in a blender and pulse until it turns to a fine powder.

2. In a medium bowl, cream together coconut sugar, butter, powdered honey, and molasses. Stir in almond milk, vanilla, and salt and mix well.

3. Add flour and stir until combined. Fold in chocolate chips.

PER SERVING (¼ cup) Calories: 278 | Fat: 14g | Protein: 3g | Sodium: 78mg | Fiber: 1g | Carbohydrates: 36g | Sugar: 19g

Cookie Dough Balls

This dough can be rolled into balls and stored in the freezer for a quick cookie dough treat on the go. Store in an airtight container for up to 1 month in the freezer. Frozen dough balls can also be added to ice cream in a blender for cookie dough milkshakes.

Dairy-Free Cinnamon Honey Butter

Healthy coconut butter is made into a sweet spread for breads of all kinds.

INGREDIENTS | MAKES ½ CUP

⅓ cup coconut butter

¼ cup honey

¼ teaspoon cinnamon

In a small bowl, whip coconut butter, honey, and cinnamon together until fluffy. Serve at room temperature.

PER SERVING (1 tablespoon) Calories: 100 | Fat: 8g | Protein: 0g | Sodium: 1mg | Fiber: 0g | Carbohydrates: 9g | Sugar: 9g

Coconut Butter

Coconut butter is even more nutritious than coconut oil because it is made of the raw meat found on the inside of the coconut. In addition to the healthy oils, coconut butter contains fiber, iron, and potassium.

Easy Chocolate Mousse

This quick and easy, completely dairy-free dessert is full of chocolaty coconut flavor. You can store the mousse in individual portions in the refrigerator for a grab-and-go snack.

INGREDIENTS | SERVES 3

1 (13.5-ounce) can full-fat coconut milk, chilled

5 tablespoons cocoa powder

1 teaspoon vanilla extract

⅛ teaspoon sea salt

1 drop liquid stevia

2 tablespoons coconut sugar

1. In a medium bowl, mix all ingredients with a handheld mixer for 2 minutes until mousse is smooth and creamy.

2. Place mousse in the freezer for 15 minutes before serving. Refrigerate leftovers.

PER SERVING Calories: 172 | Fat: 4g | Protein: 5g | Sodium: 301mg | Fiber: 9g | Carbohydrates: 41g | Sugar: 26g

Chocolate Silk Pie

Double this recipe, chill it for 30 minutes, then pour it into a prebaked pie crust to make a delicious creamy chocolate pie.

Yogurt Fruit Dip

A creamy dip to perfectly complement a tray of fresh fruit or to serve with sweet biscuits at a tea party.

INGREDIENTS | SERVES 4

⅔ cup heavy whipping cream
1 teaspoon vanilla
¼ teaspoon liquid stevia
½ cup plain Greek yogurt

1. Whip heavy cream with an electric beater until soft peaks form.

2. Add vanilla and stevia and continue beating. Fold in yogurt. Serve cold.

PER SERVING Calories: 156 | Fat: 16g | Protein: 3g | Sodium: 29mg | Fiber: 0g | Carbohydrates: 2g | Sugar: 1g

Gluten-Free Cinnamon Chips

These sweet chips can be made as crispy or soft as desired. They are a fantastic accompaniment to ice cream, or perfect all by themselves.

INGREDIENTS | SERVES 4

4 rice tortillas
3 tablespoons coconut oil, melted
3 tablespoons maple syrup
2 tablespoons ground cinnamon

Savory Chip Alternative
Try creating savory chips using the same procedure, but with sundried tomato–flavored tortillas, coconut oil, and a sprinkle of garlic and salt.

1. Preheat broiler. Line a baking sheet with parchment paper.

2. Brush tortillas with coconut oil on both sides. Cut each tortilla in half, and then in thirds, creating 6 triangles. Evenly drizzle maple syrup over the slices. Sprinkle with cinnamon.

3. Broil for about 3–4 minutes. Remove from the oven and serve immediately.

PER SERVING Calories: 229 | Fat: 12g | Protein: 3g | Sodium: 192mg | Fiber: 3g | Carbohydrates: 28g | Sugar: 9g

Chocolate Hazelnut Spread

Homemade nut spreads like these are wonderful served between graham crackers, over cupcakes or cookies, over warm pancakes, or stirred into your favorite hot drink.

INGREDIENTS | MAKES 1½ CUPS

2 cups whole roasted hazelnuts

⅓ cup coconut sugar

1½ cups sugar-free chocolate, melted and cooled

2 tablespoons coconut oil

2 teaspoons vanilla extract

¾ teaspoon sea salt

1. In a food processor, add nuts and coconut sugar. Pulse until a crumbly paste forms. Add the melted chocolate, oil, vanilla, and salt. Blend until smooth and creamy. Mixture should be thick but spreadable. Add an extra teaspoon of oil at a time if the mixture is too firm.

2. Serve at warm or at room temperature. Store leftovers covered in the refrigerator.

PER SERVING (2 tablespoons) Calories: 220 | Fat: 20g | Protein: 4g | Sodium: 150mg | Fiber: 3g | Carbohydrates: 22g | Sugar: 7g

Healthy Hazelnuts

Hazelnuts are a great source of protein and unsaturated fats. They are also high in vitamin B_6, which aids the body in creating red blood cells, helps balance hormones, and heavily supports the immune system.

Homemade Coconut Butter

Save money by making coconut butter at home. It's easy to do! It's just as delicious and even less expensive than buying it at the store. You'll love the fantastic flavor it adds to any recipe.

INGREDIENTS | MAKES 1 CUP

3 cups unsweetened shredded coconut

In a food processor or blender, process the coconut for 5 minutes, scraping sides of the bowl as needed, until mixture is smooth and creamy.

PER SERVING (1 tablespoon) Calories: 115 | Fat: 11g | Protein: 1g | Sodium: 6mg | Fiber: 3g | Carbohydrates: 4g | Sugar: 1g

Honey Mustard Dressing

This tangy and sweet dressing is perfect as a salad dressing or brushed over meats and vegetables on the grill.

INGREDIENTS | MAKES ½ CUP

3 tablespoons honey

3 tablespoons mayonnaise

2 tablespoons mustard

1 teaspoon lemon juice

½ teaspoon sea salt

1 teaspoon grapeseed oil

1. In a small mixing bowl, combine the honey, mayonnaise, and mustard. Whisk until smooth.

2. Add remaining ingredients and whisk until incorporated. Add more oil if needed. Serve immediately or refrigerate for up to 3 weeks.

PER SERVING (2 tablespoons) Calories: 138 | Fat: 10g | Protein: 0.5g | Sodium: 443mg | Fiber: 0g | Carbohydrates: 14g | Sugar: 13g

Walnut Fig Dressing

Try this sweet nutty salad dressing over sweet or savory salads. It also doubles as a meat marinade.

INGREDIENTS | MAKES 1 CUP

¾ cup olive oil

¼ cup walnut oil

3 tablespoons balsamic vinegar

1 large dried fig

3 large walnut halves

¼ teaspoon sea salt

⅛ teaspoon garlic powder

1. In a high-powered blender or food processor, combine all ingredients and blend until smooth and creamy.

2. Store covered in the refrigerator for up to 3 weeks.

PER SERVING (2 tablespoons) Calories: 252 | Fat: 27g | Protein: 0g | Sodium: 75mg | Fiber: 0g | Carbohydrates: 2g | Sugar: 1g

Raspberry Vinaigrette

This dressing is a delicious alternative to the sugary-sweet vinaigrettes found in the supermarket. It's full of healthy oils, vinegars, and mineral-packed raw honey.

INGREDIENTS | MAKES 1 CUP

1 tablespoon red wine vinegar

2 tablespoons crushed raspberries

3 tablespoons apple cider vinegar

⅓ cup olive oil

⅓ cup honey

¼ teaspoon guar gum

1. In a small bowl, whisk all ingredients together until thick.

2. Store covered in the refrigerator for up to 3 weeks.

PER SERVING (2 tablespoons) Calories: 125 | Fat: 9g | Protein: 0g | Sodium: 2mg | Fiber: 0g | Carbohydrates: 12g | Sugar: 12g

Guar Gum

Find guar gum in health food stores or online. A very small amount added to salad dressings and sauces thickens them instantly.

Dairy-Free Mayonnaise

This mayonnaise is packed with healthy protein and has a delicious light flavor. Use it as a sandwich spread or in any recipe that calls for mayonnaise.

INGREDIENTS | MAKES 1 CUP

1 cup cashews

¼ cup water

¼ cup olive oil

3 tablespoons lemon juice

2 tablespoons apple cider vinegar

¼ teaspoon sea salt

⅛ teaspoon powdered stevia

1. In a high-powered blender, grind cashews until they form a flour.

2. Add remaining ingredients and blend well.

3. Store covered in the refrigerator for up to 3 weeks.

PER SERVING (1 tablespoon) Calories: 70 | Fat: 6g | Protein: 1g | Sodium: 38mg | Fiber: 0g | Carbohydrates: 2g | Sugar: 0g

Raw Strawberry Jam

This fresh berry spread is a lovely replacement for store-bought jam. Enjoy it on bread, spread over waffles, or in any favorite recipe.

INGREDIENTS | MAKES 1 CUP

¼ cup chia seeds

3 tablespoons water

2 teaspoons vanilla extract

1½ cups sliced strawberries

1 tablespoon honey

1. In a small bowl, combine the chia seeds with the water and vanilla. Set aside for 20 minutes.

2. In a blender, add the chia mixture, strawberries, and honey. Blend until just combined and still a little chunky.

3. Pour into an airtight container and let set for 1 hour in the refrigerator. Jam will keep in the refrigerator for up to 1 week.

PER SERVING (2 tablespoons) Calories: 45 | Fat: 3g | Protein: 1g | Sodium: 0mg | Fiber: 1g | Carbohydrates: 5g | Sugar: 4g

Orange Vinaigrette

A fresh and delightful citrus dressing that enhances both green and fruit salads, this vinaigrette goes especially well with kale.

INGREDIENTS | MAKES ½ CUP

⅓ cup olive oil

2 teaspoons frozen 100% orange juice concentrate

2 teaspoons fresh lemon juice

2 teaspoons maple syrup

½ teaspoon sea salt

½ teaspoon ground black pepper

⅛ teaspoon garlic powder

1. In a small bowl, whisk all ingredients until combined.

2. Pour in a salad dressing container and serve. Refrigerate leftovers for up to 1 week.

PER SERVING (2 tablespoons) Calories: 170 | Fat: 18g | Protein: 0g | Sodium: 296mg | Fiber: 0g | Carbohydrates: 3g | Sugar: 2g

Raw Caramel Sauce

This rich and creamy sauce is perfect for a fondue party. Serve alongside chocolate fondue for a healthier dipping sauce for apples, bananas, graham crackers, marshmallows, brownie bites, and even assorted cheeses in this luscious sauce.

INGREDIENTS | SERVES 2

8 Medjool dates, pitted
1 cup water
1 tablespoon coconut butter
⅓ cup plus 1 tablespoon maple syrup
1½ teaspoons vanilla extract

Dipping Versus Pouring

This sauce is perfect for dipping, but if a thinner sauce is required—for pouring over a cake or ice cream, for example—add more date water until desired consistency is reached.

1. In a small bowl, soak dates in the water for 30 minutes. Transfer dates to a food processor, reserving the soaking liquid.

2. Add coconut butter to the dates and process until a soft paste forms. Add the maple syrup and 2 tablespoons of the date soaking water a little at a time, and process until blended. Add vanilla and pulse until smooth.

PER SERVING Calories: 320 | Fat: 6g | Protein: 1g | Sodium: 7mg | Fiber: 3g | Carbohydrates: 68g | Sugar: 59g

Sweet Poppy Seed Dressing

This dressing would go perfectly on a spinach salad served with berries, almonds, and feta cheese. The poppy seeds provide a lovely crunch.

INGREDIENTS | MAKES 1 CUP

½ cup grapeseed oil
¼ cup honey
¼ cup white vinegar
½ teaspoon sea salt
2 teaspoons poppy seeds

1. In a small bowl, whisk all ingredients together until combined.

2. Serve immediately or refrigerate for up to 3 weeks.

PER SERVING (2 tablespoons) Calories: 154 | Fat: 13g | Protein: 0g | Sodium: 148mg | Fiber: 0g | Carbohydrates: 8g | Sugar: 9g

Strawberry Sauce

This simple syrup is lovely over pancakes and salads and can be drizzled over any baked dish. For a thicker syrup, omit the almond milk.

INGREDIENTS | SERVES 2

⅓ cup frozen strawberries
1 tablespoon almond milk
½ teaspoon vanilla extract
4 drops liquid stevia

In a food processor, combine all ingredients and pulse until a syrup forms. Warm over the stove if a hot syrup is preferred.

PER SERVING Calories: 17 | Fat: 0g | Protein: 0g | Sodium: 5mg | Fiber: 1g | Carbohydrates: 4g | Sugar: 2g

Pumpkin Pie Dip

Creamy and dreamy with a touch of spice, this pumpkin dip is a fabulous spread for just about anything! Enjoy as a dip with cookies or fruit—or crumble graham crackers over it, add whipped cream, and eat it like pudding right out of the bowl.

INGREDIENTS | YIELDS 1¼ CUPS

1 cup plain Greek yogurt
¼ cup pumpkin purée
3 tablespoons maple syrup
1 teaspoon cinnamon
1 teaspoon pumpkin pie spice

In a small mixing bowl, combine all the ingredients until smooth and creamy. Serve.

PER SERVING (¼ cup) Calories: 63 | Fat: 1.5g | Protein: 3g | Sodium: 24mg | Fiber: 0g | Carbohydrates: 11g | Sugar: 9g

Syrup Substitute

Ditch the plain maple syrup on typical breakfast items for this spread instead! Enjoy the flavors of pumpkin and spice on chocolate chip pancakes or French toast.

CHAPTER 7

Drinks

Cucumber Green Drink

This raw drink is a refreshingly simple way to enjoy a daily dose of vitamins C and A and potassium. It energizes the body first thing in the morning or refuels after a workout.

INGREDIENTS | SERVES 1

1 cup spinach

1 large cucumber, peeled and sliced

½ medium frozen banana

Juice of 3 medium oranges

1 teaspoon vanilla extract

½ cup ice

Combine all ingredients in a blender and blend until smooth. Serve immediately.

PER SERVING Calories: 302 | Fat: 1g | Protein: 7g | Sodium: 31mg | Fiber: 13g | Carbohydrates: 72g | Sugar: 50g

Curious Cucumber Tips

Cucumbers are 95 percent water and still contain almost all the vitamins the body needs in a day. Cucumber skins provide great relief for a sunburn, and placing a slice of cucumber against the roof of the mouth will help with bad breath.

Easy Apple Cider

Simmering cider makes your whole house smell festive! Multiply this recipe to share with friends at a holiday party.

INGREDIENTS | SERVES 2

2 cups 100% apple juice

1 cinnamon stick

⅛ teaspoon pumpkin pie spice mix

Combine all ingredients in a saucepan over low heat. Cover and simmer 1 hour. Serve hot.

PER SERVING Calories: 149 | Fat: 0g | Protein: 0g | Sodium: 11mg | Fiber: 8g | Carbohydrates: 39g | Sugar: 24g

Green Guzzler

This monster green drink contains super greens that give an energy boost. A serving of bok choy contains 100 percent of the body's daily requirement of vitamin C and almost all of the vitamin A requirement. A hint of cinnamon in this drink helps curb sugar cravings while almond milk makes it very filling.

INGREDIENTS | SERVES 2

1½ cups chopped bok choy
1 cup defrosted frozen spinach
1½ large avocados, peeled and pitted
1 medium frozen banana
⅓ cup frozen blueberries
¼ teaspoon cinnamon
1 teaspoon vanilla extract
Juice of 1 medium lime
⅓ cup unsweetened almond milk
5 drops liquid stevia

Combine all ingredients in a blender and blend until smooth. Serve immediately.

PER SERVING Calories: 134 | Fat: 2g | Protein: 6g | Sodium: 114mg | Fiber: 6g | Carbohydrates: 28g | Sugar: 13g

Lucky Green Smoothie

This creamy and refreshing smoothie is a tasty way to drink a whole green salad. The healthy fats in the avocado allow the body to absorb all the nutrients found in kale and spinach. If you are out of avocado, coconut oil could be added in for similar benefits.

INGREDIENTS | SERVES 2

1 cup ice
1 cup chopped spinach
1 cup chopped kale
1 medium avocado, peeled and pitted
1¼ cups fresh orange juice
½ medium green apple
1 cup frozen mango
2 tablespoons maple syrup
½ teaspoon vanilla extract
¼ cup water

Combine all ingredients in a blender and blend until smooth. Serve immediately.

PER SERVING Calories: 379 | Fat: 16g | Protein: 5g | Sodium: 39mg | Fiber: 10g | Carbohydrates: 61g | Sugar: 42g

Holiday Eggnog

Spicy and sweet, thick and creamy, this holiday beverage is free of the typical sugar, high-fructose corn syrup, and artificial flavorings of store-bought eggnogs.

INGREDIENTS | SERVES 12

2½ cups xylitol

⅓ cup water

12 large eggs

1½ quarts milk

1 tablespoon vanilla extract

1 pint heavy cream, whipped

½ teaspoon nutmeg

Egg Safety

Raw eggs are common in beverages like homemade eggnog. However, if this doesn't sit well with you, try pasteurized eggs or replace the milk in this recipe with rum. Always use fresh eggs, organic and locally sourced if possible.

1. In a small saucepan over low heat, combine xylitol and water and stir until sweetener is dissolved.

2. In a large bowl, beat eggs with a hand mixer until light and fluffy. Add milk, vanilla, and xylitol mixture and continue mixing until blended.

3. Chill the mixture for 3 hours. Fold in the whipped cream and chill for another hour.

4. Dust with nutmeg and serve.

PER SERVING Calories: 387.5 | Fat: 24g | Protein: 11g | Sodium: 138mg | Fiber: 0g | Carbohydrates: 48g | Sugar: 7g

Sparkling Grape Juice

This is the perfect nonalcoholic drink for a romantic candlelit dinner. You can also make a large batch to serve in a clear beverage dispenser at a party.

INGREDIENTS | SERVES 2

2 cups 100% grape juice
1 cup sparkling water
¼ cup blueberries
1 large kiwi, peeled and sliced

In a small pitcher, mix together juice and sparkling water. Add blueberries and kiwi slices and refrigerate for 2 hours before serving. Serve within 24 hours.

PER SERVING Calories: 190 | Fat: 0g | Protein: 1.5g | Sodium: 19mg | Fiber: 2g | Carbohydrates: 47g | Sugar: 38g

Sparkling Pomegranate Lime Juice

This detoxifying juice is packed with antioxidants and vitamin C! The sparkling aspect makes it a fun and healthy alternative to soda at a party.

INGREDIENTS | SERVES 4

3 cups ice
Juice of ½ small lemon
Juice of 4 small limes
1½ cups 100% pomegranate juice
½ teaspoon liquid stevia
1 cup sparkling water

1. Combine ice, lemon juice, lime juice, pomegranate juice, and stevia in a blender and blend until smooth.

2. Add sparkling water and pulse once to incorporate. Serve immediately.

PER SERVING Calories: 57 | Fat: 0g | Protein: 1g | Sodium: 4mg | Fiber: 2g | Carbohydrates: 16g | Sugar: 9.5g

Sweet Green Juice

A large, freshly juiced drink is a great way to start the day—and saves at least $5.00 when it's homemade rather than picked up at the local juice bar.

INGREDIENTS | SERVES 1

1 bunch kale

1 large cucumber

4 green apples

3 kiwis

6 celery sticks

Process all ingredients through a juicer and stir to mix. Serve immediately.

PER SERVING Calories: 665 | Fat: 4g | Protein: 16g | Sodium: 323mg | Fiber: 27g | Carbohydrates: 161g | Sugar: 74g

Juice Benefits

Juicing a fruit (or vegetable) rather than eating it whole or putting it in a smoothie makes the fruit's vitamins and minerals extremely accessible to the body. The juice form doesn't tax the digestive system, and all of the food's nutrients remain intact.

Pumpkin Juice

Pumpkin juice is fresh, flavorful, and packed with vitamins and nutrients. Pumpkins are high in potassium and magnesium, which support immune function.

INGREDIENTS | SERVES 6

5 cups 100% apple juice

2 teaspoons cinnamon

1 teaspoon pumpkin pie spice

¼ teaspoon cloves

⅓ cup honey

1 tablespoon molasses

1 cup canned pumpkin

2 cups sparkling water, chilled

1. In a large saucepan, heat apple juice over medium-low heat. Stir in cinnamon, pumpkin pie spice, cloves, honey, and molasses. Simmer for 10 minutes. Let juice cool.

2. Whisk canned pumpkin and sparkling water into juice and pour into a large pitcher. Refrigerate for 2 hours before serving over ice.

PER SERVING Calories: 178.5 | Fat: 0g | Protein: 0g | Sodium: 15mg | Fiber: 2g | Carbohydrates: 45g | Sugar: 39g

Strawberry Peach Smoothie

A rainbow of colorful fruit plus healthy spinach combine for ultimate nutrition and refreshing satisfaction.

INGREDIENTS | SERVES 2

⅔ cup ice

1½ cups frozen sliced peaches

1 small frozen banana

1 cup sliced frozen strawberries

⅓ cup plain low-fat yogurt

2 tablespoons honey

2 tablespoons water

¼ cup spinach

Combine all ingredients in a blender and blend until smooth. Serve immediately.

PER SERVING Calories: 220 | Fat: 1g | Protein: 4g | Sodium: 35.5mg | Fiber: 5g | Carbohydrates: 53g | Sugar: 41g

Freezer Stash

Freeze summer produce to save money and have delicious fruits and vegetables on hand year-round. Smoothies are even easier to make when fruits are already washed, peeled, chopped, and frozen.

Raspberry Peach Water

An elegant and refreshing party beverage, this delicately flavored water is beautiful in color and presentation. Add ½ teaspoon liquid stevia for more sweetness if desired.

INGREDIENTS | SERVES 4

32 ounces water

¾ cup raspberries

1 large peach, peeled and thinly sliced

In a large pitcher, combine water, raspberries, and peach slices. Refrigerate for at least 2 hours to allow fruit to flavor water. Serve over ice.

PER SERVING Calories: 29 | Fat: 0g | Protein: 0g | Sodium: 7mg | Fiber: 2g | Carbohydrates: 7g | Sugar: 5g

Raspberry Mint Smoothie

While this might look like a regular green smoothie, the taste is similar to a gourmet raspberry lemonade. Mint makes this treat extremely refreshing and cleansing!

INGREDIENTS | SERVES 1

½ cup frozen chopped broccoli

½ cup chopped spinach

½ cup frozen raspberries

½ teaspoon lemon juice

½ cup ice

½ cup water

6 drops liquid stevia

4 mint leaves

Combine all ingredients in a blender and blend until smooth. Serve immediately.

PER SERVING Calories: 217 | Fat: 2g | Protein: 7g | Sodium: 115mg | Fiber: 14g | Carbohydrates: 48g | Sugar: 28g

Liquid Stevia Replacement

Three drops of liquid stevia adds about the same sweetness to a recipe as 1 teaspoon of sugar. For this recipe, that means adding 2 teaspoons of maple syrup or honey if you choose not to use stevia.

Strawberry Lemonade

This recipe boasts all the flavor of a favorite summertime beverage without the unnecessary calories from high quantities of refined sugar.

INGREDIENTS | SERVES 2

3 cups cold water

4 tablespoons lemon juice

6 whole strawberries

3 tablespoons maple syrup

1 cup ice cubes

1. In a blender pulse the water, lemon juice, 4 strawberries, and maple syrup until well blended. Chill for several hours for flavors to blend.

2. Slice remaining strawberries. Pour lemonade into glasses, add ice, and garnish with additional strawberry slices.

PER SERVING Calories: 96 | Fat: 0g | Protein: 0g | Sodium: 20mg | Fiber: .5g | Carbohydrates: 25g | Sugar: 20g

Mint Lemonade

This refreshing drink doesn't need unnecessary sugars to be satisfyingly delicious.

INGREDIENTS | SERVES 6

4½ cups water, divided
½ cup xylitol
Juice of 8 lemons
¼ cup fresh mint leaves

1. In a small saucepan on the stove, heat ½ cup of water and xylitol over low heat until xylitol has dissolved. Allow to cool and pour into a pitcher.

2. Add the lemon juice to the xylitol water. Add the remaining 4 cups of water and the mint leaves. Stir to mix, then refrigerate until chilled.

3. Serve over ice and with extra mint leaves for garnish, if desired.

PER SERVING Calories: 64 | Fat: 0g | Protein: 0g | Sodium: 8mg | Fiber: 2g | Carbohydrates: 23.5g | Sugar: 2g

Beet It Smoothie

This hot-pink drink makes a beautiful morning treat! Beets give this smoothie a unique sweet flavor and a nice dose of vitamins A, B, and C.

INGREDIENTS | SERVES 2

16 ounces cold water
½ cup chopped frozen beets
1 large frozen banana
6 strawberries
1 large apple, peeled, cored, and sliced
2 Medjool dates, pitted
1 tablespoon maple syrup

In a blender, combine the ingredients and blend on high until smooth. Enjoy immediately.

PER SERVING Calories: 188 | Fat: 0g | Protein: 2g | Sodium: 35mg | Fiber: 5.5g | Carbohydrates: 48g | Sugar: 34.5g

Carrot Mango Smoothie

Brightly colored orange drinks are usually artificially colored and flavored.
This sweet drink is all natural, refreshing, and full of beta carotene.

INGREDIENTS | SERVES 1

8 ounces unsweetened coconut milk

3 medium carrots

1 cup frozen mango chunks

1 tablespoon fresh orange juice

Place all ingredients into a blender and blend on high until smooth and frothy.

PER SERVING Calories: 217 | Fat: 4g | Protein: 5g | Sodium: 250mg | Fiber: 10g | Carbohydrates: 45g | Sugar: 32g

High-Speed Blenders

This smoothie can be made with any blender, but a high-powered blender will pulverize the carrots completely and turn this into a frothy, slightly thick drink.

"I Can't Believe It's a Green Smoothie" Smoothie

Vitamin-packed spinach is completely hidden by the decadent
flavor trio of chocolate, peanut butter, and banana.

INGREDIENTS | SERVES 1

8 ounces unsweetened coconut milk

½ cup frozen spinach

2 tablespoons cocoa powder

1 frozen medium banana

2 tablespoons natural peanut butter

2 tablespoons maple syrup

¼ teaspoon vanilla extract

1 teaspoon chia seeds

10 ice cubes

In a blender, combine all ingredients and blend until smooth. Enjoy immediately.

PER SERVING Calories: 575 | Fat: 27g | Protein: 19g | Sodium: 200mg | Fiber: 11g | Carbohydrates: 77g | Sugar: 42g

Chocolate Fix

Cocoa powder is full of fiber, iron, and magnesium. It is also high in phenethylamine, which elevates the mood. Purchasing raw cocoa powder is best because it is highest in antioxidants.

CHAPTER 8

Cakes and Cupcakes

Cake Pop Kabobs

These kabobs are the perfect way to showcase the well-loved cake pop! These require a cake pop pan and skewers. A cake pop maker can also be used.

INGREDIENTS | SERVES 10

½ cup plus 1 tablespoon whole-wheat flour

⅛ teaspoon baking soda

1 teaspoon baking powder

½ cup cocoa powder

3 tablespoons butter, softened

1⅓ cups coconut sugar

1 large egg

1 teaspoon vanilla extract

½ cup 2% milk

1 cup sugar-free chocolate chips or chunks, melted

1 medium banana, peeled and sliced

1 cup strawberry halves

½ cup pineapple chunks

Mix and Match

Cake pops have become quite popular in the last few years, and nothing makes these little cakes more fun than skewering them between assorted fruits! Make these skewers with any of your favorite fruits—try melon balls, orange sections, or slices of kiwi.

1. Preheat oven to 350°F. Lightly spray a cake pop pan with cooking spray. Alternatively, preheat a cake pop maker.

2. In a large mixing bowl, sift together the flour, baking soda, baking powder, and cocoa powder.

3. In another large bowl, cream together butter and coconut sugar until light and fluffy. Beat in egg, vanilla, and milk. Add the butter mixture to the dry mixture.

4. Pour cake batter into the bottom cake pop pan. Place top pan over the bottom pan and bake for 8–10 minutes. Remove pops from pan and cool on a wire rack.

5. Pour melted chocolate over the cake pops and allow to set. Assemble cake pops on skewers by sliding the skewer through the middle of the cake, alternating with bananas, strawberries, and pineapples.

PER SERVING Calories: 256 | Fat: 5g | Protein: 4g | Sodium: 88g | Fiber: 4g | Carbohydrates: 53g | Sugar: 32g

Carrot Cake

This cake is filled to the brim with healthy carrots and nuts. A secret ingredient, pineapple, gives unbeatable sweetness and texture. Be sure to finish this confection with Classic Cream Cheese Frosting.

INGREDIENTS | SERVES 12

2 cups coconut sugar

1½ cups grapeseed oil

4 large eggs

2 teaspoons cinnamon

1 teaspoon sea salt

2 teaspoons baking soda

2 cups white spelt flour

2½ cups grated carrot

½ cup chopped pineapple

½ cup chopped walnuts or pecans

Classic Cream Cheese Frosting (see recipe in Chapter 12)

The Zest of Life
Add 2 teaspoons of fresh orange zest to the batter and frosting for an unbeatable orange citrus flavor!

1. Preheat oven to 350°F. Lightly spray three 8" cake pans with oil and set aside.

2. Mix together the coconut sugar, oil, and eggs in a large bowl. Add the cinnamon, salt, baking soda, and spelt flour and mix until combined. Fold in the carrots, pineapple, and nuts.

3. Pour batter into prepared pans and bake for 25–35 minutes. Remove cakes from pans and cool completely on a wire rack. Fill and frost cakes with Classic Cream Cheese Frosting.

PER SERVING Calories: 633 | Fat: 37g | Protein: 5g | Sodium: 506mg | Fiber: 2g | Carbohydrates: 73g | Sugar: 53g

Chocolate Cake Waffles

Turn ordinary waffles into a dessert phenomenon! Pile them high with fresh berries for breakfast or serve with a big scoop of ice cream and all the fixings for dessert.

INGREDIENTS | SERVES 6

1 cup all-purpose flour
¼ cup cocoa powder
½ teaspoon baking powder
½ teaspoon baking soda
¼ teaspoon sea salt
⅛ teaspoon cinnamon
⅓ tablespoon honey
1 cup 2% milk
⅓ cup grapeseed oil
1 large egg
1½ teaspoons vanilla extract
½ cup sugar-free chocolate chips
or chunks

Freezer Ready!

These Chocolate Cake Waffles will keep well in the freezer for up to 2 weeks for a quick and easy dessert! Freeze in airtight containers and thaw for 1 hour before serving.

1. In a small mixing bowl, whisk together the flour, cocoa, baking powder, baking soda, salt, and cinnamon.

2. In a separate bowl, combine honey, milk, oil, egg, and vanilla. Stir in the flour mixture until just combined. Fold in chocolate chips. Be sure not to overmix the batter.

3. Pour ¼ cup of batter in a preheated waffle iron. Cook waffle according to manufacturer's instructions. Repeat with remaining batter.

PER SERVING Calories: 331 | Fat: 20g | Protein: 6g | Sodium: 274.5mg | Fiber: 3g | Carbohydrates: 40g | Sugar: 13g

Vegan Chocolate Cupcakes

Put vegan baking to the test and delight in these incredibly moist and flavorful cupcakes completely free of eggs or milk. They have an extra-full chocolate flavor when frosted with Vegan Chocolate Buttercream (see recipe in Chapter 12).

INGREDIENTS | SERVES 12

1 cup spelt flour

¾ cup plus 2 tablespoons cocoa powder

2 teaspoons baking powder

¼ teaspoon baking soda

¼ teaspoon sea salt

3 tablespoons Earth Balance Soy Free Buttery Sticks, softened

¼ cup unsweetened applesauce

1¼ cups coconut sugar

2 teaspoons vanilla extract

1 cup unsweetened almond milk

For Non-Vegans

For a non-vegan version, replace the applesauce with 2 eggs and the almond milk with 2% milk. Use regular butter instead of Earth Balance Soy Free Buttery Sticks.

1. Line a cupcake pan with cupcake liners. Preheat the oven to 350°F.

2. In a medium mixing bowl, sift together flour, cocoa, baking powder, baking soda, and salt. Set aside.

3. In a large bowl, mix Earth Balance Soy Free Buttery Sticks, applesauce, coconut sugar, and vanilla extract until well combined. Add the flour mixture alternately with the almond milk and mix to combine.

4. Fill cupcake liners a little more than ¾ full. Bake 12–14 minutes. Remove from pan and cool on a wire rack. Store cupcakes in an airtight container.

PER SERVING Calories: 180 | Fat: 4g | Protein: 3g | Sodium: 175mg | Fiber: 2.5g | Carbohydrates: 36g | Sugar: 24g

Berry Spring Crepe Cake

Unlike most crepe recipes, these crepes aren't rolled, but rather stacked on top of each other with the filling layered throughout! Bursting with fruit in every layer, this cake makes a stunning statement for Sunday brunch or a holiday breakfast.

INGREDIENTS | SERVES 8

2 cups unsweetened almond milk

3 large eggs

2 tablespoons honey

3 tablespoons grapeseed oil

1 teaspoon sea salt

1 teaspoon vanilla extract, divided

2 cups plus 2 tablespoons white spelt flour, divided

1 cup plain Greek yogurt

¾ cup powdered xylitol

½ cup sliced strawberries

½ cup blueberries

½ cup raspberries

Dairy-Free Substitutions

Dairy-free eaters can enjoy this cake with full-fat canned coconut cream in place of the Greek yogurt. Use the white portion of the cream and whip with an additional ⅓ cup flour with ¼ teaspoon liquid stevia for a sweet, firm cream. Alternately, use a thick nondairy yogurt.

1. In a small bowl, combine the almond milk, eggs, honey, oil, salt, and ½ teaspoon vanilla. Whisk in 1¾ cups flour until combined.

2. Heat a medium nonstick skillet or griddle over medium heat. Pour about 3 tablespoons of the batter onto the hot pan and immediately lift the pan off the heat and swirl the pan to make the batter form a thin circle. Flip the crepe when the edges begin to lift and darken. Remove from pan and cool on a wire rack. Repeat with remaining batter.

3. Refrigerate crepes, uncovered, for 30 minutes.

4. In a small bowl, combine yogurt, xylitol, 6 tablespoons flour, and ½ teaspoon vanilla.

5. Place two crepes on the bottom of a serving dish or plate. Top with 2 tablespoons of yogurt cream. Place two more crepes over the cream. Top crepes with 2 tablespoons of cream and layer berries over cream. Repeat with remaining ingredients, ending with a dollop of cream and berries. Refrigerate cake, uncovered, for at least 2 hours or until set. When ready to serve, slice with a sharp knife.

PER SERVING Calories: 319 | Fat: 9g | Protein: 9g | Sodium: 367mg | Fiber: 2g | Carbohydrates: 56g | Sugar: 10g

Coffee Cake

Traditional coffee cake recipes are loaded with refined sugar. This cake has all the cinnamon and sugar that streusel coffee cake enthusiasts love but is made instead with all-natural sweeteners.

INGREDIENTS | SERVES 12

3⅓ cups white whole-wheat flour, divided

4 teaspoons baking powder

¾ teaspoon sea salt

1½ cups powdered honey

1¾ cups coconut sugar, divided

1½ cups softened butter, divided

¾ cup 2% milk

½ cup sour cream

1 teaspoon vanilla extract

3 large egg whites, beaten until stiff

2 tablespoons cinnamon

2 tablespoons xylitol

⅔ cup pecans, finely chopped

⅓ cup oats

1. Preheat oven to 350°F. Lightly butter a 9" × 13" pan.

2. In a small bowl, sift together 2⅔ cups flour, baking powder, and salt. Set aside.

3. In a mixing bowl, beat together powdered honey, ½ cup coconut sugar, and ¾ cup butter. Add milk, sour cream, and vanilla extract to the butter and sugar mixture.

4. Stir flour mixture into butter mixture and mix until just combined.

5. In a separate small bowl, beat the egg whites until stiff. Fold egg whites into the batter. Pour batter into prepared pan.

6. In a small bowl, mix together ¾ cup butter, ⅔ cup flour, 1¼ cups coconut sugar, cinnamon, xylitol, pecans, and oats until crumbly. Sprinkle over coffee cake and bake for 35 minutes, or until a toothpick inserted in the center comes out clean.

PER SERVING Calories: 624.5 | Fat: 30.5g | Protein: 7g | Sodium: 351mg | Fiber: 5.5g | Carbohydrates: 88g | Sugar: 60g

Classic Chocolate Cupcakes

These basic chocolate cupcakes are the perfect go-to recipe for birthdays, parties, and holiday gatherings. Store them in an airtight container and they will last for up to 3 days.

INGREDIENTS | SERVES 16

1 cup plus 2 teaspoons white whole-wheat flour

2 teaspoons baking powder

¼ teaspoon baking soda

1 cup cocoa powder

¼ teaspoon sea salt

¼ cup butter, softened

¼ cup unsweetened applesauce

1¾ cups coconut sugar

2 teaspoons vanilla extract

2 large eggs

1 cup unsweetened almond milk

Versatility

This basic cupcake recipe is delicious for any kind of frosting recipe or ganache. This cake is also firm enough to add a cream or chocolate filling in the inner center of the cupcake: Fill a pastry bag with your filling of choice, stick the tip in the center of the cupcake, and fill with about 2 teaspoons of filling.

1. Preheat oven to 350°F. Line a cupcake pan with cupcake liners and spray liners with cooking spray.

2. In a medium bowl, sift together the flour, baking powder, baking soda, cocoa, and salt. Set aside.

3. In a large bowl, cream together butter, applesauce, and coconut sugar until light and fluffy. Add the vanilla and eggs, one at a time, beating well with each addition.

4. Alternately add the flour mixture and the almond milk to the butter mixture, beating until combined.

5. Fill the cupcake liners ¾ full. Bake for 13–15 minutes. Remove from pan and cool on a wire rack.

PER SERVING Calories: 175 | Fat: 5g | Protein: 3g | Sodium: 143mg | Fiber: 3g | Carbohydrates: 34g | Sugar: 24.5g

Gluten-Free Chocolate Cupcakes

These mouthwatering gluten-free chocolate cupcakes are just as dense, moist, and chocolaty as traditional cupcake recipes! Top with Chocolate Buttercream Frosting (see recipe in Chapter 12) for chocolate flavor to the max!

INGREDIENTS | SERVES 12

1 cup white rice flour
½ teaspoon xanthan gum
¾ cup cocoa powder
2¼ teaspoons baking powder
¼ teaspoon baking soda
¼ teaspoon sea salt
1¼ cups coconut sugar
3 tablespoons butter, softened
1 large egg
1 cup full-fat coconut milk
2 teaspoons vanilla extract

Gluten Substitute

Xanthan gum is a common gluten substitute in gluten-free baking. It's made from fermenting corn sugar into a gooey substance that can be used from baking to frozen treats like ice cream. Xanthan gum acts like a food thickener and emulsifier, so it is used as a food additive but can also be found in products like cosmetics. Xanthan gum can be purchased online or at any natural food store.

1. Preheat the oven to 350°F. Line cupcake pan with cupcake liners and spray liners with cooking spray.

2. In a medium bowl, sift together flour, xanthan gum, cocoa, baking powder, baking soda, salt, and coconut sugar. Set aside.

3. In a large bowl, mix butter, egg, coconut milk, and vanilla extract. Add the flour mixture to the bowl and stir to combine.

4. Fill prepared cupcake liners ¾ full. Bake for 14–16 minutes. Remove from pan and cool on a wire rack.

PER SERVING Calories: 219 | Fat: 8g | Protein: 3g | Sodium: 184mg | Fiber: 2g | Carbohydrates: 37g | Sugar: 22g

Lemon Mint Yogurt Cake

In the heat of summer, this lemon mint yogurt cake is sure to refresh! Yogurt keeps the cake moist without unnecessary oils. Fresh mint infuses this citrus cake for exhilarating flavor.

INGREDIENTS | SERVES 8

⅓ cup fresh mint leaves, lightly packed

⅓ cup plus 1 tablespoon grapeseed oil

¼ cup fresh lemon juice

½ cup plain low-fat yogurt

¾ cup honey

2 tablespoons lemon zest

½ teaspoon sea salt

1 teaspoon baking powder

1 teaspoon baking soda

1 cup white whole-wheat flour

½ cup white spelt flour

Baking Fresh Mint

Fresh mint bakes seamlessly into this cake if blended well with oil.

1. Preheat the oven to 350°F. Spray a 9" × 9" baking dish with cooking spray.

2. In a food processor, process mint leaves, oil, and lemon juice together until smooth.

3. In a small mixing bowl, combine mint mixture, yogurt, honey, and lemon zest. Add the salt, baking powder, and baking soda to the mixture. At this time, the batter will fizz and increase in volume.

4. Add the flours, ½ cup at a time, and mix until just combined. Pour the mixture into prepared pan and bake for 35–40 minutes or until a toothpick inserted in the center comes out clean.

5. Remove from pan and cool on a wire rack. Garnish with fresh mint leaves and serve warm or at room temperature. Store leftovers covered at room temperature.

PER SERVING Calories: 285 | Fat: 11g | Protein: 4g | Sodium: 381mg | Fiber: 2g | Carbohydrates: 45g | Sugar: 27.5g

Mexican Chocolate Ice Cream (Chapter 13)

Sour Cream Doughnuts (Chapter 2)

Chocolate Cream Sandwich Cookies (Chapter 10)

Silky Chocolate Cups (Chapter 15)

Vegan Vanilla Bean Ice Cream (Chapter 13)

Raspberry Mint Smoothie (Chapter 7)

Pumpkin Pie Dip (Chapter 6)

Vegan Lemon Bars (Chapter 11)

Tomato and Goat Cheese Pastries (Chapter 4)

Beet It Smoothie (Chapter 7)

Chia Apple Spice Pudding (Chapter 2)

Healthy Caramel Popcorn (Chapter 15)

Frozen S'mores (Chapter 13)

Lentil Lemon Cakes (Chapter 5)

Blueberry Blintzes (Chapter 2)

Chocolate Buttercream Frosting (Chapter 12)

Hazelnut Chocolate Fudge Truffles (Chapter 9)

Honey Mustard Dressing (Chapter 6)

Bakery-Style Chocolate Chip Cookies (Chapter 10)

Honey Graham Crackers (Chapter 15)

Strawberry Kale Salad (Chapter 4)

Oatmeal Cream Pies (Chapter 10)

Yogurt Fruit Dip (Chapter 6)

Sunflower Butter Cups (Chapter 9)

Oatmeal Cake

This hearty cake has a thick, dense bite with an unmistakable sweet caramel flavor from the coconut sugar. Top the cake with German Chocolate Frosting or Coconut Pecan Frosting (see recipes in Chapter 12).

INGREDIENTS | SERVES 15

1 cup rolled oats
½ cup salted butter
1¼ cups boiling water
2 cups coconut sugar
1 teaspoon baking soda
2 large eggs
½ teaspoon cinnamon
1 teaspoon vanilla extract
1⅓ cups spelt flour

1. Place oats and butter in a medium bowl and pour boiling water over them. Set aside for 20 minutes.

2. Preheat the oven to 350°F. Butter a 9" × 13" baking dish. In a large mixing bowl, stir together sugar, baking soda, and eggs. Stir in oatmeal mixture and remaining ingredients.

3. Pour batter into prepared pan. Bake for 25–30 minutes. Allow to cool for 10 minutes before cutting.

PER SERVING Calories: 237 | Fat: 7g | Protein: 3g | Sodium: 146mg | Fiber: 0g | Carbohydrates: 41g | Sugar: 29g

Peach Berry Shortcakes

These individual shortcakes are loaded with peaches, berries, and cream for a delightful summer treat. This recipe can also be doubled or tripled to serve as the perfect dish for tea parties or brunches. Use whatever fresh berries you can find.

INGREDIENTS | SERVES 6

2 cups white spelt flour

1 tablespoon baking powder

1 teaspoon sea salt

¾ cup cold butter, diced

3 large eggs, beaten, divided

1 tablespoon honey

½ cup heavy cream, chilled

2 tablespoons 2% milk

Homemade Whipped Cream (see recipe in Chapter 12)

2 large ripe peaches

½ cup blackberries

½ cup raspberries

½ teaspoon orange zest

Fresh Is Best!

Peaches, berries, and cream enhance the flavor and presentation of these healthy shortcakes. Always use fresh, seasonal fruits and be sure the heavy cream is chilled and fresh to create beautiful soft peaks.

1. Preheat the oven to 400°F. Line a baking sheet with parchment paper.

2. Combine flour, baking powder, and salt in the bowl of an electric mixer and stir in diced butter. Add in 2 eggs, honey, heavy cream, and milk and mix until just blended. Dough will be sticky.

3. On a well-floured surface, press dough until it's ¾" thick and use a cookie cutter to cut out biscuits. Lay on baking sheet 2" apart and brush with remaining egg.

4. Bake for 20–25 minutes. Remove from baking sheet and cool on a wire rack.

5. To assemble, cut the shortcakes in half, pile on whipped cream, and top with peaches, blackberries, and raspberries. Garnish with orange zest.

PER SERVING Calories: 473 | Fat: 46g | Protein: 6g | Sodium: 699mg | Fiber: 2g | Carbohydrates: 14g | Sugar: 9g

Pumpkin Chocolate Chip Cake

This recipe is loaded with chocolate chips and baked in a large 9" × 13" pan to feed a crowd. Fall spices complement the chocolate and pumpkin. Top with cream cheese or chocolate frosting for added sweetness if you wish.

INGREDIENTS | SERVES 15

1 cup butter, softened

1 (15-ounce) can pumpkin

1½ cups coconut sugar

4 extra large eggs, at room temperature

½ tablespoon vanilla extract

1 teaspoon baking soda

½ teaspoon baking powder

1 teaspoon sea salt

1 teaspoon cinnamon

½ teaspoon pumpkin pie spice

2½ cups spelt flour

1½ cups chopped sugar-free chocolate

1. Preheat the oven to 350°F. Grease a glass 9" × 13" baking dish.

2. In a large mixing bowl using an electric mixer fitted with a paddle attachment, cream together the butter, pumpkin, and sugar. Mix in eggs and vanilla, then add remaining ingredients and beat well.

3. Pour batter evenly into baking dish. Bake for 30–35 minutes or until a toothpick inserted in the center comes out clean.

PER SERVING Calories: 417 | Fat: 20g | Protein: 5.5g | Sodium: 289mg | Fiber: 3g | Carbohydrates: 55g | Sugar: 34g

Spice It Up

This cake contains the perfect spices for fall! Feel free to play around with the spices—add ginger or additional pumpkin pie spice or nutmeg for even more flavor.

Chocolate Raspberry Cake Roll

Also known as a "Log Cake," this chocolate cake with raspberry and cream filling is a classic favorite! Try substituting the raspberries with fresh oranges for a wintery treat.

INGREDIENTS | SERVES 12

5 large eggs, separated

1 cup coconut sugar

¼ cup white spelt flour

½ teaspoon sea salt

3 tablespoons cocoa powder

2 teaspoons vanilla extract, divided

1 pint heavy cream, chilled

3 drops liquid stevia

¾ cup fresh or frozen raspberries, washed and patted dry

Chocolate Buttercream Frosting (see recipe in Chapter 12)

Frozen Fruit

Using frozen fruit here allows this cake to be made at any time, regardless of the season. If using frozen fruit, pat fruit as dry as possible so the cream does not become diluted.

1. Preheat oven to 375°F. Line a jellyroll pan with parchment paper.

2. In a medium bowl, beat egg whites with a hand mixer until stiff.

3. In a separate bowl, beat the egg yolks until thick. Sift sugar, flour, salt, and cocoa into the yolks, add 1 teaspoon vanilla, and mix well.

4. Fold cocoa mixture into beaten egg whites. Spread batter evenly onto pan with a spatula. Bake for 15 minutes, then cool in pan on a rack.

5. Meanwhile, in a medium bowl, whip the heavy cream with 1 teaspoon vanilla and stevia until soft peaks form. Set aside.

6. Gently lift cooled cake from pan and peel the parchment paper off the underside of the cake. Lay flat on the pan or place on a serving platter. Spread whipped cream in a layer over the cake and dot with raspberries. Beginning with a short end of the cake, gently roll the cake up to form a large log.

7. Frost the top and sides of the log with Chocolate Buttercream Frosting.

PER SERVING Calories: 377 | Fat: 22g | Protein: 4g | Sodium: 198mg | Fiber: 1g | Carbohydrates: 43g | Sugar: 37g

Rich Chocolate Cake

If you're looking for the perfect birthday or holiday cake, this recipe is a crowd pleaser. This is also the cake to make when you are out of eggs!

INGREDIENTS | SERVES 10

2½ cups white spelt flour

1¾ cups coconut sugar

⅓ cup dark cocoa powder

1 teaspoon baking powder

1 teaspoon baking soda

1 teaspoon sea salt

1¾ cups cold water

2½ teaspoons vanilla extract

⅔ cup melted butter

2 tablespoons apple cider vinegar

1. Preheat oven to 350°F. Line two 9" cake pans with parchment paper and spray with cooking spray.

2. In a large bowl, combine the flour, sugar, cocoa, baking powder, baking soda, and salt until thoroughly combined. Add water, vanilla, butter, and vinegar. Stir until just combined.

3. Pour into prepared pan and bake for 25–30 minutes, until a toothpick inserted in center comes out clean. Cool for 30 minutes in the pans before removing.

PER SERVING Calories: 379 | Fat: 13g | Protein: 4g | Sodium: 425.5mg | Fiber: 2g | Carbohydrates: 63.5g | Sugar: 38g

Single Serving Chocolate Cake

This recipe will absolutely curb a craving for something warm, gooey, and chocolaty. This cake is the perfect excuse to indulge—it doesn't yield a whole pan's worth of temptation and there is very little clean up! Top it with a little Dark Chocolate Fudge Sauce (see recipe in Chapter 12).

INGREDIENTS | SERVES 1

2 tablespoons rinsed, drained, and puréed chickpeas

3 tablespoons coconut sugar

¼ cup cocoa

¼ teaspoon baking powder

¼ teaspoon sea salt

½ teaspoon vanilla extract

¼ cup unsweetened almond milk

3 tablespoons chocolate chips

1. Mix all the ingredients in a small bowl. Pour into a microwave-safe dish.

2. Microwave for 2 minutes. Let cool for 1 minute and enjoy.

PER SERVING Calories: 485 | Fat: 15g | Protein: 10g | Sodium: 699mg | Fiber: 11g | Carbohydrates: 87g | Sugar: 64g

Microwave Safe

This cake is cooked in a short amount of time in the microwave. Be sure to use a microwave-safe bowl or dish.

Strawberry Shortcake

A summertime classic gets a natural makeover with powdered honey and xylitol. Fresh orange zest enhances the flavor and makes this cake topped with strawberries and cream irresistible!

INGREDIENTS | SERVES 6

1 cup plus 3 tablespoons spelt flour

1 teaspoon cornstarch

2½ teaspoons baking powder

1 teaspoon sea salt

1½ sticks butter, softened

¼ cup ricotta cheese or sour cream

1 cup powdered honey

½ cup xylitol

3 large eggs

1 teaspoon vanilla extract

2 tablespoons almond extract

1½ teaspoons orange zest

1 pint fresh strawberries, sliced

Homemade Whipped Cream (see recipe in Chapter 12)

Cake Flour Substitute

This recipe utilizes cornstarch mixed with healthy spelt flour as a natural cake flour substitute. Regular cake flour could be substituted for the flour and cornstarch.

1. Preheat oven to 350°F. Butter an 8" × 8" baking dish.

2. In a mixing bowl, whisk together the flour, cornstarch, baking powder, and salt.

3. In a separate bowl, beat the butter, cheese, honey, xylitol, and eggs until fluffy. Add vanilla, almond extract, and orange zest to the mixture.

4. Stir flour mixture into the cheese mixture until just combined. Pour batter into prepared pan.

5. Cover cake with foil and bake for 30 minutes. Remove foil and bake for an additional 18–22 minutes, or for about 50 minutes in all. Cool cake completely before serving with strawberries and whipped cream.

PER SERVING Calories: 681 | Fat: 39g | Protein: 8g | Sodium: 660mg | Fiber: 2g | Carbohydrates: 85g | Sugar: 49g

Vanilla Pound Cake

The sophisticated taste of vanilla is spotlighted in this moist sweet cake. Healthy additions like protein powder, yogurt, and spelt flour make this cake high in protein and low in fat.

INGREDIENTS | SERVES 8

⅔ cup yogurt

¾ cup unsweetened applesauce

3 tablespoons coconut oil, melted

2 tablespoons vanilla extract

½ teaspoon liquid stevia

2 cups white spelt flour

⅔ cup powdered honey

1 teaspoon cornstarch

2 tablespoons unsweetened vanilla protein powder

1½ teaspoons baking powder

½ teaspoon baking soda

½ teaspoon sea salt

Baking with Protein Powder

Protein powder in baked goods is an easy way to sneak in extra protein when not using eggs or nut butters.

1. Preheat the oven to 325°F. Line a 9" × 5" loaf pan with parchment paper and gently spray with cooking spray.

2. In a large mixing bowl, combine yogurt, applesauce, coconut oil, vanilla extract, and stevia.

3. In another large bowl, mix the flour, powdered honey, cornstarch, protein powder, baking powder, baking soda, and salt. Slowly add the flour mixture to the yogurt mixture, gently folding together to combine. Be careful not to overmix the batter.

4. Spoon the batter into prepared loaf pan. It will be fairly thick. Place in the center of oven and bake 30–32 minutes. Remove from pan and cool on a wire rack.

PER SERVING Calories: 285 | Fat: 6g | Protein: 5g | Sodium: 329mg | Fiber: 1g | Carbohydrates: 52g | Sugar: 27g

Vegan Lemon Cupcakes

These delicious citrus cupcakes are packed with bright lemon flavor! They are ideal for warmer months and are superb with a vegan cream cheese frosting.

INGREDIENTS | SERVES 12

1¾ cups spelt flour

1 cup maple sugar

½ teaspoon sea salt

1¼ teaspoons baking powder

1 teaspoon baking soda

½ cup plus 1 tablespoon unsweetened almond milk

½ cup fresh lemon juice

¼ cup grapeseed oil

2 teaspoons vanilla extract

1 teaspoon fresh lemon zest

1. Preheat oven to 350°F. Line a cupcake pan with liners and spray liners with cooking spray.

2. In a medium mixing bowl, whisk together flour, maple sugar, salt, baking powder, and baking soda.

3. In a small dish, combine the almond milk with the lemon juice. Add the milk mixture to the flour mixture. Add the oil, vanilla extract, and lemon zest. Gently mix to combine.

4. Use a ⅓ cup measuring cup to scoop out batter. Fill the prepared cupcake liners almost completely full. Bake for 14–16 minutes. Remove from pan and cool on a wire rack.

PER SERVING Calories: 183 | Fat: 5g | Protein: 2g | Sodium: 263mg | Fiber: 0g | Carbohydrates: 35g | Sugar: 24g

Chocolate Chip Cookie Cupcakes

Gourmet cupcakes are easy to create with this moist, thick batter that smells and tastes just like a chocolate chip cookie! Chocolate frosting doubles the fudgy goodness.

INGREDIENTS | SERVES 12

½ cup butter, softened

¾ cup coconut sugar

3 large egg whites

½ cup half-and-half

½ tablespoon vanilla extract

1 teaspoon baking powder

½ teaspoon sea salt

1 teaspoon cornstarch

½ cup white spelt flour

⅔ cup sugar-free chocolate chips

Chocolate Buttercream Frosting (see recipe in Chapter 12)

Perfectly Uniform

Use a large spring-release ice cream scoop for scooping batter into cupcake liners. This creates evenly baked and professional-looking treats. A small spring release scoop can be used when making cookies to achieve the same uniform results.

1. Preheat the oven to 350°F. Line a muffin tin with cupcake liners and spray liners with cooking spray.

2. In a large mixing bowl, cream butter and coconut sugar together with a hand mixer until smooth.

3. Add egg whites, half-and-half, vanilla, baking powder, salt, and cornstarch, mixing well. Add flour and mix until just combined. Fold in chocolate chips.

4. Pour batter into prepared cupcake liners, filling ¾ of the way full.

5. Bake for 15 minutes or until a toothpick inserted in the center comes out clean. Remove from pan and cool on a wire rack. Frost cupcakes with Chocolate Buttercream Frosting.

PER SERVING Calories: 332 | Fat: 17g | Protein: 3g | Sodium: 212mg | Fiber: 1g | Carbohydrates: 44g | Sugar: 36g

Walnut Chocolate Chip Cake

Date syrup sweetens this thick, hearty cake. Dotted with chocolate chips and walnuts, this cake has wonderful texture in every bite!

INGREDIENTS | SERVES 15

1½ cups boiling water

1 cup lightly packed pitted Medjool dates

1¾ teaspoons baking soda, divided

¾ cup unsalted butter

½ cup honey

½ cup coconut sugar

2 large eggs

½ teaspoon sea salt

2 cups spelt flour

½ cup walnuts

1 cup sugar-free chocolate chips

Not Your Typical Fruitcake

Do not be frightened by the thought of dried fruits and cake combined. This is nothing like the ubiquitous fruitcake. In this recipe, boiling the dates dissolves them into a syrup, making them a wonderful natural sweetener!

1. Pour boiling water over dates in a medium bowl. Add 1 teaspoon baking soda and stir. Set aside to cool.

2. Preheat oven to 350°F. Butter a 9" × 13" baking pan.

3. With a mixer, combine butter, honey, and sugar. Add eggs and beat until fluffy. Add remaining baking soda and the salt. Add the flour, alternating with the dates, adding all the date liquid as well. Beat until smooth. There will still be chunks of dates, but they will bake away in the oven.

4. Pour batter into the buttered dish. Top with walnuts and chocolate chips.

5. Bake for 15 minutes uncovered, and another 20–25 minutes covered with foil. (The top browns quickly; the foil helps keep it from browning too much.) A toothpick inserted should come out *almost* clean. Do not overbake. Enjoy warm or at room temperature.

PER SERVING Calories: 350 | Fat: 16.5g | Protein: 4g | Sodium: 240mg | Fiber: 3g | Carbohydrates: 49g | Sugar: 32g

Flourless Devil's Food Pudding Cake

This flourless version of a favorite rich, pudding-like cake is completely guilt-free. Everyone will rave over this tempting chocolate cake and will never guess that it contains antioxidant-rich black beans.

INGREDIENTS | SERVES 8

4 tablespoons chia seeds

¾ cup unsweetened chocolate almond milk

1½ cups rinsed and drained canned black beans

1½ tablespoons vanilla extract

½ teaspoon sea salt

6 tablespoons coconut oil, softened

1 cup coconut sugar

½ cup cocoa powder

¾ teaspoon baking powder

½ teaspoon baking soda

Baking Black Beans

Using black beans creates a healthy flour and egg replacement in baked goodies. Top this cake with a complementary chocolate fudge icing to add to the rich chocolate flavor for those guests who are nervous about a bean flavor.

1. Preheat the oven to 350°F. Spray an 8" × 8" baking dish with cooking spray.

2. In a small bowl, combine chia seeds with almond milk and set aside for 10 minutes until the mixture becomes thick.

3. In a blender or food processor, combine chia mixture, black beans, vanilla extract, salt, coconut oil, sugar, cocoa powder, baking powder, and baking soda. Process until smooth and totally combined.

4. Pour the batter into prepared baking dish. Bake 40–50 minutes, or until a toothpick inserted in the center comes out clean. Let the cake cool in pan completely.

PER SERVING Calories: 292 | Fat: 13g | Protein: 5g | Sodium: 436mg | Fiber: 5g | Carbohydrates: 41g | Sugar: 30g

CHAPTER 9

Candy

Easy Banana Bites

With just four simple ingredients, these banana bites are a snap to whip up. They're cute and delicious, and kids of all ages enjoy making and eating them!

INGREDIENTS | SERVES 4

2 large bananas, peeled

⅓ cup natural creamy peanut butter

⅓ cup chopped sugar-free vegan chocolate

3 tablespoons crushed raw peanuts

Browned Bananas

These banana bites are perfect for parties or other events, and best made and eaten the day of the event. Store leftover assembled banana bites in the fridge to keep bananas from browning.

1. Slice bananas into ¾" thick pieces. Spread about ½ teaspoon peanut butter on each slice. Place on a baking sheet and freeze for 30 minutes.

2. While the banana bites are chilling, carefully melt the chocolate in the microwave. Remove the bananas from the freezer and gently pour a little chocolate over each piece, spreading the chocolate down around the edges to form a nice coating.

3. Sprinkle with nuts and serve.

PER SERVING Calories: 322 | Fat: 19g | Protein: 9g | Sodium: 101mg | Fiber: 5g | Carbohydrates: 33g | Sugar: 20g

Honey Cinnamon Almonds

These honey-sweetened almonds are the perfect energy boost! Honey and cinnamon help eliminate unhealthy cravings and protein can help boost energy. These nuts store well in airtight containers for an on-the-go snack.

INGREDIENTS | SERVES 4

1 cup unsalted almonds

6 tablespoons honey

2 tablespoons coconut oil

1/16 teaspoon sea salt

2 teaspoons cinnamon

1. Preheat broiler. Line a baking sheet with parchment paper.

2. Mix all ingredients in a small bowl. Spread the mixture out onto baking sheet. It will be sticky and clumpy but will be the perfect texture when baked.

3. Broil for 3 minutes. Stir, then broil for another 2–4 minutes, until almonds are bubbly and lightly browned and the honey has caramelized. Cool for at least 5 minutes before serving.

PER SERVING Calories: 296 | Fat: 18.5g | Protein: 5g | Sodium: 38mg | Fiber: 3.5g | Carbohydrates: 32g | Sugar: 27g

Almond Butter Cups

This peanut-allergy-friendly rendition of a peanut butter cup is at least as delicious as the original! Enjoy these fresh, frozen, or crushed and mixed into your favorite frozen yogurt or ice cream.

INGREDIENTS | SERVES 15

½ cup natural creamy almond butter

⅓ cup honey

1⁄16 teaspoon sea salt

1¼ cups melted sugar-free chocolate

1. Line a mini muffin pan with muffin liners and very lightly spray liners with cooking spray.

2. In a small bowl, combine the almond butter, honey, and salt. Mix well.

3. Spoon about ¾ teaspoon of chocolate into the bottom of each muffin liner. Spread the chocolate to coat the bottom and sides of the liner.

4. Next, drop about 1 teaspoon of the almond butter mixture on top of the melted chocolate.

5. Fill the cups with remaining chocolate to cover all the almond butter. Freeze for 30 minutes.

PER SERVING Calories: 141 | Fat: 8.5g | Protein: 3g | Sodium: 51mg | Fiber: 1g | Carbohydrates: 17g | Sugar: 15g

Almond Coconut Chocolate Candies

These little candies are delicious, easy to make, and totally addicting! Unsweetened coconut and raw almonds provide a healthy dose of nutrients as well. Try using dark chocolate for an extra-rich candy.

INGREDIENTS | MAKES 12

1 cup shredded unsweetened coconut

¾ cup honey

2 large egg whites

12 almonds

1¼ cups chopped sugar-free chocolate, melted

Unsweetened Only

There are many sweetened shredded coconut products available. To control sweetness and to avoid unhealthy sugars, make sure to use unsweetened shredded coconut.

1. Preheat oven to 350°F. Spray a mini muffin tin with cooking spray.

2. In a large mixing bowl, mix together coconut and honey.

3. In a separate bowl, beat the egg whites until light and fluffy. Mix egg whites with the coconut and honey mixture.

4. Place 1 almond in each section of the muffin tin. Add a bit of batter over the almond to completely cover.

5. Bake for 18–20 minutes. Transfer the tray to the freezer for 15 minutes. Remove the candies from the tray and coat with melted chocolate.

PER SERVING (2 candies) Calories: 436 | Fat: 18g | Protein: 4g | Sodium: 23.5mg | Fiber: 5g | Carbohydrates: 68g | Sugar: 60.5g

Buckeyes

This famous Ohio treat is an easy, delicious peanut butter fudge truffle with a delectable chocolate coating. Coconut sugar sweetens the peanut butter fudge portion for a healthier rich, creamy bite.

INGREDIENTS | SERVES 6

½ cup creamy natural peanut butter

½ cup coconut sugar

1 teaspoon vanilla extract

2 tablespoons unsweetened vanilla protein powder

⅓ cup melted sugar-free chocolate

Natural Peanut Butter

Natural peanut butter is often a bit harder to work with than regular peanut butter because the natural oils can separate and leave the remainder hard at the bottom of the jar. A little mixing is all that's required, and the reward is a delicious peanut butter free of hydrogenated oils and sugar.

1. Line a baking sheet with parchment paper.

2. In a mixing bowl, combine peanut butter, sugar, vanilla, and protein powder and mix well.

3. Chill the mixture for 10 minutes, then roll into balls. Dip the balls into the melted chocolate, covering completely. Place on the prepared baking sheet.

4. Return to the refrigerator for another 5 minutes, or until chocolate has hardened.

PER SERVING Calories: 252 | Fat: 14g | Protein: 8g | Sodium: 105mg | Fiber: 2g | Carbohydrates: 29g | Sugar: 25g

Candied Pecans

Candied nuts are the easiest candies to make. This recipe uses coconut oil, egg whites, and coconut sugar to create the most tantalizing caramelized coating!

INGREDIENTS | SERVES 4

1 extra-large egg white
1 tablespoon melted coconut oil
3 cups pecans
¾ cup coconut sugar
½ teaspoon sea salt
½ teaspoon cinnamon

Egg Whites

Egg whites create a perfect coating on the nuts while creating a sticky layer for the other ingredients to adhere to. Use an extra large egg for optimal coverage.

1. Preheat oven to 300°F. Line a baking sheet with parchment paper.

2. In a mixing bowl, beat the egg white and oil until soft peaks form.

3. Add pecans to the egg whites and coat well. Add coconut sugar, salt, and cinnamon. Continue stirring until nuts are well coated.

4. Spread nuts in a single layer on the prepared baking sheet and bake for 30 minutes, stirring every 10 minutes. Cool before serving.

PER SERVING Calories: 756 | Fat: 62g | Protein: 8g | Sodium: 320mg | Fiber: 8g | Carbohydrates: 52g | Sugar: 43g

Chocolate Nut Truffles

The combination of walnuts and cashews creates a fabulously nutty flavor in these simple truffles. Dates sweeten this confection while chocolate rounds out the flavors for a truly sweet finish.

INGREDIENTS | SERVES 4

1⅓ cups dates, pitted
½ cup whole cashews
½ cup whole walnuts
¼ cup cocoa powder
⅔ cup chopped sugar-free chocolate, melted

Raw Nuts

Use raw nuts when possible because they blend well and have the most nutritional value.

1. In a food processor, blend dates until they are smooth and the purée comes together and forms a ball. Add nuts and cocoa powder, mixing until nuts are chopped well and cocoa is well distributed.

2. Form dough into 1" balls. Dip truffles into melted chocolate. Refrigerate until chocolate is set, about 10 minutes.

PER SERVING Calories: 409 | Fat: 19g | Protein: 6g | Sodium: 6mg | Fiber: 9g | Carbohydrates: 67g | Sugar: 53g

Chocolate-Covered Raisin Fudge

Raisins give such a wonderful sweet flavor to this treat that no additional sweeteners are needed. This no-bake fudge has just 6 ingredients and is a quick and fruity treat!

INGREDIENTS | SERVES 2

1⅓ cups raisins
1 tablespoon water
¾ cup plus 2 tablespoons cocoa
1½ tablespoons vanilla extract
¼ teaspoon sea salt
½ cup chopped sugar-free chocolate, melted

Benefits of Raisins

Raisins contain a good amount of iron and fiber, helping blood pressure and good digestion. Enjoy them raw for maximum nutritional benefits.

1. In a food processor or blender, mix the raisins and water until the mixture forms a smooth paste. Add cocoa, vanilla, and salt and mix until well incorporated.

2. Press the batter into two large ramekins. Chill in the freezer for 10 minutes. Pour the melted chocolate over the bars and freeze another 10 minutes. Serve in the ramekin and eat with a spoon. Store leftovers in an air-tight container in the refrigerator.

PER SERVING Calories: 607 | Fat: 18g | Protein: 12g | Sodium: 320mg | Fiber: 19g | Carbohydrates: 126.5g | Sugar: 82g

Cinnamon Baking Chips

These cinnamon chips work beautifully in any baked good, giving the perfect burst of cinnamon to a recipe! Snickerdoodles, cinnamon rolls, and even chocolate chip cookies will benefit from these soft cinnamon nuggets.

INGREDIENTS | MAKES 1 CUP

⅓ cup coconut sugar
2 tablespoons cinnamon
1 tablespoon coconut oil
1 tablespoon maple syrup

1. Preheat the oven to 300°F. Line an 8" × 8" baking dish with parchment paper.

2. In a small bowl, combine all ingredients. Spread the mixture into baking dish and bake for 18 minutes.

3. The mixture will be slightly bubbly. Allow chips to cool for 30 minutes, place in freezer to firm for 15 minutes, cut into small slices and enjoy.

4. If not using right away, store in the refrigerator. The chips will soften and may fuse together if not kept cold.

PER SERVING (1 tablespoon) Calories: 29 | Fat: 0g | Protein: 0g | Sodium: 1mg | Fiber: 0g | Carbohydrates: 6g | Sugar: 5g

Dark Chocolate Coconut Truffles

The pure ingredients of dark chocolate, healthy oils, and unsweetened coconut fuse together in these delectable raw truffles. Sweetened with raw honey, these chocolate bites are as rich as they are sweet!

INGREDIENTS | SERVES 8

¾ cup cocoa powder
6 tablespoons honey
2 tablespoons coconut oil, softened
2 teaspoons vanilla extract
½ teaspoon sea salt
2 tablespoons agave inulin
¼ cup unsweetened shredded coconut

1. In a small bowl, mix together cocoa powder, honey, and coconut oil.

2. Add vanilla, salt, and agave inulin and mix until well combined. The mixture will be a very thick paste. Form mixture into a ball. Chill the mixture for 10 minutes.

3. Place coconut in a shallow bowl. Remove chocolate mixture from the refrigerator. Roll chocolate mixture into 8 small balls and coat with shredded coconut. Serve immediately or store in an airtight container in the refrigerator.

PER SERVING Calories: 112.5 | Fat: 5g | Protein: 2g | Sodium: 150mg | Fiber: 4.5g | Carbohydrates: 20g | Sugar: 13g

Oatmeal Raisin Cookie Dough Truffles

Bite into a healthy, no-bake truffle version of your favorite cookie! Enjoy the warm spice of cinnamon with the refreshing pop of raisins. With a delicious flavor and a soft texture, these are definitely a guilt-free treat!

INGREDIENTS | SERVES 8

½ cup unsalted cashews
½ cup rolled oats
1⅓ cups Medjool dates, pitted and lightly packed
1½ teaspoons vanilla extract
¼ teaspoon sea salt
1 teaspoon cinnamon
¼ cup raisins

1. Line a baking sheet with parchment paper.

2. In a food processor, pulse cashews and oats until mixture has a rough sandy texture. Add the dates, vanilla, salt, and cinnamon and mix until smooth and combined.

3. Add raisins and pulse for a few seconds to incorporate. The dough will be a little sticky.

4. Divide the dough into 8 equal parts. Roll into balls and place on prepared baking sheet. Refrigerate for 30 minutes before serving.

PER SERVING Calories: 197 | Fat: 7g | Protein: 4g | Sodium: 77mg | Fiber: 4g | Carbohydrates: 34g | Sugar: 22g

Easy Chocolate Fudge

The base of this no-bake fudge contains a surprising ingredient. Melted chocolate fuses with avocado to create a silky soft fudge no one can pass up.

INGREDIENTS | SERVES 4

1 medium ripe avocado, peeled and pitted

2 tablespoons natural creamy almond butter

⅔ cup sugar-free chocolate chips, melted

1½ teaspoons vanilla extract

¼ teaspoon liquid stevia

Melted and Cooled

When working with melted chocolate, allow it to cool slightly so the hot chocolate doesn't melt the other ingredients.

1. Line a 9" × 5" loaf pan with parchment paper.

2. In a food processor, mix all ingredients, scraping the sides of the bowl as needed to get everything well incorporated.

3. Scoop out the mixture and press into the bottom of the loaf pan.

4. Place in the freezer for 30 minutes. Remove from freezer and cut into 8 equal pieces. Serve immediately or keep covered in the refrigerator for up to 4 days.

PER SERVING Calories: 325.5 | Fat: 21g | Protein: 5g | Sodium: 41mg | Fiber: 6g | Carbohydrates: 31g | Sugar: 21g

Green Mint Fudge

Enjoy a cool mint treat that resembles a mint cream! An avocado base creates the perfect soft texture while turning this confection naturally green!

INGREDIENTS | SERVES 4

1 large ripe avocado

2 tablespoons coconut butter

¾ cup powdered xylitol

⅓ cup rice flour

1½ teaspoons peppermint extract

Natural Food Coloring

For a bright green treat, try adding 1 or 2 drops of spirulina or natural food dye made from natural food sources.

1. Line a small baking dish or mini bread pan with parchment paper.

2. In a food processor, combine avocado, coconut butter, xylitol, and rice flour. Blend until smooth. Add the extract and mix until incorporated.

3. Scoop out the fudge and spread in the prepared baking dish.

4. Freeze for 30 minutes until set. Remove from freezer and cut into 8 pieces.

PER SERVING Calories: 189 | Fat: 6g | Protein: 0g | Sodium: 0mg | Fiber: 0g | Carbohydrates: 46.5g | Sugar: 0g

Graham Cracker Toffee

Everyone loves homemade toffee, but nobody loves the time-consuming process of making it. Graham cracker toffee gives the delicious taste of toffee without the hassle. Sweetened with coconut sugar and lots of chocolate, this is another holiday favorite.

INGREDIENTS | SERVES 5

20 Mi-Del All Natural Honey Grahams
1 cup coconut sugar
1 cup butter
1 teaspoon vanilla extract
1 cup sugar-free chocolate, melted
¾ cup chopped almonds

Honey Graham Crackers

This recipe can also be made using home-made Honey Graham Crackers (see recipe in Chapter 15) instead of store-bought ones for a really special treat.

1. Preheat oven to 350°F. Line the bottom of a 9" × 13" baking dish with graham crackers.

2. In a small saucepan over medium-high heat, combine coconut sugar, butter, and vanilla extract. Cook, stirring occasionally until mixture comes to a full boil. Cook for 4 minutes, stirring vigorously. Remove from heat and pour evenly over the crackers in the baking dish. Place in oven and bake for 10–12 minutes, until bubbly.

3. Remove from the oven. Pour melted chocolate over toffee and spread evenly. Sprinkle with almonds. Let cool. Break crackers into authentic freeform broken toffee piece shapes and serve.

PER SERVING Calories: 456 | Fat: 12g | Protein: 3g | Sodium: 95mg | Fiber: 2g | Carbohydrates: 40g | Sugar: 17g

Healthy Fudge Truffles

Decrease the unhealthy fats in traditional fudge by substituting coconut cream to yield the same creamy texture. This fudge is best rolled in sweet or salty toppings.

INGREDIENTS | SERVES 8

3 cups coconut sugar

⅓ cup unsweetened cocoa

¼ cup roughly chopped unsweetened baking chocolate

½ cup canned coconut milk

2 tablespoons coconut oil

2 teaspoons vanilla extract

¼ teaspoon sea salt

Endless Coatings

Roll finished fudge truffles in cocoa powder, unsweetened shredded coconut, nuts, natural sprinkles, coconut sugar, or chocolate chips to create a variety of textures and flavors.

1. Line an 8" × 8" baking dish with parchment paper.

2. In a medium bowl, mix together the coconut sugar, cocoa, and chopped chocolate.

3. In a medium saucepan over medium-high heat, combine coconut milk and coconut oil. Bring to a boil, stirring constantly. Be careful not to burn the mixture as it heats.

4. When the mixture reaches a boil, reduce heat to low and add the chocolate mixture. Mix well until chocolate is melted and well incorporated. Remove from heat and add the vanilla and salt.

5. Pour the batter into the prepared baking dish. Refrigerate until cool and firm, about 2 hours. Scoop out and roll into 1½" balls.

PER SERVING Calories: 419 | Fat: 9g | Protein: 1g | Sodium: 100mg | Fiber: 2g | Carbohydrates: 88g | Sugar: 83g

Honey Fudge Rolls

A candy thermometer will help ensure the perfect texture for these bite-size nuggets. Reminiscent of a classic roll candy, they can be individually wrapped in parchment paper with twisted ends to keep them closed.

INGREDIENTS | SERVES 3

1 teaspoon butter
½ cup honey
½ teaspoon vanilla extract
½ cup unsweetened vanilla protein powder
¼ cup cocoa powder

1. Butter a 12" piece of wax paper.

2. Cook honey over medium-low heat in a small sauce-pan until it reaches hard-ball stage, about 250°F. Remove from heat. Stir in vanilla.

3. In a small bowl, combine protein powder and cocoa. Add to the honey and vanilla extract mixture. Spoon/pour onto buttered paper. Coat your hands with butter and begin pulling the mixture like taffy until it cools completely.

4. On buttered paper, roll the candy into a rope shape. Cut the rope into 1" pieces. Wrap pieces in individual pieces of wax paper or store in an airtight container at room temperature.

PER SERVING Calories: 275 | Fat: 3g | Protein: 15.5g | Sodium: 4mg | Fiber: 3g | Carbohydrates: 53g | Sugar: 47g

Healthy Coconut Chocolate Mounds

These sweet chocolate-covered morsels are bursting with fresh coconut and maple syrup flavors. Baked to perfection, then covered with chocolate, they are hard to resist.

INGREDIENTS | SERVES 10

¾ cup whole cashews

¾ cup unsweetened shredded coconut

2 tablespoons coconut oil

2 tablespoons maple syrup

1 teaspoon vanilla extract

⅛ teaspoon sea salt

⅓ cup chopped sugar-free dark chocolate

1. Line a baking sheet with parchment paper.

2. Process cashews in a food processor to form a rough powder. Add coconut, coconut oil, maple syrup, vanilla, and salt. Pulse mixture to combine.

3. Using a small 1½" ice cream scoop, form the mixture into balls and place on the baking sheet. Freeze for about 30 minutes. Meanwhile, melt the chocolate.

4. Dip each mound into the chocolate until completely covered. Place the baking sheet back in the freezer to set another 5 minutes until hardened. Keep chilled until ready to serve.

PER SERVING Calories: 96 | Fat: 7g | Protein: 0g | Sodium: 31mg | Fiber: 1g | Carbohydrates: 8.5g | Sugar: 7g

Hazelnut Chocolate Fudge Truffles

Rich and decadent, these truffles are not for the chocolate faint of heart! Keep these truffles in the refrigerator for best results.

INGREDIENTS | SERVES 8

Chocolate Hazelnut Spread (see recipe in Chapter 6)

6 ounces sugar-free chocolate

1. Line a large plate with parchment paper.

2. Pour the Chocolate Hazelnut Spread into candy molds. When the molds are filled, place in the freezer to chill for at least 1 hour.

3. Remove truffles from the molds. Dip or pour melted chocolate over the tops and place on prepared plate. The frozen candies will harden the chocolate, allowing you to enjoy them immediately.

PER SERVING Calories: 101 | Fat: 6g | Protein: 0g | Sodium: 2mg | Fiber: 1g | Carbohydrates: 13g | Sugar: 11g

White Chocolate Chips

No-bake chips are easy to make and easy to bake with! For a really special treat, try using vanilla beans instead of vanilla extract. For best results, store them in the refrigerator so they are ready at a moment's notice.

INGREDIENTS | MAKES ⅔ CUP

1 cup unsweetened shredded coconut

1 cup cacao butter chunks, melted

1½ teaspoons vanilla extract

2 tablespoons protein powder

2 teaspoons liquid stevia

Chip or Chunk?

If desired, use candy chip molds to create authentic baking chips. This recipe can also be poured into candy bar molds for white chocolate on the go!

1. In a food processor, process the coconut for about 6–7 minutes, scraping the inside bowl periodically. The coconut needs to be blended until smooth to form coconut butter.

2. Once coconut butter is smooth, add the cacao butter. Add vanilla, protein powder, and stevia and mix well.

3. Pour the mixture into a small flat dish, about 5" wide, or into candy molds. Place in the freezer for 30 minutes. Remove from the freezer and cut into little squares or remove from molds.

PER SERVING (1 tablespoon) Calories: 229 | Fat: 24.5g | Protein: 1g | Sodium: 2mg | Fiber: 0g | Carbohydrates: 1.5g | Sugar: 0g

Salted Honey Caramels

Caramelized honey becomes absolutely dreamy in these lush salted caramel squares.
Use a good quality coarse sea salt to really bring out the sweet caramel flavors.

INGREDIENTS | SERVES 4

2 teaspoons vanilla extract
3 tablespoons butter, divided
1 cup honey
¾ cup heavy cream
1 tablespoon coarse sea salt

1. Measure out vanilla extract and butter and set near the stove. Grease an 8" × 8" baking dish with 1 tablespoon of the butter.

2. Combine honey and cream in a saucepan over medium-high heat and bring to a boil. Stir occasionally while mixture cooks until it reaches soft ball stage, about 250°F on a candy thermometer. Remove pan from the heat and immediately stir in vanilla and remaining butter. Stir until butter is completely melted and incorporated.

3. Pour into prepared dish. Sprinkle with salt. Place in the freezer to harden for 30 minutes.

4. Cut into squares or scoop out balls with a spoon. Keep leftovers in the fridge or freezer and keep cold when serving. Caramels will melt and become sticky in high humidity and hot temperatures.

PER SERVING Calories: 495 | Fat: 25g | Protein: 1g | Sodium: 1,790mg | Fiber: 0g | Carbohydrates: 71g | Sugar: 70g

Peanut Butter Granola Cups

Enjoy the taste of peanut butter candies with a healthy granola twist. These cups are perfect for care packages and gifts when stored in individual storage cups.

INGREDIENTS | SERVES 5

3½ ounces melted sugar-free chocolate
1 cup pitted chopped dates
¼ cup salted natural peanut butter
¼ cup honey
1 cup chopped roasted almonds
¼ cup shredded unsweetened coconut
¼ cup dry-roasted peanuts
1 cup oats
½ teaspoon vanilla extract

1. Line a mini muffin tin with paper liners.

2. Spoon 1 teaspoon melted chocolate into each of the mini muffin cups (or small candy cup molds). Lift and roll the muffin tin to coat the cups or use a mini spatula for additional help. Refrigerate chocolate cups for 30 minutes.

3. Process dates in a food processor until smooth. Add peanut butter, honey, almonds, coconut, peanuts, oats, and vanilla. Pulse to combine.

4. Scoop out about 2 teaspoons of nut mixture to fill each chocolate cup. Gently press the mixture into the cup. Place pan in the freezer for at least 30 minutes.

5. Remove the peanut butter cups from the pan and serve.

PER SERVING Calories: 508 | Fat: 24g | Protein: 11g | Sodium: 65mg | Fiber: 9g | Carbohydrates: 71g | Sugar: 50g

Easy Hazelnut Chocolate Balls

These simple no-bake balls are an easy sweet treat to make when a chocolate craving strikes!

INGREDIENTS | SERVES 6

½ cup hazelnuts
½ cup pitted chopped dates
2 tablespoons maple syrup
1 teaspoon vanilla extract
⅛ teaspoon sea salt
⅓ cup cocoa powder
¼ cup sugar-free chocolate, melted

1. Line a baking sheet with parchment paper.

2. Put the hazelnuts and dates in a food processor and pulse until a rough crumbly mixture forms. Add maple syrup, vanilla, salt, and cocoa powder and pulse until smooth and well combined. Roll mixture into 1" balls and place on prepared baking sheet.

3. Top with melted chocolate, and refrigerate for 15 minutes to harden chocolate.

PER SERVING Calories: 166 | Fat: 9g | Protein: 3g | Sodium: 52mg | Fiber: 4g | Carbohydrates: 24.5g | Sugar: 18g

Orange Spice Truffles

Need a healthy and delicious snack but want to leave the guilt factor at the door? Try these decadent-tasting little truffles for a burst of festive fruity flavor.

INGREDIENTS | SERVES 2

⅓ cup chopped walnuts
¼ cup pitted chopped dates, lightly packed
1 tablespoon honey
½ teaspoon pumpkin spice
½ teaspoon cinnamon
1 teaspoon vanilla extract
⅛ teaspoon sea salt
2 teaspoons orange zest

1. In a food processor, blend walnuts until crumbly. Add dates, honey, pumpkin spice, cinnamon, vanilla extract, sea salt, and orange zest.

2. Pulse until everything is incorporated. Roll into 1" balls and serve.

PER SERVING Calories: 232 | Fat: 13g | Protein: 4g | Sodium: 149mg | Fiber: 3g | Carbohydrates: 29g | Sugar: 24g

Molasses Cookie Dough Bites

Enjoy these soft, safe-to-eat cookie dough bites! Intensely spiced and sweetened only with dates and molasses, these are the perfect wintertime treat.

INGREDIENTS | SERVES 5

½ cup oats
½ cup pitted chopped Medjool dates
¼ cup chopped pecans
1 tablespoon molasses
½ teaspoon vanilla extract
½ teaspoon cinnamon
⅛ teaspoon nutmeg
1/16 teaspoon cloves
⅛ teaspoon sea salt

Slow As Molasses

Molasses adds a wonderful richness to these truffles. Make sure to add the molasses with the spices so this thick sweetener does not become stuck in the walls of the processor.

1. In a food processor, add the oats and pulse until it becomes a fine flour. Add the dates and pecans and pulse until crumbly. Add the molasses, vanilla, cinnamon, nutmeg, cloves, and salt and mix well.

2. Roll into 1" balls. Store leftovers in an airtight container in the refrigerator.

PER SERVING Calories: 133 | Fat: 5g | Protein: 2g | Sodium: 61mg | Fiber: 3g | Carbohydrates: 23g | Sugar: 14g

Peanut Butter Cups

It's easier (and healthier) to make these peanut butter cups at home than to drive to the store to get the sugar-loaded version! These four simple ingredients yield mouthwatering results.

INGREDIENTS | SERVES 10

½ cup natural creamy peanut butter
⅓ cup honey
¼ teaspoon sea salt
1¼ cups sugar-free chocolate, melted

1. Line a mini muffin pan with liners and very lightly spray with cooking spray.

2. In a small bowl, combine the peanut butter, honey, and salt. Mix well.

3. Spoon about ¾ teaspoon of chocolate into the bottom of each muffin liner. Spread the chocolate to coat the sides and bottom of the liner. Place about 2 teaspoons of the peanut butter mixture on top of the chocolate.

4. Fill the remaining cups with chocolate to cover all the peanut butter. Freeze for 30 minutes and serve.

PER SERVING Calories: 211 | Fat: 13g | Protein: 4g | Sodium: 121mg | Fiber: 2g | Carbohydrates: 25g | Sugar: 22g

Sunflower Butter Cups

These chocolate candies are perfect for people with peanut allergies—and for those without! Sunflower butter is a tasty peanut butter substitute and creates candies that are nothing short of amazing.

INGREDIENTS | SERVES 12

⅓ cup sunflower seed butter

2 tablespoons honey

¼ teaspoon sea salt

½ teaspoon vanilla extract

1 cup chopped sugar-free chocolate, melted

No Sunflower?

Almond butter or cashew butter could also be used as a replacement for peanut butter in any of your favorite recipes. There are great nutritional benefits to consuming a wide variety of nuts, so experimenting with different nut butters is an easy way to reap a variety of health benefits.

1. Line a mini muffin pan with muffin liners and spray liners with cooking spray.

2. In a small bowl, combine the sunflower seed butter with the honey. Add the salt and vanilla to the mixture.

3. Generously coat the bottom of each liner with chocolate. Place a small 1 teaspoon-size ball of nut mixture into each cup. Top with remaining melted chocolate. Place in the fridge to set for 10 minutes.

PER SERVING Calories: 150 | Fat: 8g | Protein: 3g | Sodium: 82.5mg | Fiber: 2g | Carbohydrates: 17g | Sugar: 13g

Loaded Chocolate-Covered Strawberries

Regular chocolate-covered strawberries get a promotion in this recipe with sweet ingredients added to their chocolate coatings. Pick large, juicy strawberries with healthy green stems for ease of assembling and eating.

INGREDIENTS | SERVES 4

1 pint fresh strawberries
⅓ cup unsweetened shredded coconut
2 tablespoons xylitol
10 ounces sugar-free chocolate, melted

1. Line a dinner plate with wax paper. Wash and dry strawberries. In a small bowl, combine the unsweetened shredded coconut with xylitol. Place melted chocolate in another small bowl.

2. Dip strawberries into the melted chocolate. Sprinkle or dip strawberries in coconut mixture and lay fruit on the prepared plate.

3. Refrigerate for 15–20 minutes or until chocolate is hardened.

PER SERVING Calories: 398 | Fat: 23g | Protein: 4g | Sodium: 10mg | Fiber: 6g | Carbohydrates: 57g | Sugar: 10g

CHAPTER 10

Cookies

Almond Butter Chocolate Chip Cookies

These almond butter cookies use whole-wheat flour and are packed with chocolate chips for full almond-chocolate flavor. Enjoy a soft, velvety textured cookie without a speck of butter!

INGREDIENTS | MAKES 24

½ cup whole-wheat flour

1½ teaspoons baking soda

¾ cup coconut sugar

⅛ teaspoon sea salt

1 cup natural almond butter

1 teaspoon molasses

¼ cup unsweetened applesauce

2 teaspoons vanilla extract

1 cup sugar-free chocolate chips

1. Preheat oven to 350°F. Line a baking sheet with parchment paper.

2. In a medium bowl, mix together the flour, baking soda, coconut sugar, and salt until well combined.

3. Add the almond butter, molasses, unsweetened applesauce, and vanilla and mix all the ingredients together until smooth. Gently mix in the chocolate chips.

4. Roll into about 1" balls and place on baking sheet 2" apart. Bake for 7–8 minutes. Remove from baking sheet and cool on a wire rack.

PER SERVING (2 cookies) Calories: 254 | Fat: 16g | Protein: 7g | Sodium: 280mg | Fiber: 3g | Carbohydrates: 34g | Sugar: 15g

Almond Chocolate Cookies

Chocolate cookies with chopped almonds are a nice alternative to the typical chocolate chip cookie. Cocoa and vanilla enhance these crispy, crunchy cookies.

INGREDIENTS | SERVES 12

½ cup butter
1 cup powdered honey
1 large egg
½ teaspoon vanilla extract
½ teaspoon sea salt
½ teaspoon baking soda
1 cup spelt flour
½ cup almonds, chopped

1. Preheat oven to 375°F. Line a baking sheet with parchment paper.

2. In a mixing bowl, cream together butter and powdered honey. Beat mixture until light and airy.

3. Beat in egg and vanilla. Add in salt, baking soda, and flour. Add chopped almonds and mix.

4. Roll into small 1½" balls and place on baking sheet 2" apart. Bake for 10 minutes, or for 12–13 minutes if you want extra crunchy cookies. Remove from baking sheet and cool on a wire rack.

PER SERVING Calories: 178 | Fat: 10g | Protein: 3g | Sodium: 155mg | Fiber: 2g | Carbohydrates: 20g | Sugar: 10g

Chewy Ginger Cookies

These soft chewy cookies are delectable with a cup of regular or chocolate milk. Delicious spices give them just a touch of heat with the perfect amount of sweetness.

INGREDIENTS | MAKES 24

½ cup unsalted butter
¼ cup coconut oil
1 cup coconut sugar
1 large egg
¼ cup molasses
2¼ cups spelt flour
2 teaspoons ginger
1 teaspoon cinnamon
1 teaspoon baking soda
¼ teaspoon sea salt

1. Preheat oven to 350°F. Line a baking sheet with parchment paper.

2. In a large bowl, cream together the butter, coconut oil, and coconut sugar until light and fluffy. Beat in egg. Stir in the molasses.

3. In a separate bowl, sift flour, ginger, cinnamon, baking soda, and salt together. Gradually stir flour mixture into the butter mixture.

4. Scoop out small 1½" balls, place 2" apart on baking sheet, and cook for 8–10 minutes. Cool on baking sheet 5 minutes. Remove from baking sheet and cool on a wire rack.

PER SERVING (2 cookies) Calories: 295 | Fat: 13g | Protein: 3.5g | Sodium: 165mg | Fiber: 3g | Carbohydrates: 43g | Sugar: 21g

Maple Jam Thumbprint Cookies

These cookies get their name from the large thumb impression in the center of the cookie. This thumbprint becomes the perfect well to fill with delicious sugar-free jam.

INGREDIENTS | MAKES 24

1½ cups almond meal

1½ cups white rice flour

¼ teaspoon xanthan gum

½ teaspoon sea salt

½ teaspoon cinnamon

⅓ cup grapeseed oil

½ cup maple syrup

3 tablespoons unsweetened almond milk

1 teaspoon vanilla extract

⅓ cup sugar-free jam of choice

1. Preheat oven to 350°F. Line a baking sheet with parchment paper and set aside.

2. In a large mixing bowl, combine the almond meal, rice flour, xanthan gum, salt, and cinnamon. Stir to combine. Add the rest of the ingredients except the jam and stir until well combined.

3. With wet hands, roll dough into about 1" balls. Place on baking sheet 2" apart and indent the middle of each cookie with your thumb or finger.

4. Fill the indent with jam (about 1 teaspoon or so per cookie). Bake for 8–9 minutes and cool 5 minutes before removing from baking sheet and placing on a wire rack.

PER SERVING (2 cookies) Calories: 252 | Fat: 13g | Protein: 4g | Sodium: 105mg | Fiber: 2g | Carbohydrates: 34g | Sugar: 9g

Lemon Love Notes

Similar to lemon bars, these lovely cookies have a shortbread base with a lemon-custard filling. The buttery cookie base complements the smooth lemon centers perfectly!

INGREDIENTS | MAKES 35

½ cup xylitol, divided
½ cup honey, divided
1 large egg
¼ teaspoon vanilla extract
3 tablespoons lemon juice
¾ teaspoon lemon zest, divided
2 tablespoons organic cornstarch
¾ teaspoon sea salt, divided
1 teaspoon guar gum
2 cups spelt flour
1 cup unsalted butter, softened
½ teaspoon baking powder

1. Preheat oven to 350°F. Line a baking sheet with parchment paper.

2. Combine ¼ cup xylitol, ¼ cup honey, egg, and vanilla in a small bowl. Whisk until smooth. Add lemon juice, ¼ teaspoon lemon zest, cornstarch, ¼ teaspoon salt, and guar gum. Mix until there are no lumps and the batter is completely smooth. Set aside.

3. In a medium bowl, combine flour, butter, ¼ cup xylitol, ¼ cup honey, ½ teaspoon salt, baking powder, and ½ teaspoon lemon zest. Roll the dough into 1" balls or scoop dough with a 1" ice cream scoop.

4. Place balls on the prepared baking sheet. Indent the centers with your finger or the back of the cookie scoop, making sure the indention is fairly large without breaking the cookie edge. Bake cookies for 4–6 minutes or until edges are just baked.

5. Remove cookies from the oven. If the centers have puffed up, pat down slightly as needed. Pour about 2 teaspoons of filling into centers of each cookie or enough to fill. Place filled cookies back in oven for another 5 minutes or until centers are no longer liquid, but still a little jiggly. Cool completely before serving.

PER SERVING (2 cookies) Calories: 185 | Fat: 10g | Protein: 2g | Sodium: 117mg | Fiber: 1g | Carbohydrates: 18g | Sugar: 8g

Cherry Nut Blossoms

Inspired by the cherry blossoms in the Washington D.C. area, these cookies are the perfect welcome to spring. Three different types of flour make these cookies healthy and hearty. Dried cherries provide pops of natural sweetness in each bite.

INGREDIENTS | MAKES 24

1¾ cups spelt flour
¼ cup coconut flour
½ cup almond flour
½ teaspoon baking powder
¼ teaspoon sea salt
¾ cup unsalted butter
1 cup coconut sugar
1 large egg
2 teaspoons orange zest
1 teaspoon vanilla extract
½ cup dried cherries, chopped
½ cup walnuts, chopped

In Full Bloom

It's possible to dry and eat the actual cherry blossoms off of cherry trees! In Japan this is known as sakura and it's used as a flavoring in many snack foods such as chips, ice cream, and drinks. Using dried cherries and extracts in these cookies is an easy way to create a similar floral flavor.

1. Preheat oven to 350°F and line a baking sheet with parchment paper.

2. In a large bowl, whisk together flours, baking powder, and salt and set aside.

3. In a separate bowl, cream butter and coconut sugar together until light and fluffy. Add egg and beat well. Beat in orange zest and vanilla.

4. Gradually add the flour mixture to the butter mixture and mix until well blended. Gently add in the cherries and walnuts and mix to combine.

5. Scoop out 1½" cookie dough balls with a small ice cream scoop or spoon and place on baking sheet 2" apart. Bake for 8–10 minutes. Remove from baking sheet and cool on a wire rack.

PER SERVING (2 cookies) Calories: 324 | Fat: 19g | Protein: 5g | Sodium: 78mg | Fiber: 3g | Carbohydrates: 36g | Sugar: 18g

Dark Chocolate Brownie Cookies

High in protein and bursting with two kinds of chocolate, these cookies are both healthy and delicious. Even though they contain black beans, the scent, flavor, and appearance is unmistakably chocolate.

INGREDIENTS | MAKES 4 DOZEN

1 (15-ounce) can black beans, drained and mashed

6 ounces unsweetened chocolate, melted

¾ cup maple syrup

¾ cup xylitol

¼ coconut oil, softened

¼ cup unsweetened applesauce

2 teaspoons vanilla extract

1½ cups white whole-wheat flour

½ teaspoon baking soda

1 teaspoon baking powder

½ teaspoon sea salt

1¾ cups sugar-free chocolate chips or chopped chocolate

1. Line a baking sheet with parchment paper. Preheat oven to 375°F.

2. In a high-speed blender, combine the black beans and melted chocolate. Blend until completely smooth and creamy.

3. Add maple syrup, xylitol, coconut oil, unsweetened applesauce, and vanilla. Blend until combined. It should look like a chocolate frosting.

4. Add flour, baking soda, baking powder, and salt. Stir in the chocolate chips and mix well.

5. Scoop out 1½" balls and place on baking sheet 1" apart. Bake for 8–10 minutes. Remove from baking sheet and cool on a wire rack.

PER SERVING (2 cookies) Calories: 263 | Fat: 13g | Protein: 5g | Sodium: 200mg | Fiber: 5g | Carbohydrates: 50g | Sugar: 16g

Double Chocolate Cookies

Honey is the secret ingredient to keeping these rich chocolate cookies sweet and soft. For a truly enticing confection, sandwich these cookies with Dark Chocolate Fudge Sauce (see recipe in Chapter 12).

INGREDIENTS | MAKES 48

1 cup butter, softened
¾ cup honey
¾ cup coconut sugar
2 large eggs
2 teaspoons vanilla extract
2 cups white whole-wheat flour
½ cup cocoa
1 teaspoon baking soda
½ teaspoon sea salt
1 cup sugar-free chocolate chips

1. Preheat oven to 350°F. Line a baking sheet with parchment paper.

2. In a medium bowl, cream together butter, honey, and coconut sugar. Add eggs and vanilla and mix together.

3. In a separate bowl, mix together flour, cocoa, baking soda, and salt. Add flour mixture to butter mixture and stir to combine. Add the chocolate chips and mix.

4. Drop 1" balls on baking sheet 2" apart and bake for 8–9 minutes. Cookies will still be soft when done, so do not overbake. Slide the parchment paper off the baking sheet and allow to cool. Store cookies in an airtight container for up to 3 days.

PER SERVING (2 cookies) Calories: 197 | Fat: 11g | Protein: 3g | Sodium: 110mg | Fiber: 2g | Carbohydrates: 30g | Sugar: 15g

Chocolate Sugar Cookies

Traditional sugar cookies are even better in chocolate form, especially when piled high with rich chocolate buttercream! Sour cream in the cookie dough makes a thick, soft sugar cookie to really sink your teeth into.

INGREDIENTS | MAKES 30

1 cup unsalted butter, softened

1¼ cups coconut sugar

2 large eggs, at room temperature

½ cup sour cream

1 teaspoon vanilla extract

1 teaspoon baking powder

½ teaspoon baking soda

¼ teaspoon sea salt

½ cup unsweetened cocoa

3 cups white whole-wheat flour, plus more for rolling out

Chocolate Buttercream Frosting (see recipe in Chapter 12)

Small Cookies

Depending on the cookie cutter size, baking times will vary. For larger cookies, no more than 11 minutes will be needed. For mini cookies, bake for 7–8 minutes.

1. Preheat oven to 350°F. Line a baking sheet with parchment paper.

2. In an electric stand-mixer, whip butter and coconut sugar together until fluffy. Add eggs, sour cream, vanilla, baking powder, baking soda, and salt. Mix well until completely combined.

3. Add cocoa and flour, 1 cup at a time, until incorporated.

4. On a lightly floured work surface, roll out dough to about ¼" thickness. Cut out cookies with desired cookie cutter and place on a baking sheet 2" apart.

5. Bake cookies for 8–10 minutes depending on your cookie cutter size. Remove from baking sheet and cool on a wire rack. Let cookies cool completely before frosting them.

PER SERVING (2 cookies) Calories: 580 | Fat: 31g | Protein: 7g | Sodium: 159mg | Fiber: 7g | Carbohydrates: 79g | Sugar: 53g

Cinnamon Pecan Cookies

Cinnamon and pecans blend wonderfully in these sweet chewy cookies. Try using almonds or walnuts instead of pecans if you'd like to enjoy a different nutty flavor.

INGREDIENTS | MAKES 24

1 cup unsalted butter, softened
1 cup coconut sugar
1 large egg
1 teaspoon baking soda
1 teaspoon vanilla extract
1 teaspoon sea salt
1 tablespoon cinnamon
2¼ cups spelt flour
¼ cup very finely chopped pecans

1. Preheat oven to 350°F. Line a baking sheet with parchment paper.

2. In a medium mixing bowl, cream together butter and coconut sugar. Add the egg and mix until incorporated. Add baking soda, vanilla extract, salt, cinnamon, flour, and chopped nuts. Mix until combined.

3. Roll into 1" balls. Place the balls on prepared baking sheet 2" apart and bake for 16–20 minutes. Remove from baking sheet and cool on a wire rack.

PER SERVING (2 cookies) Calories: 320 | Fat: 18g | Protein: 4g | Sodium: 310mg | Fiber: 3g | Carbohydrates: 38g | Sugar: 17g

Classic Gingerbread Cookies

Traditional ginger cookies are even tastier with all-natural sweeteners and flours. These wonderfully spiced cookies are egg-free and contain healthy ingredients such as ground flaxseed and unsweetened applesauce.

INGREDIENTS | MAKES 20

2 tablespoons ground flaxseed

4 tablespoons unsweetened applesauce

½ cup butter, at room temperature

½ cup coconut sugar

⅔ cup molasses

½ teaspoon sea salt

¾ teaspoon baking soda

1 tablespoon ginger

2 teaspoons cinnamon

¼ teaspoon nutmeg

¼ teaspoon cloves

3 cups white spelt flour, plus more for rolling and cutting out dough

Gingerbread Men

This fantastic versatile dough is the perfect recipe for all your gingerbread men cookie cutouts. You'll get great gingerbread men of any size or shape that are sturdy and firm enough to withstand holiday decorations and toppings.

1. Preheat oven to 350°F. Line a baking sheet with parchment paper.

2. In a small bowl, combine the ground flaxseed with the applesauce and set aside.

3. In a large bowl, cream together the butter and coconut sugar. Add ground flaxseed mixture and molasses and mix until well combined.

4. Mix in salt, baking soda, ginger, cinnamon, nutmeg, and cloves. Gradually add the flour until completely combined.

5. Wrap the dough in plastic wrap and chill in the freezer for 30 minutes.

6. Roll out dough on a lightly floured work surface to about ¼" thick. Cut out shapes with cookie cutters and place on baking sheet, about 1" apart.

7. Bake for 8–12 minutes, or until cookies are puffed up and golden. These cookies will harden once out of the oven, so be sure to remove them when they look puffy. Remove from baking sheet and cool on a wire rack.

PER SERVING (2 cookies) Calories: 350 | Fat: 10g | Protein: 5g | Sodium: 224mg | Fiber: 5g | Carbohydrates: 62g | Sugar: 24g

Apple Pie Cookies

Enjoy the natural simplicity of pure apples with warm spices to create a flavor near to apple pie.

INGREDIENTS | SERVES 8

1 medium sweet apple, peeled and finely chopped
1 large egg
¾ cup powdered honey
½ teaspoon vanilla extract
1 tablespoon molasses
1 cup plus 1 tablespoon spelt flour
½ teaspoon baking soda
½ teaspoon sea salt
1 teaspoon cinnamon
¼ teaspoon nutmeg

Apple of the Day

Fresh apples in these cookies make them soft and moist. Enjoy them the same day you make them so they do not become overly soggy.

1. Preheat oven to 350°F. Line a baking sheet with parchment paper.

2. In a large bowl, add apple, egg, and powdered honey and mix well. Add vanilla and molasses. Add the flour, baking soda, salt, cinnamon, and nutmeg and mix until combined.

3. Spoon 1 tablespoon amount of dough balls onto baking sheet 2" apart. Bake for 9–11 minutes, until cookies are browned. Remove from baking sheet and cool on a wire rack. Store in an airtight container.

PER SERVING Calories: 140 | Fat: 1g | Protein: 3g | Sodium: 237mg | Fiber: 2g | Carbohydrates: 31g | Sugar: 15g

Super Soft Gluten-Free Peanut Butter Cookies

Looking for that ultra pillow-soft peanut butter cookie? Gluten-free flours create the softest, peanut butter cookie yet.

INGREDIENTS | MAKES 36

1¼ cups natural creamy peanut butter

1 cup coconut oil, softened

1⅓ cups coconut sugar

1½ tablespoons vanilla extract

1 large egg

1 large egg yolk

1 cup rice flour

⅔ cup gluten-free oat flour

½ teaspoon guar gum

1 tablespoon cornstarch

1¼ teaspoons baking soda

1 teaspoon baking powder

1/16 teaspoon cinnamon

1 teaspoon sea salt

Just Baked

These cookies need to bake until just set and will continue to cook and firm as they cool. If you want super-soft cookies, don't overbake them.

1. Line two baking sheets with parchment paper.

2. In a large bowl, cream together peanut butter and coconut oil until light and fluffy, about 5 minutes. Beat in coconut sugar and vanilla. Add the egg and egg yolk and beat for another minute. Add the flours, guar gum, cornstarch, baking soda, baking powder, cinnamon, and sea salt, and mix until just combined.

3. For each cookie, scoop out about 2 tablespoons of batter, roll into a ball, and place on prepared baking sheet. Cover cookie dough balls with plastic wrap and place in the freezer for 45 minutes or in the refrigerator for up to 3 days.

4. Preheat oven to 350°F. Place 10–12 cookies on second lined baking sheet 2" apart and bake cookies for 7–8 minutes.

5. Remove from baking sheet and cool on a wire rack. Store cooled cookies in an airtight container for up to 3 days at room temperature.

PER SERVING (2 cookies) Calories: 326 | Fat: 22g | Protein: 6g | Sodium: 334mg | Fiber: 2g | Carbohydrates: 29g | Sugar: 17g

Black and White Chocolate Chip Cookies

Why choose between white chocolate chips and dark chocolate chips? Use both! Double the chocolate is double the delicious flavor in these somewhat traditional chocolate chip cookies.

INGREDIENTS | MAKES 36

1½ cups unsalted butter, softened

3 cups coconut sugar

2 large eggs

1 large egg yolk

2 teaspoons baking soda

2 teaspoons vanilla extract

1½ teaspoons sea salt

5 cups spelt flour, divided

1 cup sugar-free dark chocolate chips

1 cup White Chocolate Chips (see recipe in Chapter 9)

1. Preheat oven to 375°F. Line a baking sheet with parchment paper.

2. In a large bowl, cream together butter and coconut sugar. Add the eggs and egg yolk, baking soda, vanilla, and salt.

3. Add 4 cups flour and mix well. Add both of the chocolate chips with the fifth cup of flour and mix well.

4. Scoop out balls with small 1" ice cream scoop and place on baking sheet 2" apart. Bake for 7–10 minutes. Remove from baking sheet and cool on a wire rack.

PER SERVING (2 cookies) Calories: 469 | Fat: 22g | Protein: 6g | Sodium: 350mg | Fiber: 5g | Carbohydrates: 76g | Sugar: 34g

Homemade Fortune Cookies

Complete with homemade fortunes, these cute little cookies are the perfect ending to any dinner party. Serve them after an Asian-style meal, such as Chinese Lemon Chicken (see recipe in Chapter 5).

INGREDIENTS | SERVES 12

¼ cup butter, softened

4 tablespoons coconut sugar

1 large egg white, at room temperature

½ teaspoon vanilla extract

⅔ cup spelt flour, divided

1½ tablespoons water

Folding Tip

If you get interrupted while folding these delicate cookies and they become too brittle to fold, return them to the oven for several seconds to soften so they will become pliable again.

1. Type or write up your custom fortunes on white paper and cut them into small strips. Fold them in half twice to fit inside the fortune cookies later.

2. Preheat oven to 400°F. Grease a baking sheet. Cut a sheet of parchment paper and set aside.

3. In a small mixing bowl, mix together butter and coconut sugar. Add egg white, vanilla, and ⅓ cup flour. Add water and mix until smooth.

4. Make a flour outline on the greased baking sheet as a guide for pouring the cookie batter. To do this, dip the rim of a 3" round cookie cutter or cup in a plate with ⅓ cup of flour and press firmly onto baking sheet 2" apart. Spread 1 teaspoon of the batter within each of the flour outlines. Bake for 4–5 minutes.

5. Remove cookies from oven quickly and remove from baking sheet. Place cookies on parchment paper so the bottoms of the cookies are facing up. Place paper fortunes in the center.

6. Gently fold the cookie in half and hold edges together while bending the cookie in the middle to form a fortune cookie shape. Cool on a wire rack.

PER SERVING Calories: 80 | Fat: 4g | Protein: 1g | Sodium: 5mg | Fiber: 1g | Carbohydrates: 10g | Sugar: 4g

Apple Coconut Cookies

For a delicious sweet apple treat with lots of spice, try these easy cookies. Filled with coconut, nuts, and oats, they make the perfect afternoon snack. These cookies also freeze well and are good for packing in lunchboxes.

INGREDIENTS | MAKES 24

½ cup honey
½ cup unsalted butter
1 teaspoon vanilla extract
1 teaspoon baking powder
½ teaspoon sea salt
1 teaspoon ginger
1 teaspoon cinnamon
½ cup unsweetened shredded coconut
1 cup chopped sweet apple
1 cup white spelt flour
1 cup rolled oats
⅔ cup walnuts, roughly chopped

Wonders of Walnuts

Walnuts and walnut oil are nutrient dense. They contain the highest levels of antioxidants and omega-3 fatty acids of any tree nut. They have been shown to lower cholesterol and support heart health, and they're packed with B vitamins.

1. Preheat the oven to 350°F. Line a baking sheet with parchment paper and set aside.

2. In a large mixing bowl, cream together the honey, butter, and vanilla until smooth. Add the baking powder, salt, ginger, and cinnamon. Add the coconut, apples, flour, oats, and nuts until all combined.

3. Scoop out 1½" dough balls and place on prepared pan 2" apart. Bake for 12–15 minutes, or until firm. Remove from baking sheet and cool on a wire rack. Store cookies in an airtight container at room temperature for up to 3 days or 2 weeks in the freezer.

PER SERVING (2 cookies) Calories: 258 | Fat: 15g | Protein: 4g | Sodium: 143mg | Fiber: 3g | Carbohydrates: 29g | Sugar: 13g

Almond Butter Chocolate Chip Oatmeal Cookies

Naturally vegan and gluten-free, these oatmeal cookies are easy and healthy!
Try adding dark chocolate chips to really intensify the chocolate flavor.

INGREDIENTS | SERVES 12

¼ cup unsweetened applesauce

1 tablespoon ground flaxseed

1 cup natural creamy almond butter, softened

½ cup coconut sugar

½ teaspoon sea salt

2 teaspoons vanilla extract

1 teaspoon baking soda

¾ cup rolled oats

⅔ cup sugar-free vegan chocolate chips

Natural Nut Butter

Natural almond butter has no added sugar or oils and should be refrigerated after opening. Sometimes nut butters are easiest to mix into a recipe if they have been allowed to come to room temperature first, however.

1. Preheat the oven to 350°F. Line a baking sheet with parchment paper.

2. In a small bowl, combine the applesauce and flaxseed and set aside.

3. In a small mixing bowl, cream together the almond butter and coconut sugar. Add the salt, vanilla, and applesauce mixture. Mix in the baking soda and oats. Add the chocolate chips and mix until everything is combined.

4. For each cookie, scoop out about 1 tablespoon of dough and shape into a ball. Place balls on baking sheet 2" apart and bake for 8–9 minutes. Cookies will firm more when cooled, so don't overbake! Remove from baking sheet and cool on a wire rack.

PER SERVING Calories: 221 | Fat: 15g | Protein: 7g | Sodium: 300mg | Fiber: 3g | Carbohydrates: 25g | Sugar: 10g

Super Healthy Chocolate Chip Cookies

The coconut butter in these cookies acts as a secret ingredient to create a wonderful flavor and texture. Loads of chocolate chips and natural butter extract will make these cookies disappear from the cookie jar in no time.

INGREDIENTS | SERVES 12

2 tablespoons coconut butter

2 tablespoons grapeseed oil

⅔ cup coconut sugar

2 tablespoons xylitol

¼ cup unsweetened applesauce

1 teaspoon vanilla extract

½ teaspoon natural butter extract

¼ teaspoon sea salt

½ teaspoon baking soda

¼ teaspoon baking powder

1 cup plus 3 tablespoons white spelt flour, divided

⅔ cup sugar-free chocolate chips

Coconut Butter Versus Coconut Oil

Coconut butter is made by removing the meat of the coconut and whipping it into butter. It contains all the health benefits of the oil as well as those of the meat, such as protein, fiber, and additional vitamins. Coconut oil is simply the oil alone. Both are incredible products that do wonders for your energy level, skin, and immune system, among other benefits.

1. Preheat oven to 350°F. Line a baking sheet with parchment paper.

2. In a small bowl, combine coconut butter and oil and mix well. Add the coconut sugar, xylitol, and applesauce and stir to combine.

3. Add the vanilla, butter extract, salt, baking soda, and baking powder. Stir the batter to combine well.

4. Add ½ cup of flour and stir to combine. Then add the chocolate chips with the remaining flour. The dough should be a bit sticky.

5. Spoon out rounded teaspoons of dough onto baking sheet 2" apart. Bake for 8–10 minutes. Remove from baking sheet and cool on a wire rack.

PER SERVING Calories: 175 | Fat: 8g | Protein: 2g | Sodium: 113mg | Fiber: 2g | Carbohydrates: 33g | Sugar: 11g

Bakery-Style Chocolate Chip Cookies

These chocolate chip cookies bake up into beautifully large and chewy confections. No one will believe they are naturally sugar-free! Add ¾ cup walnuts or pecans for an extra gourmet taste and appearance.

INGREDIENTS | MAKES 26

1½ cups butter, melted and cooled

2 cups coconut sugar

1 cup powdered honey

1½ teaspoons baking soda

¾ teaspoon baking powder

1 teaspoon cornstarch

2 teaspoons vanilla extract

½ teaspoon almond extract

2 large eggs, at room temperature

1 large egg yolk, at room temperature

4¾ cups spelt flour, divided

2 cups sugar-free semisweet chocolate chips or chunks

Freeze!

These cookies last well in an airtight container in the freezer for up to 6 weeks.

1. Preheat oven to 375°F. Line a baking sheet with parchment paper.

2. In an electric mixer, combine the butter with the coconut sugar and honey powder. Add baking soda, baking powder, cornstarch, vanilla extract, and almond extract. Add the eggs and egg yolk one at a time.

3. Add 4 cups of flour, then add the last ¾ cup with the chocolate chips. Mix until just combined. The dough should be smooth and shiny but not sticky. Add an extra tablespoon or two of flour to the dough if it is too sticky.

4. Scoop out cookies with a small or large ice cream scoop and place on baking sheet 3" apart.

5. Bake 7–8 minutes for smaller cookies (small cookie scoop) or 9–11 minutes for larger cookies (large ice cream scoop). Remove from baking sheet and cool on a wire rack. Store cookies in an airtight container at room temperature or freeze for up to 6 weeks.

PER SERVING (2 cookies) Calories: 612 | Fat: 31g | Protein: 8g | Sodium: 193mg | Fiber: 7g | Carbohydrates: 97g | Sugar: 40g

Healthy Peanut Butter Cookies

One bowl and spoon are all the utensils needed to whip up these delicious, soft peanut butter cookies! Butter-free and egg-free, these cookies are filled with healthy protein.

INGREDIENTS | SERVES 12

1½ teaspoons baking soda
½ cup rice flour
¼ teaspoon xanthan gum
¾ cup coconut sugar
1 cup natural creamy peanut butter
1 teaspoon molasses
¼ cup unsweetened applesauce
¼ teaspoon sea salt
2 teaspoons vanilla extract

1. Preheat oven to 350°F. Line a baking sheet with parchment paper.

2. In a medium bowl, mix together the baking soda, rice flour, xanthan gum, and coconut sugar until well combined.

3. Add the peanut butter, molasses, applesauce, salt, and vanilla extract and mix all the ingredients together until smooth.

4. Roll into 1" balls and place on baking sheet 2" apart. Bake in preheated oven for 7–8 minutes. Remove from baking sheet and cool on a wire rack.

PER SERVING Calories: 205 | Fat: 11g | Protein: 6g | Sodium: 306mg | Fiber: 1.5g | Carbohydrates: 23g | Sugar: 15g

Honey Chocolate Glaze Cookies

To satisfy a dark chocolate craving, these honey-sweetened chocolate cookies are the ultimate indulgence. Each cookie is finished off with a delectable chocolate-glazed center.

INGREDIENTS | MAKES 24

2 large eggs

½ teaspoon sea salt

4½ teaspoons vanilla extract, divided

2 tablespoons butter, softened

4½ ounces unsweetened chocolate, melted and cooled, divided

1 cup honey, divided

½ teaspoon baking soda

1 teaspoon baking powder

2 tablespoons cocoa powder

1⅓ cups spelt flour

6 drops liquid stevia

Milk or Dark?

If you prefer a sweeter, milk chocolate flavor for these cookies, increase the stevia in the chocolate glaze to ½ teaspoon.

1. Preheat oven to 350°F. Line a baking sheet with parchment paper.

2. In a small bowl, combine eggs, salt, and 2 teaspoons vanilla. Mix until well combined. Add the butter, 3 ounces chocolate, and ¾ cup honey. Beat until incorporated. Add baking soda, baking powder, cocoa powder, and flour and beat until just combined.

3. Roll batter into 1½" size balls and place on baking sheet 2" apart. Bake for 7–8 minutes.

4. While the cookies bake, mix together 1½ ounces melted chocolate, ¼ cup honey, 2½ teaspoons vanilla, and stevia in a small bowl.

5. When the cookies are finished baking, gently indent the very center of each cookie by pressing with a spoon. Pour about ½–1 teaspoon of the chocolate glaze into each center. Remove from baking sheet and cool on a wire rack.

PER SERVING (2 cookies) Calories: 204 | Fat: 6g | Protein: 3.5g | Sodium: 206mg | Fiber: 2.5g | Carbohydrates: 43g | Sugar: 23g

Lemon Cookies

Moist lemon cookies are even more scrumptious when topped with an easy lemon glaze. The glaze adds most of the citrus flavor to these cookies and provides a sparkling finish!

INGREDIENTS | MAKES 42

1¼ cups unsalted butter, at room temperature

¼ cup unsweetened applesauce

1 cup powdered honey

¾ cup plus 1 tablespoon xylitol, divided

2 large eggs

1 teaspoon vanilla extract

1 tablespoon lemon zest

¾ cup plus 2 tablespoons fresh lemon juice, divided

3 tablespoons coconut milk

1 teaspoon baking soda

1 teaspoon baking powder

½ teaspoon sea salt

½ teaspoon xanthan gum

4 cups white rice flour

1. Preheat oven to 350°F. Line a baking sheet with parchment paper.

2. In a large bowl, beat together butter, applesauce, powdered honey, and ½ cup xylitol until combined.

3. Blend in the eggs, vanilla, lemon zest, and 6 tablespoons lemon juice. Add the coconut milk and mix well.

4. Add baking soda, baking powder, salt, xanthan gum, and flour. Stir just until combined.

5. In a small bowl, whisk ½ cup fresh lemon juice and 5 tablespoons xylitol.

6. Spoon rounded teaspoons of dough onto baking sheet 2" apart. Bake for 8–9 minutes. Allow to cool slightly, for about 1–2 minutes, then drizzle the lemon glaze over the tops of the cookies. Remove from baking sheet and cool on a wire rack.

PER SERVING (2 cookies) Calories: 263 | Fat: 12g | Protein: 3g | Sodium: 150mg | Fiber: 1g | Carbohydrates: 38g | Sugar: 6g

Linzer Schnitten Cookies

No holiday cookie tray is complete without these lovely cookies. They are packed with cinnamon and cloves, enhanced with a tinge of lemon, and finished with sugar-free jam and a sweet glaze.

INGREDIENTS | MAKES 50

2 large eggs

1½ cups powdered honey

¾ cup coconut oil, melted

1½ teaspoons vanilla extract, divided

3⅔ cups spelt flour, plus more for rolling out

½ teaspoon sea salt

1 teaspoon baking powder

2 teaspoons cinnamon

1 teaspoon cloves

Juice and zest of 1 large lemon

⅔ cup sugar-free seedless jam of your choice

1 egg white

¾ cup xylitol

3 drops lemon juice

Lemon Power

Eating raw egg whites poses the risk of foodborne illness. However, the citric acid in a couple of drops of lemon juice neutralizes the egg and makes it safe to eat. Do not skip this step, especially if serving to young children, the elderly, or pregnant women.

1. In a large bowl with an electric mixer, beat eggs until light and frothy. Add the powdered honey to the eggs and mix. Gradually add melted oil. Add 1 teaspoon vanilla and stir to combine.

2. In a separate mixing bowl, mix together flour, salt, baking powder, cinnamon, and cloves.

3. In a small bowl, mix together lemon juice and zest.

4. Add the lemon mixture alternately with the flour mixture to the egg mixture until all are incorporated together. Cover the dough and refrigerate for 45 minutes.

5. Remove dough from the refrigerator and preheat oven to 375°F. Line a baking sheet with parchment paper.

6. Knead dough and roll out on a lightly floured surface to ¼" thick. Cut the dough into strips about 1½" wide, then into diagonals for diagonal shaped cookies. Or use cookie cutters to create desired cookie shape. Make a groove in the center of the cookie. Fill each groove with 1 teaspoon jam.

7. Place cookies on baking sheet 2" apart and bake for 12–14 minutes. While cookies are baking, mix up the egg white, xylitol, 3 drops of lemon juice, and ½ teaspoon vanilla extract. Spoon over cookies. Remove from baking sheet and cool on a wire rack.

PER SERVING (2 cookies) Calories: 173 | Fat: 7g | Protein: 3g | Sodium: 78mg | Fiber: 2g | Carbohydrates: 35g | Sugar: 7g

Molasses Oatmeal Spice Cookies

Warm up with these cookies and a hot cup of tea. Given a wonderful soft texture by the molasses, these cookies are just like the ones Grandma used to make.

INGREDIENTS | MAKES 24

½ cups spelt flour

¾ cup rolled oats

1 cup coconut sugar

1 teaspoon baking soda

1 teaspoon ginger

½ teaspoon cloves

½ teaspoon cinnamon

½ teaspoon sea salt

½ cup butter, melted and cooled

¼ cup unsweetened applesauce

¼ cup molasses

A Sprinkle of Sugar

For crispier, sweeter cookies, sprinkle tops with 3 tablespoons of coconut sugar before baking.

1. Preheat oven to 375°F. Line a baking sheet with parchment paper.

2. In a mixing bowl, whisk together the flour, oats, coconut sugar, baking soda, ginger, cloves, cinnamon, and salt. Add the melted butter, applesauce, and molasses and mix until just combined.

3. Spoon rounded tablespoons of dough onto baking sheet 2" apart. Gently press the balls down to form little fat disks.

4. Bake in the oven for 8–9 minutes. Remove from baking sheet and cool on a wire rack.

PER SERVING (2 cookies) Calories: 197 | Fat: 8g | Protein: 1g | Sodium: 208mg | Fiber: 1g | Carbohydrates: 30g | Sugar: 21g

No-Bake Chocolate Chunk Peanut Butter Cookies

These easy, fuss-free cookies are delicious, with big chunks of chocolate in every bite. Use creamy peanut butter for a delightful soft cookie or crunchy peanut butter for a nice crispy bite.

INGREDIENTS | SERVES 6

½ cup creamy or chunky natural peanut butter

¾ cup plus 1 tablespoon Kamut or quinoa puffs, finely crushed

¼ cup maple syrup

1 teaspoon vanilla extract

½ teaspoon cinnamon

⅛ teaspoon sea salt

2 tablespoons chopped sugar-free chocolate or chocolate chunks

1. Line a baking sheet with parchment paper.

2. Mix together peanut butter and crushed puffs in a medium mixing bowl until smooth. Add remaining ingredients and mix until completely combined. Dough should be soft and pliable.

3. Roll dough into 1" balls and place on baking sheet. Flatten balls into cookie shapes. Serve immediately or store in an airtight container.

PER SERVING Calories: 257 | Fat: 13g | Protein: 9g | Sodium: 150mg | Fiber: 3g | Carbohydrates: 30g | Sugar: 10g

No-Bake Carrot Cookies

Get a taste of all the delicious flavors of carrot cake in these healthy no-bake cookie balls. Sweet carrot, coconut, and applesauce sweeten these cookies naturally, and coconut sugar adds a faint taste of brown sugar.

INGREDIENTS | SERVES 14

2 tablespoons coconut oil, softened

¼ cup unsweetened applesauce, at room temperature

2 tablespoons ground flaxseed

⅓ cup coconut sugar

⅓ cup unsweetened shredded coconut

1 teaspoon vanilla extract

2 teaspoons cinnamon

¼ cup chopped walnuts

½ cup grated carrots

1 cup rolled oats

1. Line a baking sheet with parchment paper.

2. Combine all ingredients in a medium mixing bowl. Roll dough into 1 tablespoon-size balls and place on baking sheet. Chill for 15 minutes. Store covered in the refrigerator for up to 3 days.

PER SERVING Calories: 94 | Fat: 5g | Protein: 1.5g | Sodium: 4mg | Fiber: 2g | Carbohydrates: 11g | Sugar: 6g

No-Bake Mexican Chocolate Cookies

These cookies look innocent enough on the outside, but they're laced with a touch of chili pepper to create a warm heat that enhances the cookie's chocolate flavor immensely.

INGREDIENTS | SERVES 10

1 cup white whole-wheat flour
¼ cup cocoa powder
1 teaspoon cream of tartar
½ teaspoon sea salt
1 stick unsalted butter, softened
¾ cup plus 1 tablespoon coconut sugar
½ teaspoon vanilla extract
¾ teaspoon cinnamon
¼ teaspoon chili powder
1 tablespoon unsweetened almond milk

1. In a small bowl, mix together the flour, cocoa, cream of tartar, and salt.

2. In another bowl, cream together the butter, coconut sugar, vanilla, cinnamon, and chili powder.

3. Add the flour mixture to the butter mixture. Beat in almond milk until smooth and blended.

4. With floured hands, roll dough into a large log, about 1½" thick, on a work surface. Cover log with plastic wrap and freeze for 30–45 minutes.

5. Remove dough from refrigerator and slice log into cookies. Keep cookies in an airtight container in the refrigerator or freezer for up to 3 days.

PER SERVING Calories: 193 | Fat: 10g | Protein: 2g | Sodium: 122mg | Fiber: 2g | Carbohydrates: 27g | Sugar: 16g

No-Bake Quinoa Cookies

Leftover pre-cooked quinoa becomes the perfect dessert in these chocolate chip quinoa cookies. Instead of using quinoa in a savory dish, try enjoying it next time in these easy no-bake cookies.

INGREDIENTS | MAKES 14

½ cup natural peanut butter

2 tablespoons unsweetened applesauce

¼ cup honey

1 tablespoon vanilla extract

½ teaspoon sea salt

⅓ cup whole-wheat flour

1½ cups cooked quinoa

⅓ cup sugar-free dark chocolate chips

Protein Punch

Quinoa, peanut butter, and whole-wheat flour in these cookies make them high in protein. Enjoy as a quick breakfast, post-workout power snack, or healthy dessert.

1. Line a baking sheet with parchment paper.

2. In a small bowl, combine the peanut butter, applesauce, honey, vanilla, and salt.

3. Add the flour, quinoa, and chocolate chips and mix until combined.

4. Spoon rounded tablespoons of cookies on baking sheet. Place in the freezer to set, about 20 minutes. Store any leftovers in an airtight container.

PER SERVING (2 cookies) Calories: 250 | Fat: 13g | Protein: 8g | Sodium: 257mg | Fiber: 4g | Carbohydrates: 34g | Sugar: 12g

Chocolate Cream Sandwich Cookies

Traditional junk food gets a homemade, healthy twist with all-natural sweeteners and whole-food ingredients. Enjoy these chocolate cookies with or without the vanilla cream filling!

INGREDIENTS | MAKES 20

1¼ cups wheat flour
½ cup unsweetened dark cocoa powder
2 teaspoons cornstarch
1 teaspoon baking soda
¼ teaspoon baking powder
½ teaspoon sea salt
1¼ cups coconut sugar
⅔ cup organic butter, softened
1 teaspoon vanilla extract
1 large egg
1 large egg yolk
Vanilla Cream Filling (see recipe in Chapter 12)

1. Preheat oven to 375°F. Line a baking sheet with parchment paper.

2. In a large bowl, combine the flour, cocoa powder, cornstarch, baking soda, baking powder, and salt. Mix well.

3. Add coconut sugar and softened butter. Add vanilla, egg, and egg yolk and mix until incorporated.

4. Roll dough out on a flat, lightly floured surface and cut out cookies with cookie cutters. Alternatively, scoop out about tablespoon-size amounts of dough, roll into smooth spheres, and very lightly flatten to a round shape. Place cookies on baking sheet 2" apart and bake for 7–9 minutes. Smaller size cookies may just need 6–7 minutes if you want them extra soft. Remove from baking sheet and cool on a wire rack.

5. Once cookies are cooled, spread or pipe about a ¼" thick layer of Vanilla Cream Filling on a cookie and place another cookie on top to form a cookie sandwich. Repeat until all are assembled. Store cookies in an airtight container at room temperature for up to 2 days, or up to 3 weeks in the freezer.

PER SERVING (2 cookie sandwiches) Calories: 530 | Fat: 32g | Protein: 6g | Sodium: 310mg | Fiber: 3g | Carbohydrates: 65g | Sugar: 26g

Oatmeal Raisin Pillow Cookies

These cookies are so healthy, you can eat them for breakfast guilt-free! Small and soft, they contain lots of texture and health benefits in their little bites.

INGREDIENTS | MAKES 12

¾ cup unsalted butter

1¼ cups coconut sugar

1 teaspoon baking powder

¼ teaspoon baking soda

¾ teaspoon cinnamon

2 large eggs, at room temperature

2 teaspoons molasses

1 teaspoon vanilla extract

½ teaspoon sea salt

1 cup whole-wheat flour

2 cups oats

1 cup raisins

1. Preheat oven to 375°F. Line a baking sheet with parchment paper.

2. In a large bowl, beat butter until soft and fluffy. Add coconut sugar and beat until incorporated. Add baking powder, baking soda, and cinnamon.

3. Add the eggs one at a time and beat well. Add molasses and vanilla. Add salt, flour, oats, and raisins and mix until well combined.

4. Roll dough into about 1" balls and place on baking sheet 2" apart. Bake for 8–9 minutes. Remove from baking sheet and cool on a wire rack.

PER SERVING (2 cookies) Calories: 642 | Fat: 27g | Protein: 9g | Sodium: 364mg | Fiber: 6g | Carbohydrates: 96g | Sugar: 58g

Peanut Butter Oatmeal Chocolate Chip Cookies

Don't waste a minute debating whether to make peanut butter, chocolate chip, or oatmeal cookies. Treat yourself to all three flavors in these wonderfully chewy cookies! Use crunchy peanut butter for an even more diverse selection of textures.

INGREDIENTS | MAKES 30

½ cup honey

⅓ cup coconut sugar

½ cup unsalted butter

½ cup natural peanut butter

1 teaspoon vanilla extract

1 large egg

1¾ cups white whole-wheat flour

½ cup rolled oats

1 teaspoon baking powder

¼ teaspoon sea salt

1 cup sugar-free chocolate chips

Don't Burn Your Honey!

Honey bakes more quickly than regular sugar. These cookies bake quickly and may become burned or too brittle by 11 minutes, so watch carefully toward the end of baking time.

1. Preheat oven to 350°F. Line a baking sheet with parchment paper.

2. In a large bowl, mix together honey, coconut sugar, butter, peanut butter, vanilla, and egg until well combined.

3. Add flour, oats, baking powder, and salt. Mix in the chocolate chips. Dough will look damp, but do not add more flour.

4. Use a 1" ice cream scoop to make uniform balls and place on baking sheet 2" apart. Bake for 8–10 minutes. Remove from baking sheet and cool on a wire rack.

PER SERVING (2 cookies) Calories: 265 | Fat: 15g | Protein: 6g | Sodium: 118mg | Fiber: 4g | Carbohydrates: 37g | Sugar: 14g

Classic Peanut Butter Cookies

Extra soft, slightly salty, and extremely delightful, these cookies are a winner every time. Serve with a big glass of cold milk and try not to eat every last one.

INGREDIENTS | MAKES 18

1 cup natural creamy peanut butter, softened

⅔ cup unsalted butter, softened

¾ cup coconut sugar

⅓ cup xylitol

1 large egg, at room temperature

3 tablespoons milk

1 teaspoon vanilla extract

¾ teaspoon baking powder

½ teaspoon sea salt

1½ cups spelt flour

Bake in a 360°F Oven

Proteins get extra tender and soft when baked at low temperatures. Since these cookies are extra large and thick, a temperature slightly hotter than 350°F will ensure that these cookies bake perfectly.

1. Preheat oven to 360°F. Line a baking sheet with parchment paper.

2. In a large bowl, cream together the peanut butter, butter, coconut sugar, and xylitol until well combined.

3. Mix in the egg. Add the milk and vanilla. Add the baking powder, salt, and spelt flour and mix all together. Dough will look damp.

4. Roll dough into large (1½–2") balls and place on baking sheet 3" apart. Bake for 10–12 minutes. Remove from baking sheet and cool on a wire rack.

PER SERVING (1 cookie) Calories: 348 | Fat: 15g | Protein: 9g | Sodium: 159mg | Fiber: 5g | Carbohydrates: 49g | Sugar: 10g

Pumpkin Chocolate Chip Cookies

These cookies are a fall favorite! Packed with coconut sugar and powdered honey, they are light and pillowy with a soft touch of brown sugar flavor.

INGREDIENTS | MAKES 36

1 cup unsalted butter, softened

2 cups canned pumpkin

1½ cups powdered honey

½ cup coconut sugar

4 large eggs

1 teaspoon vanilla extract

4 cups spelt flour, divided

2 teaspoons baking soda

1½ teaspoons sea salt

1 teaspoon cinnamon

½ teaspoon pumpkin pie spice

2 cups sugar-free chocolate chips or chunks

1. Preheat oven to 350°F. Line a baking sheet with parchment paper.

2. In a large mixing bowl using an electric mixer fitted with a paddle attachment, cream together the butter, pumpkin, powdered honey, and coconut sugar. Add eggs and vanilla and mix well.

3. Add 3 cups flour, baking soda, salt, cinnamon, and pumpkin pie spice. Stir in chocolate chips with remaining cup of flour.

4. Spoon 1½" mounds of dough onto baking sheet 2" apart. Bake for 12–14 minutes. Remove from baking sheet and cool on a wire rack.

PER SERVING (2 cookies) Calories: 471 | Fat: 18g | Protein: 6g | Sodium: 357mg | Fiber: 6g | Carbohydrates: 85g | Sugar: 42g

Raw Chocolate Cookies

This recipe uses a dehydrator to create raw cookies with a firm, yet soft texture.
Maple syrup fuses with chocolate for an amazing sweet flavor.

INGREDIENTS | SERVES 10

2¼ cups cashew flour

2 cups oat flour

½ cup cocoa powder

¾ cup maple syrup

¼ cup water

1 tablespoon vanilla extract

1 teaspoon sea salt

½ cup chopped walnuts

Make Your Own Flours

You can buy cashew and oat flour, but if you prefer, simply blend 3 cups cashews and 2½ cups oats in a blender until fine to use in this recipe.

1. Mix cashew flour, oat flour, and cocoa in a large bowl. Add remaining ingredients and beat until combined.

2. Form small balls and press flat, creating ¼" thick cookies. Place these cookies on dehydrator trays 1½" apart from each other. Dehydrate at 105°F for 8–9 hours until no longer sticky or damp, but still very soft and moist. Store cookies in an airtight container.

PER SERVING Calories: 349 | Fat: 19g | Protein: 10g | Sodium: 243mg | Fiber: 6g | Carbohydrates: 40g | Sugar: 16g

Chocolate Oatmeal Cookies

Delectable oatmeal cookies made with common pantry items give those chocolate cravings a delicious, healthy fix. Whipped honey and butter form a base for creating the most amazing chocolate oatmeal cookies yet.

INGREDIENTS | MAKES 20

½ cup unsalted butter, softened

⅔ cup honey

1 large egg, beaten

1¼ teaspoons vanilla extract

¼ cup cocoa powder

1/16 teaspoon cinnamon

1 cup plus 2 tablespoons white whole-wheat flour

½ teaspoon baking powder

½ teaspoon sea salt

1 cup rolled oats

½ cup chopped sugar-free chocolate

1. Preheat oven to 350°F. Line a baking sheet with parchment paper.

2. In a large bowl, mix together softened butter and honey. Add egg and vanilla.

3. Add cocoa powder, cinnamon, flour, baking powder, salt, oats, and chocolate chips. Stir to combine.

4. Drop 1 tablespoon-rounded spoonfuls onto baking sheet 2" apart. Bake for 10–12 minutes. Remove from baking sheet and cool on a wire rack.

PER SERVING (2 cookies) Calories: 260 | Fat: 13g | Protein: 4g | Sodium: 154mg | Fiber: 4g | Carbohydrates: 41g | Sugar: 18g

Snickerdoodles

Healthy snickerdoodles utilize cream of tartar for a familiar classic flavor. Even though these are sugar-free, each cookie is rolled in a thick layer of cinnamon and "sugar"!

INGREDIENTS | MAKES 24

2½ cups white spelt flour

2 teaspoons cream of tartar

1 teaspoon baking soda

1 teaspoon cornstarch

½ teaspoon sea salt

½ cup unsalted butter

1 teaspoon vanilla extract

1½ cups maple sugar

2 large eggs

¼ cup xylitol

2 teaspoons cinnamon

1. Preheat oven to 375°F. Line a baking sheet with parchment paper.

2. In a medium bowl, combine flour, cream of tartar, baking soda, cornstarch, and salt.

3. In a large bowl, combine butter, vanilla, maple sugar, and eggs. Stir in flour mixture and mix until smooth.

4. In a shallow dish, combine the xylitol and cinnamon.

5. Scoop out 1½" dough balls and roll in the xylitol and cinnamon mixture. Place dough on baking sheet 2" apart. Bake for 8–10 minutes. Remove from baking sheet and cool on a wire rack.

PER SERVING (2 cookies) Calories: 298 | Fat: 9g | Protein: 4g | Sodium: 215mg | Fiber: 3g | Carbohydrates: 53g | Sugar: 25g

Sugar-Free Ginger Cookies

For a full-flavored ginger treat, these are sure to please! These cookies have a crisp edge and a moist, soft center.

INGREDIENTS | MAKES 12

2 cups spelt flour
1 tablespoon ground ginger
½ teaspoon sea salt
½ teaspoon cinnamon
1 teaspoon baking soda
⅔ cup xylitol
1 large egg
1½ tablespoons fresh grated ginger
1 tablespoon fresh lemon zest
½ cup coconut oil
½ teaspoon natural butter extract
½ teaspoon vanilla extract

1. Preheat oven to 375°F. Line a baking sheet with parchment paper.

2. In a medium mixing bowl, whisk together flour, ginger, salt, cinnamon, and baking soda.

3. In a small bowl, combine xylitol, egg, ginger, lemon zest, oil, butter extract, and vanilla. Add the dry ingredients to the wet and mix until incorporated.

4. Roll dough into small balls about 1 tablespoon sized and place on prepared baking sheet 2" apart. Bake for 7–9 minutes.

PER SERVING (2 cookies) Calories: 400 | Fat: 20g | Protein: 6g | Sodium: 420mg | Fiber: 5g | Carbohydrates: 60g | Sugar: 0g

Thin Chocolate Mint Cookies

Sweet chocolate cookies are covered in melted mint-infused dark chocolate. The dough is gluten-free and can be cut into any size or shape desired.

INGREDIENTS | MAKES 32

½ cup unsalted butter, at room temperature

½ cup powdered honey

¾ teaspoon vanilla extract

1 tablespoon unsweetened almond milk

½ cup cocoa

½ teaspoon sea salt

¼ teaspoon xanthan gum

¾ cup white rice flour, plus more for rolling out

1¼ cups melted sugar-free dark or semisweet chocolate

1¼ teaspoons peppermint extract

Patience Is a Virtue

After these cookies are coated in chocolate, be patient and let them properly set up in the freezer. Plus, these are delicious chilled!

1. In a large bowl of an electric mixer, cream butter and powdered honey until fluffy. Add vanilla, almond milk, cocoa, and salt. Mix on low to continue creaming until mixture looks like thick frosting.

2. Add xanthan gum and rice flour and mix on low until batter is smooth. Gather the dough into a ball, wrap in plastic wrap, and chill for 15 minutes.

3. Preheat oven to 350°F. Line two baking sheets with parchment paper. Remove dough from the freezer and roll out to ⅛" thickness on a lightly floured surface. With cookie cutter, cut out cookies, no bigger than 2½" diameter.

4. Place the cookies on the prepared baking sheets 2" apart. Bake for 9 minutes. Remove from baking sheet and cool on a wire rack.

5. In a small bowl, combine melted chocolate and peppermint extract. Dip cookies into chocolate to cover.

6. Place coated cookies on a parchment-lined baking sheet and place in the freezer for 20 minutes to set and harden.

PER SERVING (2 cookies) Calories: 163 | Fat: 10g | Protein: 2g | Sodium: 77mg | Fiber: 2g | Carbohydrates: 20g | Sugar: 11g

Vanilla Crinkle Cookies

A chocolate crinkle cookie remake—these cookies are soft and chewy but without the unnecessary dusting of powdered sugar. A full tablespoon of vanilla extract creates unmistakable flavor.

INGREDIENTS | MAKES 16

½ cup unsalted butter
¾ cup maple sugar
1 tablespoon vanilla extract
1 large egg
1 large egg yolk
½ teaspoon sea salt
1¼ cups rice flour
¼ teaspoon xanthan gum
½ teaspoon baking soda
¼ teaspoon cream of tartar

1. Preheat oven to 350°F. Line a baking sheet with parchment paper.

2. In a large bowl, beat together the butter, maple sugar, and vanilla until light and fluffy. Add the egg and egg yolk, one at a time, and mix to combine.

3. Add salt, flour, xanthan gum, baking soda, and cream of tartar. Mix until just incorporated.

4. Spoon 1 tablespoon-size dough balls onto the parchment lined baking sheet, about 2" apart onto baking sheet and bake for 10–12 minutes. Remove from baking sheet and cool on a wire rack.

PER SERVING (2 cookies) Calories: 395 | Fat: 13g | Protein: 4.5g | Sodium: 238mg | Fiber: 1g | Carbohydrates: 63g | Sugar: 19g

Vanilla Wafers

Re-create a classic, simple vanilla cookie! These wafers use unsweetened applesauce to decrease the fat and keep a soft texture. They're best served with ice cream.

INGREDIENTS | MAKES 24

¼ cup unsweetened applesauce

2 tablespoons vanilla extract

¼ cup grapeseed oil

½ teaspoon sea salt

⅓ cup powdered honey

¼ cup xylitol

¾ teaspoon baking powder

¼ teaspoon baking soda

1 cup plus 1 tablespoon spelt flour, plus more for rolling if needed

1. Preheat oven to 325°F. Line a baking sheet with parchment paper.

2. In a large mixing bowl, combine applesauce, vanilla, and oil. Add salt, powdered honey, xylitol, baking powder, and baking soda and mix.

3. Mix in the flour until the batter is smooth. For each cookie, scoop out a scant tablespoon of dough, roll into a smooth ball (with lightly floured hands if needed), flatten to a ¼" disc, and place on the baking sheet 2" apart.

4. Bake for about 12 minutes for softer cookies or 15–16 minutes for more crisp wafers. The cookies will firm more as they cool; do not bake more than 16 minutes.

5. When the cookies are still warm, gently press down on them to lightly flatten, if needed. Remove from baking sheet and cool on a wire rack. Store any leftover cookies in an airtight container.

PER SERVING (2 cookies) Calories: 117 | Fat: 5g | Protein: 1g | Sodium: 155mg | Fiber: 1g | Carbohydrates: 18g | Sugar: 4g

Sunflower Butter Oatmeal Chocolate Chip Cookies

Sunflower butter shines in these soft, flourless cookies. Oats give them a nice shape and healthy flavor.

INGREDIENTS | MAKES 18

¼ cup unsweetened applesauce

1 tablespoon ground flaxseed

1 cup natural sunflower butter

½ cup plus 1 tablespoon coconut sugar

2 teaspoons vanilla extract

1 teaspoon baking soda

½ teaspoon sea salt

¾ cup oats

½ cup sugar-free chocolate chips

1. Preheat oven to 350°F. Line a baking sheet with parchment paper.

2. In a small dish, combine applesauce and ground flaxseed and set aside.

3. In a small mixing bowl, combine sunflower butter, coconut sugar, vanilla, and applesauce mixture. Mix in baking soda, salt, and oats. Add chocolate chips and mix until combined.

4. For each cookie, scoop out about 1 tablespoon of dough and shape into a ball on baking sheet about 2" apart. Bake for 8–9 minutes. Cookies will firm when cooled, so don't overbake! Remove from baking sheet and cool on a wire rack.

PER SERVING (2 cookies) Calories: 317 | Fat: 18g | Protein: 9g | Sodium: 403mg | Fiber: 3.5g | Carbohydrates: 32g | Sugar: 23g

Whole-Wheat Peanut Butter Sandwich Cookies

This recipe features a delightfully creamy peanut butter filling sandwiched between two soft peanut butter cookies. These cookies resemble peanut–butter flavored whoopie pies.

INGREDIENTS | MAKES 12

¾ cup unsalted butter, at room temperature, divided

1 cup natural creamy peanut butter, divided

2¼ cups coconut sugar, divided

½ teaspoon molasses

2 large eggs

1½ teaspoons vanilla extract, divided

½ teaspoon baking soda

¼ teaspoon baking powder

½ teaspoon sea salt

⅛ teaspoon cinnamon

½ cup rolled oats

¾ cup whole-wheat flour

¼ cup agave inulin

3 tablespoons heavy cream

Agave Inulin

Agave inulin is a nutritional supplement that aids in promoting good intestinal health and has probiotic benefits. It's a natural fiber source, derived from the agave plant, and dissolves well in drinks, smoothies, and frostings. If you do not have this product on hand, protein powder can be substituted.

1. Preheat oven to 350°F. Line a baking sheet with parchment paper.

2. In the bowl of a stand mixer or a large bowl, beat ½ cup butter, ½ cup peanut butter, 1 cup coconut sugar, and molasses until light and fluffy. Add eggs and 1 teaspoon vanilla.

3. In a small bowl, whisk together baking soda, baking powder, salt, cinnamon, oats, and flour.

4. Slowly add the flour mixture to the peanut butter mixture. Roll into 1" balls and place on baking sheet 2" apart. Bake for 9–12 minutes. Remove from baking sheet and cool on a wire rack.

5. While cookies are baking, cream together ¼ cup butter and ½ cup peanut butter in a bowl until creamy and smooth. Place 1¼ cup coconut sugar and agave inulin in a blender and blend until a smooth powder. Add this to the peanut butter mixture. Add ½ teaspoon vanilla extract and beat until smooth.

6. Add cream slowly to the frosting mixture until desired consistency is reached. Spread frosting on the bottom of cooled cookies and top with remaining cookies until all cookie sandwiches have been assembled.

PER SERVING (2 cookie sandwiches) Calories: 890 | Fat: 50g | Protein: 16g | Sodium: 550mg | Fiber: 9g | Carbohydrates: 104g | Sugar: 80g

Oatmeal Cream Pies

Soft chewy oatmeal cookies sandwich a delightful vanilla cream filling for ultimate satisfaction. Each bite contains oats, cinnamon, and tasty cream for the perfect cookie pie.

INGREDIENTS | MAKES 12

½ cup butter, softened

½ cup coconut oil, softened

1 cup plus 2 tablespoons coconut sugar

1 tablespoon molasses

2 large eggs

1½ teaspoons vanilla extract

2 teaspoons cornstarch

1 teaspoon baking powder

½ teaspoon baking soda

1¼ cups white whole-wheat flour

½ teaspoon sea salt

¾ teaspoon cinnamon

¼ teaspoon nutmeg

¼ teaspoon ginger

1½ cups rolled oats, blended to very rough meal

Vanilla Cream Filling (see recipe in Chapter 12)

1. Preheat the oven to 350°F. Line a baking sheet with parchment paper.

2. In a large mixing bowl, cream together butter, coconut oil, coconut sugar, and molasses until smooth and fluffy.

3. Add eggs, vanilla, cornstarch, baking powder, and baking soda.

4. Mix in flour, salt, cinnamon, nutmeg, ginger, and oats until just combined. Dough will be sticky, but should form a ball easily.

5. Roll into 1" balls and place on baking sheet 1½" apart. Bake for 10–11 minutes, until cookies are golden and puffy. Allow to cool completely on baking sheet.

6. Once cookies are cool, apply about 1–2 tablespoons of vanilla cream filling on the underside of one cookie. Place another cookie on top of the cream to form a sandwich. Store cookies in an airtight container at room temperature for up to 3 days.

PER SERVING (1 cookie sandwich) Calories: 525 | Fat: 35g | Protein: 5g | Sodium: 210mg | Fiber: 3g | Carbohydrates: 56g | Sugar: 20g

Dessert Bars

Apricot Oat Bars

Spiced apricot bars are sure to become a fall favorite. Enjoy these chewy, naturally sweet bars, packed with both apricot jam and dried apricots for maximum flavor in each bite.

INGREDIENTS | SERVES 12

10 dried apricots, chopped coarsely

1¼ cups sugar-free apricot jam

⅔ cup plus 1 tablespoon honey, divided

1¾ cups spelt flour

¾ cup plus 1 tablespoon coconut sugar, divided

1½ teaspoons cinnamon

1 teaspoon sea salt

¾ teaspoon baking soda

1¾ cups plus 1 tablespoon oats, divided

¾ cup coarsely chopped walnuts

1 cup unsalted butter, melted

1 room-temperature large egg, beaten

1½ teaspoons vanilla extract

1. Preheat oven to 350°F. Lightly spray a 9" × 13" baking dish with cooking spray and set aside.

2. In a small mixing bowl, mix apricots, jam, and 1 tablespoon of honey. Set aside.

3. In a medium mixing bowl, mix together flour, ¾ cup coconut sugar, cinnamon, salt, baking soda, 1¾ cup oats, and walnuts. Stir in the rest of the honey. Add butter, egg, and vanilla and stir until well combined.

4. With clean fingers, press half of the crust mixture firmly in the bottom of the baking dish. Spread the apricot jam filling all over the crust. Cover the apricot filling with the remaining crust mixture and press lightly to flatten and firm.

5. Sprinkle remaining coconut sugar and oats over the mixture. Bake 28–32 minutes. Allow to cool for 15 minutes before cutting.

PER SERVING Calories: 468 | Fat: 22g | Protein: 6g | Sodium: 300mg | Fiber: 5g | Carbohydrates: 81g | Sugar: 34g

Peanut Butter Chocolate Chip Brownies

These thick, dense brownies are rich with peanut butter flavor and have a generous helping of sweet chocolate chips scattered throughout. These may be the richest brownies around.

INGREDIENTS | SERVES 15

1 cup unsalted butter, softened

1 cup natural creamy peanut butter

1½ cups coconut sugar

1 cup maple sugar

1 tablespoon molasses

4 large eggs, at room temperature

1 tablespoon vanilla extract

3 cups spelt flour

1½ teaspoons baking powder

½ teaspoon cinnamon

½ teaspoon sea salt

1½ cups sugar-free coarsely chopped chocolate

1. Preheat oven to 350°F and grease a 9" × 13" baking dish.

2. In the bowl of an electric mixer, cream butter and peanut butter together until fluffy. Add coconut sugar and maple sugar and mix until combined. Add the molasses, eggs, and vanilla. Mix on low speed until incorporated.

3. Keeping the mixer on low speed, add the flour, baking powder, cinnamon, salt, and chocolate chips slowly. Mix until everything is combined. Using a spatula, pour the batter into prepared dish.

4. Bake in center of oven for 25 minutes or until edges are golden brown and a toothpick inserted in the center comes out clean. Let cool for about 5 minutes before cutting.

PER SERVING Calories: 512 | Fat: 28g | Protein: 10g | Sodium: 230mg | Fiber: 5g | Carbohydrates: 71g | Sugar: 36g

Chocolate Chip Energy Bars

Covered with a thick slab of chocolate, these no-bake, nut-based bars provide a delicious mid-afternoon energy boost.

INGREDIENTS | SERVES 8

1 cup raw whole walnuts

1 cup raw whole cashews

2 tablespoons coconut shreds

½ cup pitted dates

1½ teaspoons vanilla extract, divided

1 tablespoon maple syrup

1 tablespoon water

¼ cup sugar-free chocolate chips or chunks

1 cup coconut oil

½ cup cocoa powder

⅓ cup maple syrup

Melting Bars

If you plan to take these for lunch or as a travel snack, freeze the bars beforehand to keep the chocolate cold so they don't melt in transit. Keep leftovers in the refrigerator or freezer.

1. In a food processor, place nuts and coconut and pulse until ingredients are blended. Add the dates, 1 teaspoon vanilla, maple syrup, and water and mix until mixture comes together and looks like cookie dough. Mix in the chocolate chips by hand.

2. Line an 8" × 8" baking dish with parchment paper and spread the dough out in the dish.

3. In a small bowl, combine the coconut oil with the cocoa. Add maple syrup and remaining vanilla and mix until smooth. Pour the chocolate over the cookie dough bars.

4. Cover dish and place in freezer to chill for 1 hour. Remove from freezer, cut into squares, and enjoy.

PER SERVING Calories: 512 | Fat: 46g | Protein: 6g | Sodium: 5mg | Fiber: 5g | Carbohydrates: 32g | Sugar: 18g

Chocolate Krispy Rice Bars

Enjoy the chocolaty, chewy crunch of these puffed cereal bars. Chocolate chips create an extra level of texture and sweetness.

INGREDIENTS | SERVES 8

2 cups 100% puffed rice cereal

½ cup rolled oats

¼ teaspoon sea salt

½ cup coconut sugar

3 tablespoons honey

2 teaspoons water

1 ounce unsweetened chocolate, chopped

1½ teaspoons vanilla extract

1½ tablespoons cocoa powder

1. Prepare an 8" × 8" baking dish by either lining it with parchment paper or lightly greasing it; set aside. Combine puffed rice cereal, oats, and sea salt in a large bowl.

2. In a small microwave-safe bowl, combine the coconut sugar, honey, and water. Microwave for 1 minute, stirring every 10 seconds. The mixture will bubble up, but this is okay. After 1 minute, add the chopped chocolate and stir. Microwave for another 5 seconds or so until the chocolate is completely melted.

3. Add the vanilla extract and cocoa powder to the chocolate mixture. The mixture should look like a chocolate ganache. Quickly pour over the rice and oats mixture while it is still warm. Work quickly to stir and coat everything evenly.

4. Pour the mixture in prepared baking dish. Press firmly with damp hands to smooth out the mixture into the pan. Place in the refrigerator for 15 minutes until the mixture has become firm. Remove from the refrigerator and cut into slices with a sharp knife.

PER SERVING Calories: 140 | Fat: 2g | Protein: 2g | Sodium: 135mg | Fiber: 1.5g | Carbohydrates: 30g | Sugar: 20g

Chocolate Hazelnut Shortbread Bars

Soft shortbread, hazelnuts, and chocolate are all rolled into one delicious bar. This winning combination cannot be beat.

INGREDIENTS | SERVES 9

½ cup whole hazelnuts

½ cup unsalted butter

½ cup coconut sugar

1 teaspoon vanilla extract

¼ teaspoon sea salt

1 cup plus 2 tablespoons flour

1 cup sugar-free chopped chocolate, melted

2 tablespoons crushed hazelnuts, optional

Flour Power

Please use a white flour in this recipe, such as white spelt flour, to create a moist and buttery shortbread. Any other flour may create a shortbread that is too dry and grainy.

1. Preheat oven to 350°F. Butter a 9" × 9" baking dish. In a food processor, pulse hazelnuts until nuts are a coarse meal; set aside.

2. With an electric mixer, cream together butter and coconut sugar until smooth. Add vanilla and salt and mix to combine. Add the flour and processed hazelnut mixture to the butter mixture and mix on low until fully incorporated.

3. Scoop out the mixture and press into the buttered baking dish. Bake for 15 minutes. Be sure not to overbake—the middle should be light and have puffed up from baking. Remove from the oven.

4. Spread the chocolate evenly over the warm bars. Sprinkle with crushed hazelnuts, if desired. Place bars in the refrigerator until hardened, about 30 minutes. Cut into squares and enjoy!

PER SERVING Calories: 291 | Fat: 21g | Protein: 4g | Sodium: 70mg | Fiber: 2g | Carbohydrates: 36g | Sugar: 12g

Dairy-Free, Gluten-Free Brownies

These allergy-friendly brownies are almost better than traditional brownies! They are fudgy, rich, and chewy, and everything else a good brownie should be.

INGREDIENTS | SERVES 15

3 ounces unsweetened chocolate, melted

1 cup grapeseed oil

2½ cups coconut sugar

4 large eggs

½ teaspoon natural butter extract

2 teaspoons vanilla extract

¾ teaspoon sea salt

½ teaspoon cornstarch

⅓ cup cocoa

2 tablespoons almond flour

1. Preheat the oven to 350°F. Line a 7" × 11" pan with parchment paper or spray with cooking spray and set aside.

2. In a large mixing bowl, combine melted chocolate, oil, and coconut sugar. Mix to combine. Gradually mix in the eggs. Add the butter extract, vanilla, and salt and whisk to combine.

3. Sift together the cornstarch, cocoa, and flour and then add to the mixture.

4. Pour mixture in the prepared pan and bake for 30–35 minutes. Allow to cool before cutting into bars.

PER SERVING Calories: 316 | Fat: 18 | Protein: 2g | Sodium: 138mg | Fiber: 1g | Carbohydrates: 38g | Sugar: 37g

Flourless Cinnamon Oatmeal Blondies

Garbanzo beans create a fiber-rich base to these delicious flourless dessert bars. Have no fear, however, because sweet coconut sugar and spicy cinnamon cover up any trace of bean flavor perfectly.

INGREDIENTS | SERVES 15

1 (15-ounce) can garbanzo beans, drained and thoroughly rinsed

3 tablespoons coconut oil

4 tablespoons unsweetened applesauce

2 tablespoons almond milk

½ teaspoon baking powder

⅛ teaspoon baking soda

1½ teaspoons vanilla extract

½ teaspoon butter extract

¼ teaspoon sea salt

¾ cup plus 3 tablespoons coconut sugar, divided

¾ cup plus 2 tablespoons oats, divided

2½ teaspoons cinnamon, divided

Baked Beans

Garbanzo beans give these dessert bars an excellent source of protein while decreasing the amount of unhealthy fats that you find in traditional brownies. Using beans eliminates the need for eggs, creating a dish that is vegan and gluten-free if using gluten-free oats.

1. Preheat oven to 350°F. Grease a 9" × 9" baking dish.

2. In a food processor or blender, process the garbanzo beans, coconut oil, applesauce, and almond milk until the mixture looks like a very smooth hummus.

3. Add the baking powder, baking soda, vanilla, butter extract, salt, ¾ cup coconut sugar, ¾ cup oats, and 2 teaspoons cinnamon and blend until smooth and fully incorporated.

4. Pour batter in pan. In a small bowl, combine remaining coconut sugar, oats, and cinnamon. Sprinkle mixture over the top of the bars and bake for 22–25 minutes. The center should be firm but still soft and moist. Let cool 10 minutes before serving.

PER SERVING Calories: 130 | Fat: 3g | Protein: 2g | Sodium: 145mg | Fiber: 2g | Carbohydrates: 23g | Sugar: 13g

Halfway Cookie Bars

These delicious cookie bars feature warm melted chocolate and silky, naturally sweet meringue. They should absolutely be accompanied with a glass of milk!

INGREDIENTS | SERVES 15

2 cups spelt flour

1 teaspoon sea salt

½ teaspoon baking soda

1 teaspoon baking powder

⅓ cup butter

3 tablespoons unsweetened applesauce

⅓ cup honey

1½ cups coconut sugar, divided

3 large egg yolks

1 teaspoon vanilla extract

1 cup sugar-free chocolate chips or chunks

4 large egg whites

⅛ teaspoon cream of tartar

½ teaspoon cornstarch

1. Preheat oven to 350°F. Line a glass 9" × 13" baking dish with parchment paper so enough hangs off the sides that you can easily lift the bars out after they are baked. Spray with cooking spray.

2. In a medium bowl, combine flour, salt, baking soda, and baking powder.

3. In another bowl, cream together the butter, applesauce, honey, and 1 cup coconut sugar. Add egg yolks and vanilla and mix until combined. In 3 batches, stir in the flour mixture.

4. Press the dough in the prepared pan. Sprinkle chocolate chips over the dough.

5. Wipe out bowl that was used for the dry ingredients. Place the 4 egg whites in the bowl and begin whisking, gradually increasing speed until they look very frothy and light in color. Add the cream of tartar and cornstarch and beat for another minute. Add in the remaining coconut sugar and beat until sugar is dissolved and the mixture is smooth and slightly glossy. The meringue should hold a soft peak and be light in color. Spread the mixture over the bars.

6. Cover the pan with foil. Bake for 20 minutes. Remove the foil cover and bake for an additional 5–7 minutes until the meringue is golden brown. Let cool 15 minutes before lifting parchment paper from the pan to remove the bars to slice and serve.

PER SERVING Calories: 268 | Fat: 9g | Protein: 4g | Sodium: 250mg | Fiber: 3g | Carbohydrates: 52g | Sugar: 27g

Sugar Cookie Bars

Traditional sugar cookies are baked into a thick bar and topped with a generous layer of sweet frosting! Add food coloring to the frosting to fit any festive occasion.

INGREDIENTS | SERVES 15

½ cup unsalted butter, at room temperature

1 cup powdered honey

2 large eggs, at room temperature

1 teaspoon vanilla extract

½ teaspoon sea salt

¼ teaspoon baking soda

⅛ teaspoon baking powder

2½ cups white spelt flour

Vanilla Cream Filling (see recipe in Chapter 12)

Sugar Cookies As Easy As 1-2-3!

Forgo rolling and cutting cookie dough and piping frosting on each individual cookie with these easy bars! Simply spread frosting over the intact cake, then slice and serve!

1. Preheat oven to 375°F. Grease a 9" × 13" baking dish.

2. In a large bowl of an electric mixer, cream together the butter and powdered honey until fluffy. Add eggs, one at a time, and mix until well combined.

3. Add vanilla, salt, baking soda, and baking powder. Add in the flour, half a cup at a time, mixing on low until all the flour is incorporated.

4. Spread the dough out into greased pan. Bake for 10–15 minutes. Be careful not to overbake! The bars should be light and golden. Let cool completely before cutting and frosting with cream filling.

PER SERVING Calories: 460 | Fat: 22g | Protein: 4g | Sodium: 139mg | Fiber: 2.5g | Carbohydrates: 65g | Sugar: 44g

No-Bake Cookie Dough Cheesecake Bars

Cheesecake has never been so easy. This recipe creates a thick layer of luscious healthy cheesecake with a naturally sweet graham cracker base.

INGREDIENTS | SERVES 9

⅓ cup rolled oats

1 cup natural graham cracker crumbs

½ cup Earth Balance Shortening Sticks, softened, divided

¼ cup maple syrup, divided

½ cup xylitol

8 ounces vegan cream cheese, at room temperature

1½ teaspoons vanilla extract, divided

¾ cup plus 1 tablespoon white spelt flour, divided

⅓ cup coconut sugar

½ teaspoon sea salt

⅓ cup sugar-free chocolate chips

Natural Graham Crackers

Refined sugar-free graham crackers can be expensive or hard to find. For a truly made-from-scratch dessert, try making Honey Graham Crackers (see recipe in Chapter 15) for this recipe instead of using store-bought.

1. Line an 8" × 8" baking dish with parchment paper and set aside.

2. In a food processor or blender, combine the oats with graham cracker crumbs. Mix until crumbly. Pour into a small mixing bowl, and combine with ¼ cup shortening and 3 tablespoons of maple syrup. Mix until moist and well combined. Wet your hands and gently press the mixture into the bottom of pan. Place in the freezer for 10 minutes.

3. Empty crumbs out of food processor and add the xylitol. Process the xylitol until powdery. Add the soft cream cheese, 1 teaspoon of vanilla, and 1 tablespoon of flour. Mix until creamy.

4. Remove crust from freezer and spread the cream cheese filling over the crust, reserving 2 tablespoons for the cookie dough. Return to the freezer for another 10 minutes.

5. Combine the 2 tablespoons cream cheese filling, remaining shortening, and coconut sugar and mix well. Add the rest of the ingredients the 1 tablespoon maple syrup, salt, ½ teaspoon vanilla extract, ¾ cup spelt flour, and chocolate chips and mix well. Spread the cookie dough over the cream cheese filling and return the pan to the refrigerator to set for 30 minutes. Cut into squares. Keep any leftovers in the refrigerator.

PER SERVING Calories: 375 | Fat: 21g | Protein: 3g | Sodium: 310mg | Fiber: 2.5g | Carbohydrates: 48g | Sugar: 19g

No-Bake Peanut Butter Pretzel Granola Bars

These no-bake granola bars are chewy and sweet thanks to delicious dates. The rich salty peanut butter flavor is enhanced with nutritional yeast and complemented with a healthy helping of chocolate chips.

INGREDIENTS | SERVES 9

¼ cup soaked dates

⅓ cup honey

⅓ cup creamy salted natural peanut butter

1 teaspoon vanilla extract

2 tablespoons nutritional yeast

1⅓ cups oats

⅓ cup chocolate chips or chopped chocolate

½ cup chopped pretzels

Soaked Dates

Soaking dates rehydrates and softens them for optimal texture in no-bake recipes or baked goodies. Soak dates for this recipe for 1 hour in just enough water to cover.

1. Line an 8" × 8" baking dish with parchment paper.

2. Chop soft dates until fine and the dates become a very rough paste.

3. In a medium mixing bowl, combine honey, peanut butter, vanilla, and dates. Add the nutritional yeast, oats, chocolate, and pretzels and mix well.

4. Press mixture into the pan. Place in freezer to set for 30 minutes. Cut into slices. Store leftovers in an airtight container in the refrigerator.

PER SERVING Calories: 228 | Fat: 8g | Protein: 6g | Sodium: 274mg | Fiber: 3g | Carbohydrates: 35g | Sugar: 19g

Orange Bars

These delightful treats are a refreshing twist on a classic lemon bar. Enjoy the soft, luscious texture of these citrus-infused treats.

INGREDIENTS | SERVES 9

½ cup unsalted butter, at room temperature

1 cup powdered honey, divided

1 cup white rice flour, divided

½ cup oat flour

½ teaspoon xanthan gum

⅛ teaspoon sea salt

3 large eggs, at room temperature

⅓ cup xylitol

Zest of 1 large orange

6 tablespoons fresh orange juice

2 tablespoons fresh lemon juice

½ teaspoon almond extract

1. Grease an 8" × 8" baking dish.

2. In an electric mixer with the paddle attachment, cream together the softened butter and ⅓ cup powdered honey until light and fluffy.

3. Sift together ⅓ cup rice flour, oat flour, xanthan gum, and salt and add to the mixture. Mix until just combined.

4. Pour the dough into baking dish and press down, creating a ¼" edge of dough up the sides of pan. Preheat oven to 350°F. Place dough in freezer while oven heats. Bake the crust for 10 minutes.

5. In a medium bowl, whisk together the eggs, ⅔ cup powdered honey, xylitol, orange zest, orange and lemon juice, and almond extract. Mix until well combined. Add the ⅔ cup rice flour and mix.

6. Pour over the baked crust and bake covered for 30–32 minutes. Be careful not to overbake. It's okay if the very middle is a bit wiggly—the filling will set completely when cooled. Slice into squares and garnish with fresh orange zest if desired.

PER SERVING Calories: 279 | Fat: 13g | Protein: 4g | Sodium: 60mg | Fiber: 1g | Carbohydrates: 40g | Sugar: 14g

Peanut Butter Delight

These peanut butter chocolate oat bars are chewy and sweet, and resemble peanut butter Rice Krispies bars. Use crunchy peanut butter for extra crunch and texture in these truly decadent dessert bars.

INGREDIENTS | SERVES 9

¼ cup butter
2 cups coconut sugar
½ cup full-fat canned coconut milk
⅓ cup cocoa powder
1 tablespoon vanilla extract
¾ cup natural peanut butter
2¾ cups rolled oats

Butter-Free

To create a dairy-free version of this recipe, a neutral oil, such as grapeseed or light coconut oil, with ¼ teaspoon natural butter extract can be used in place of the butter.

1. Grease an 8" × 8" baking dish and set aside.

2. In a small saucepan, combine the butter, coconut sugar, and coconut milk. Mix until the sugar has dissolved. Add the cocoa powder and bring to a boil over low heat. Allow to boil for 4–5 minutes, stirring frequently so the mixture does not burn. Remove pan from heat and stir in the vanilla and peanut butter.

3. Stir in oats and mix until the oats are completely incorporated. Pour the mixture into baking dish, spreading evenly. Place in the refrigerator for about 25 minutes or until firm. Slice into bars and enjoy.

PER SERVING Calories: 480 | Fat: 21g | Protein: 10g | Sodium: 110mg | Fiber: 5g | Carbohydrates: 68g | Sugar: 47g

Peanut Butter Protein Bars

Whey protein powder and peanut butter create valuable energy-sustaining protein to fuel the body. Chocolate melted over these bars make them an irresistible healthy breakfast or snack.

INGREDIENTS | SERVES 9

¾ cup honey

1 cup rolled oats

¾ cup whey protein powder

1 cup natural peanut butter

2 teaspoons vanilla extract

2 cups crispy rice cereal

2 ounces sugar-free chocolate, chopped

1. Heat the honey over medium heat in a 3-quart saucepan. The honey should boil slightly, with bubbles at the edges only. If it comes to a rapid boil, the final product will be very brittle. Once honey is hot, immediately remove from heat and mix in the oats, protein powder, peanut butter, and vanilla. Add the rice cereal and stir well.

2. Use a spatula to press mixture into an 8" × 8" baking dish. Add chocolate on top of hot bars and spread with a spatula. The heat will melt the chocolate pieces for easy spreading of the chocolate.

3. After the chocolate is evenly spread, take a sharp knife and cut into bars. Refrigerate for 30 minutes to set. Keep covered in the refrigerator for up to 7 days.

PER SERVING Calories: 390 | Fat: 17g | Protein: 20g | Sodium: 230mg | Fiber: 3g | Carbohydrates: 47g | Sugar: 27g

Raspberry Crumble Bars

These tasty raspberry bars are hearty enough for breakfast and sweet enough for dessert. They are thick and chewy, with raspberry jam layered between oats and buttery pecans.

INGREDIENTS | SERVES 9

1¾ cups wheat flour
1 cup maple sugar
½ teaspoon sea salt
1 cup pecans, chopped
¾ cup cold butter
2 large eggs
1 cup sugar-free raspberry jam
1 teaspoon vanilla extract

1. Preheat the oven to 350°F. Line a 9" × 9" baking pan with parchment paper so enough hangs off the sides that you can easily lift the bars out after they are baked.

2. In a large mixing bowl, whisk together the flour, maple sugar, salt, and pecans. Cut the butter and the eggs into the mixture. Scoop out 3 cups of the mixture into prepared baking pan and gently press down in an even layer.

3. In a small bowl, combine the raspberry jam and vanilla. Spread the jam mixture over the crust. Sprinkle the remaining flour mixture over the jam, creating a crumb topping. Bake for 40 minutes or until browned. Allow the bars to cool in the pan before slicing.

PER SERVING Calories: 412 | Fat: 25 | Protein: 5g | Sodium: 162mg | Fiber: 2g | Carbohydrates: 59g | Sugar: 14g

Raw Triple Chocolate Bars

Three different delectable layers of chocolate provide an intense chocolate bar. These bars are no-bake, vegan, and naturally sweetened—a winning combination!

INGREDIENTS | SERVES 9

¾ cup plus 5 tablespoons oat flour, divided

⅔ cup plus 2 tablespoons cocoa powder, divided

6 tablespoons maple syrup, divided

2 tablespoons water

1½ cups coconut sugar

⅓ cup ripe avocado

1½ teaspoons vanilla extract, divided

⅛ teaspoon sea salt

1. Lightly spray an 8" × 8" baking dish with cooking spray.

2. Combine ¾ cup flour, ⅓ cup cocoa powder, and 4 tablespoons maple syrup in a small bowl. Add the water slowly, 1 tablespoon at a time until it becomes a smooth mixture but does not become sticky. It's okay if only 1 tablespoon of water is needed. Press into prepared baking dish. Place in the freezer for 10 minutes.

3. In a food processor, pulse the coconut sugar until it turns to powder. Add the avocado, 1 teaspoon vanilla, salt, ⅓ cup cocoa, and remaining flour. Spread the mixture over the chilled crust.

4. In a small bowl, whisk together 2 tablespoons of cocoa powder, 2 tablespoons maple syrup, and ½ teaspoon vanilla until smooth. Pour the glaze over the top of the bars and refrigerate for 30 minutes. Cut bars with a sharp knife and remove from pan.

PER SERVING Calories: 237 | Fat: 3g | Protein: 3g | Sodium: 38mg | Fiber: 4g | Carbohydrates: 55g | Sugar: 42g

Secretly Vegan Brownies

These brownies are so dense and fudgy, it's hard to believe they are full of healthy ingredients like avocado, wheat flour, and coconut sugar!

INGREDIENTS | SERVES 9

1 large ripe avocado
¾ cup unsweetened almond milk
1½ cups coconut sugar
½ cup maple syrup
1 teaspoon vanilla extract
½ teaspoon baking powder
⅛ teaspoon sea salt
¾ cup cocoa powder
½ cup white whole-wheat flour
¾ cup sugar-free vegan chocolate chips or chunks

Extra Fudge

These brownies are very much like fudge, with a thick, moist texture. Brownies will still be moist when they are finished baking.

1. Preheat oven to 350°F. Grease a glass 9" × 9" baking dish.

2. In a large bowl, beat together the avocado and almond milk until very smooth and creamy. Add the coconut sugar and maple syrup. Add the vanilla and mix until very smooth.

3. Add the baking powder, salt, cocoa powder, and flour together and mix until just incorporated. Add the chocolate chips or chunks.

4. Pour mixture into the prepared dish. Cover and bake for 30–35 minutes. A toothpick inserted in the center should come out clean. Store any leftovers in the refrigerator.

PER SERVING Calories: 320 | Fat: 10g | Protein: 4g | Sodium: 75mg | Fiber: 6g | Carbohydrates: 70g | Sugar: 45g

Shortbread Bars

A simple shortbread recipe becomes spectacular with melted chocolate and chopped nuts. Few ingredients and a simple procedure make these the perfect quick treat.

INGREDIENTS | SERVES 9

1½ cups butter, softened

¾ cup coconut sugar

3 cups spelt flour

3 ounces sugar-free chocolate chips, melted

¼ cup whole almonds, chopped

Bite-Size

This recipe can be doubled and cut into smaller bite-size squares for a fun finger dessert for a crowd.

1. Preheat oven to 350°F. Butter a 9" × 9" baking dish.

2. In a medium mixing bowl, cream together butter and coconut sugar thoroughly. Add flour and mix well. Spread into the prepared dish and bake for 15–20 minutes.

3. Remove from oven and spread chocolate over the intact cake. Sprinkle with chopped almonds and slice into bars to serve warm or allow to cool before enjoying. Store in an airtight container.

PER SERVING Calories: 550 | Fat: 35g | Protein: 6g | Sodium: 6mg | Fiber: 6g | Carbohydrates: 60g | Sugar: 17g

Blondie Bars

Blondies are the vanilla version of a classic chocolate brownie. These blondies have a thick, chewy cookie bar base made of healthy spelt flour and coconut sugar.

INGREDIENTS | SERVES 15

2 cups spelt flour

1 teaspoon baking powder

⅛ teaspoon baking soda

1 teaspoon sea salt

½ cup plus 3 tablespoons unsalted butter, melted

1 tablespoon molasses

1¼ cups coconut sugar

¾ cup powdered honey

2 large eggs, beaten

2 tablespoons vanilla extract

Chocolate Chips

Sprinkle ½ cup chocolate chips over bars when they are warm to create a chocolate chip cookie flavor if desired.

1. Preheat oven to 325°F. Butter a glass 7" × 11" baking dish.

2. In a medium mixing bowl, mix together flour, baking powder, baking soda, and salt. Set aside.

3. In a large bowl, add melted and cooled butter, molasses, coconut sugar, and powdered honey. Mix well until combined. Add beaten eggs and vanilla. Stir until incorporated.

4. Pour batter into the prepared dish. Bake for 35–40 minutes, or until browned, covering with foil halfway into baking. Be careful not to overbake. Allow to cool for 15 minutes before cutting into bars.

PER SERVING Calories: 250 | Fat: 9g | Protein: 3g | Sodium: 212mg | Fiber: 2g | Carbohydrates: 39g | Sugar: 24g

Strawberry Oat Bars

Undeniably delicious and completely vegan, these oat bars are packed with strawberries, nuts, and grains in a healthy dessert bar that also satisfies a sweet tooth.

INGREDIENTS | SERVES 12

1⅓ cups Earth Balance Buttery Baking Sticks

1 cup coconut sugar

1½ teaspoons baking powder

½ teaspoon sea salt

⅓ cup crushed walnuts

1½ cups rolled oats

1½ cups whole-wheat flour

12 ounces sugar-free strawberry jam

1 teaspoon vanilla extract

1. Preheat oven to 350°F. Spray a 9" × 13" glass baking dish with cooking spray.

2. In a medium mixing bowl, mix together Earth Balance Buttery Baking Sticks, coconut sugar, baking powder, and sea salt. Add the crushed walnuts, oats, and flour and mix until combined. The mixture should be soft and pliable and not sticky.

3. In a small bowl, combine the jam with the vanilla.

4. Scoop out about half of the dough mixture and press into the bottom of the baking dish. Spread the jam over the dough. Gently crumble the remaining dough over the jam and press very slightly to flatten a bit.

5. Bake in the oven for 20–25 minutes or until the top has become a golden color and the jam is bubbling slightly. Let cool before cutting.

PER SERVING Calories: 383 | Fat: 23g | Protein: 4g | Sodium: 405mg | Fiber: 3g | Carbohydrates: 55g | Sugar: 17g

Vegan Lemon Bars

This traditionally egg-rich confection is easy to make egg-free. Agar-agar powder creates a custard that is vegan-friendly and contains less fat. Sprinkle powdered xylitol over the tops of these bars right before serving in true classic lemon bar style.

INGREDIENTS | YIELDS 15 BARS

2⅓ cups white spelt flour

¾ cup maple sugar

¼ teaspoon baking powder

⅛ teaspoon sea salt

1⅓ cups Earth Balance Buttery Baking Sticks

½ teaspoon natural butter extract

1 tablespoon agar-agar powder

2 cups water

1¼ cups xylitol

1 tablespoon liquid stevia

2 tablespoons cornstarch

1½ cups fresh lemon juice

2 tablespoons fresh lemon zest

1 teaspoon vanilla extract

3 drops natural yellow food coloring (optional)

Powdered xylitol, for dusting

Agar-Agar Powder

Agar-agar is a seaweed-based gelatin substitute. Make sure to use agar powder, not agar-agar flakes, in this recipe.

1. Preheat oven to 350°F. Spray a 9" × 13" dish with cooking spray.

2. In a large bowl, combine the flour, maple sugar, baking powder, and salt. Mix well to combine. Cut in the Earth Balance Buttery Baking Sticks and butter extract until the mixture looks like a moist pie dough. Scoop out the mixture and press into prepared pan. Press dough gently up the sides of the pan to create a small edge so the filling will hold well. Place in the freezer for 5 minutes.

3. Bake crust for 20 minutes. Remove the pan from the oven and allow to cool.

4. In a small saucepan, soak the agar-agar and water for 2 minutes. When it has dissolved, turn on heat to high, bring to a boil, and boil for 2 minutes. The mixture will bubble up, so just lift the pan from the heat if it rises too much. Mix in xylitol and stevia.

5. Turn heat down to low and whisk in cornstarch, lemon juice, and lemon zest. Whisk constantly over a low simmer until the mixture thickens slightly and everything is dissolved, about 4–5 minutes. Turn off heat, whisk in the vanilla extract and the food coloring, if desired.

6. Pour filling over the baked crust. Refrigerate for about 30 minutes or until the filling has set. Bars become extra firm when chilled but soften more at room temperature. Sprinkle tops with powdered xylitol before serving. Store any leftovers in an airtight container in the refrigerator.

PER SERVING Calories: 299 | Fat: 16g | Protein: 3g | Sodium: 224mg | Fiber: 2g | Carbohydrates: 43g | Sugar: 7g

Buckeye Brownies

Thick and densely rich, these peanut butter brownies are the best of both worlds. Use dark melted chocolate for an extra decadent treat.

INGREDIENTS | YIELDS 15 BARS

Dairy-Free, Gluten-Free Brownies (see recipe in this chapter)

1 cup creamy natural peanut butter

⅔ cup coconut sugar

1 teaspoon vanilla extract

3 tablespoons almond milk

½ teaspoon grapeseed oil

8 ounces sugar-free chocolate, melted

1. Prepare brownies according to directions. Let cool completely.

2. In a small mixing bowl, combine the peanut butter, coconut sugar, and vanilla and stir to combine. Add the almond milk, a little at a time, until the mixture is smooth, creamy, and spreadable.

3. Spread peanut butter layer onto the brownies and set in the freezer for 10 minutes while preparing the chocolate.

4. Add oil to the warm melted chocolate and mix to combine. Remove brownies from the freezer, pour and spread the chocolate evenly over the bars and place in the fridge for 5 minutes for chocolate to set. Slice and serve.

PER SERVING Calories: 495 | Fat: 31g | Protein: 7g | Sodium: 220mg | Fiber: 3g | Carbohydrates: 61g | Sugar: 48g

No-Bake Pumpkin Cheesecake Bars

Here is a plush cheesecake treat with loads of flavor. A gluten-free crust gives texture to the slightly tangy cream cheese and pumpkin spread.

INGREDIENTS | SERVES 9

1½ cups gluten-free oats

¼ cup raw walnuts

4 Medjool dates, pitted

½ cup honey, divided

½ cup cream cheese

½ cup powdered xylitol

1½ teaspoons vanilla extract, divided

⅔ cup pumpkin purée

½ teaspoon cinnamon

¼ teaspoon pumpkin spice mix

¼ cup gluten-free oat flour

1. In a food processor, pulse the oats until they become a rough flour. Add the walnuts, dates, and ¼ cup honey and pulse until a ball starts to form. Transfer the dough to an 8" × 8" baking dish, spreading and pressing to the bottom of the pan.

2. In a small mixing bowl, mix together the cream cheese, xylitol, and ½ teaspoon vanilla. Gently spread over the base layer and place in the freezer.

3. In the same bowl, combine the pumpkin, ¼ cup honey, cinnamon, pumpkin spice mix, and 1 teaspoon vanilla. Add the flour to the mixture and mix until the batter is smooth and thickened.

4. Spread the pumpkin layer over the cheesecake layer and then place in the freezer for another 30 minutes. Cut into squares and enjoy immediately for a chilled treat, or allow to sit out for 10 minutes for a softer bar. Store covered in the freezer for up to 2 weeks or keep in the fridge for 1 week.

PER SERVING Calories: 250 | Fat: 8g | Protein: 4g | Sodium: 45mg | Fiber: 3g | Carbohydrates: 45g | Sugar: 19g

CHAPTER 12

Frostings, Glazes, and Toppings

Classic Cream Cheese Frosting

This creamy soft icing is the perfect topping for an endless assortment of desserts. Try it over chocolate cupcakes, pumpkin bread, sugar cookies, or even graham crackers.

INGREDIENTS | MAKES 2½ CUPS

1 (8-ounce) package cream cheese, at room temperature

½ cup unsalted butter

1 cup maple sugar, finely powdered

3 cups xylitol, finely powdered

3 teaspoons cornstarch

2 teaspoons vanilla extract

2 tablespoons heavy cream

Powdered Only, Please!

To achieve the smoothest frosting, sugars need to be completely powdered. Use a blender or food processor and blend on high power until there are no more sugar granules.

1. In a medium bowl, beat cream cheese and butter with a hand-held mixer until whipped.

2. Add the powdered sweeteners, cornstarch, and vanilla and beat until incorporated.

3. Slowly add the heavy cream and beat until desired consistency is reached. Store covered in the refrigerator.

PER SERVING (⅛ cup) Calories: 198 | Fat: 9g | Protein: 1g | Sodium: 37mg | Fiber: 0g | Carbohydrates: 40g | Sugar: 10g

German Chocolate Frosting

Chocolate icing gets an intense flavor and texture enhancement with shredded coconut in this thick, flavorful frosting.

INGREDIENTS | MAKES 2 CUPS

1 cup unsweetened almond milk

1 cup coconut sugar

3 large egg yolks

½ cup unsalted butter, softened

1 teaspoon vanilla extract

1⅓ cups shredded unsweetened coconut

1 cup chopped pecans

1. In a medium saucepan over medium heat, pour almond milk, sugar, and egg yolks and heat, stirring, to thicken.

2. Remove from heat and add softened butter, vanilla extract, shredded coconut, and chopped pecans. Stir until well combined. Cool before using.

PER SERVING (⅛ cup) Calories: 189 | Fat: 14g | Protein: 2g | Sodium: 11mg | Fiber: 1g | Carbohydrates: 16g | Sugar: 14g

Easy Vanilla Glaze

For muffins, cookies, or anything that would benefit from a little extra sweetness, this vanilla glaze is easy to make and instantly gives a gourmet look to desserts.

INGREDIENTS | MAKES ⅓ CUP

3 tablespoons unsweetened almond milk

3 tablespoons vanilla protein powder

½ teaspoon liquid stevia

½ teaspoon vanilla extract

1. In a small bowl, whisk together the almond milk and protein powder. Add the stevia and vanilla and mix until smooth and combined.

2. Use immediately or store covered in the refrigerator.

PER SERVING (2 tablespoons) Calories: 65 | Fat: 0.5g | Protein: 13g | Sodium: 32mg | Fiber: 0g | Carbohydrates: 2g | Sugar: 1g

Chocolate Buttercream Frosting

This buttercream rivals even bakery-style chocolate frostings thanks to pure coconut sugar's fantastic sweetness and flavor.

INGREDIENTS | MAKES 2½ CUPS

2⅔ cups coconut sugar

1½ tablespoons cornstarch

1 cup unsalted butter, softened

1⅔ cups cocoa

⅛ teaspoon sea salt

2 teaspoons vanilla extract

6 tablespoons heavy cream

Coconut Sugar

While coconut sugar contains roughly the same amount of calories and carbohydrates as refined white sugar, it's lower on the glycemic index and contains much less fructose than regular sugar. It also has many vitamins and minerals still intact after production, making it a beneficial sweetener.

1. In a blender, blend coconut sugar and cornstarch for a few minutes, scraping the bowl occasionally, until it turns into a fine powder.

2. In a large bowl, using a hand-held mixer, cream together the powdered sugar mix and the butter. Add in cocoa, salt, and vanilla.

3. Slowly add the heavy cream and whip until desired consistency is reached.

PER SERVING (⅛ cup) Calories: 220 | Fat: 12g | Protein: 1.5g | Sodium: 20mg | Fiber: 2g | Carbohydrates: 32g | Sugar: 27g

Vegan Chocolate Buttercream

This frosting has the same taste and appearance as other chocolate buttercream recipes, but is made without dairy.

INGREDIENTS | MAKES 1¾ CUPS

¾ cup Earth Balance Shortening Sticks

1⅓ cups coconut sugar, finely powdered

⅛ teaspoon sea salt

½ cup cocoa powder

1 teaspoon vanilla extract

⅛ teaspoon natural butter extract

2 teaspoons rice flour

Thick or Thin?

To create a very thick frosting, add an extra 1–2 teaspoons of flour to the frosting and place in the refrigerator for 30 minutes before using.

1. In a medium mixing bowl, add shortening, powdered coconut sugar, and salt. Cream together using a hand-held mixer until smooth and combined.

2. Add the cocoa, vanilla, and butter extract and mix until creamy.

3. Mix in the rice flour until frosting is creamy and smooth. Use immediately or store covered in an airtight container in the refrigerator.

PER SERVING (⅛ cup) Calories: 170 | Fat: 10g | Protein: 1g | Sodium: 135mg | Fiber: 1g | Carbohydrates: 21g | Sugar: 19g

Peanut Butter Fudge Frosting

This thick frosting is not for the peanut butter faint of heart! Thick like fudge, yet creamy like frosting, this recipe is packed with amazing peanut butter flavor.

INGREDIENTS | YIELDS 3 CUPS

⅔ cup natural salted peanut butter

3 tablespoons Earth Balance Shortening Sticks

2 teaspoons vanilla extract

3 cups coconut sugar

¼ cup white spelt flour

4 tablespoons full-fat coconut cream

1. In a small bowl, combine the peanut butter, shortening, and vanilla. Using a hand-held mixer, mix to combine.

2. Add the powdered coconut sugar and flour and beat until smooth.

3. Add the coconut cream, 1 tablespoon at a time, until the frosting is smooth and pliable. It will be thick and fudge-like; add as much or as little cream as needed to reach desired consistency. Store covered in the refrigerator.

PER SERVING (2 tablespoons) Calories: 170 | Fat: 5.5g | Protein: 2g | Sodium: 50mg | Fiber: 0.5g | Carbohydrates: 29g | Sugar: 27g

Dairy-Free Cream Cheese Frosting

For lactose-intolerant guests or for anyone who prefers to omit dairy, this recipe creates a delicious sweet frosting with a touch of tang.

INGREDIENTS | MAKES 1½ CUPS

¼ cup Earth Balance Buttery Baking Sticks

⅓ cup coconut butter

1 tablespoon fresh lemon juice

1 teaspoon vanilla extract

1¾ cups powdered xylitol

1 tablespoon spelt flour

1 tablespoon unsweetened almond milk

Coconut Butter

It is important to use pure coconut butter in this recipe. Coconut oil can not be substituted and will not yield the same results. If coconut butter is unavailable, any vegan cream cheese product will do the trick.

1. In a mixing bowl, mix together Earth Balance Buttery Baking Sticks and coconut butter using a hand-held mixer.

2. Add lemon juice, vanilla extract, xylitol, and flour and mix. The batter may be a little crumbly.

3. Add almond milk slowly and beat until smooth and silky or to desired consistency. Store in an airtight container in a cool place.

PER SERVING (⅛ cup) Calories: 213 | Fat: 9g | Protein: 0g | Sodium: 46mg | Fiber: 0g | Carbohydrates: 53g | Sugar: 0g

Dreamy Chocolate Fudge Frosting

Divinely chocolaty, this frosting pairs well with any cake or cupcake or could even be used as a delectable appetizer dip.

INGREDIENTS | MAKES ¾ CUP

⅔ cup cocoa powder

⅓ cup coconut oil, melted

½ cup maple syrup

1 teaspoon vanilla extract

2 tablespoons unsweetened chocolate almond milk

¼ teaspoon liquid stevia

1. In a small bowl, combine the cocoa powder and coconut oil. Add maple syrup and vanilla. Slowly add almond milk to desired consistency. Add stevia to taste.

2. Whisk the ingredients together until the consistency of smooth frosting. Store leftovers in an airtight container in the refrigerator.

PER SERVING (⅛ cup) Calories: 203 | Fat: 13g | Protein: 2g | Sodium: 7mg | Fiber: 3g | Carbohydrates: 24g | Sugar: 16g

Soften at Room Temperature

Allow this frosting to come to room temperature if it's been stored in the refrigerator. Coconut oil is solid when cold, so to make it a spreadable frosting, make sure it's been out of the refrigerator for 30 minutes.

Dark Chocolate Fudge Sauce

Dip, drizzle, or spread this rich sauce on anything imaginable! This chocolate sauce is rich and creamy and is perfect on an ice cream sundae.

INGREDIENTS | MAKES 1 CUP

¾ cup cocoa powder

⅓ cup grapeseed oil

1 teaspoon vanilla extract

⅛ teaspoon sea salt

1 cup maple syrup

1. In a small mixing bowl, combine the cocoa, grapeseed oil, vanilla, sea salt, and maple syrup. Blend until completely smooth.

2. Serve immediately or refrigerate for 1 hour for fudge sauce to thicken.

PER SERVING (2 tablespoons) Calories: 205 | Fat: 10g | Protein: 1.5g | Sodium: 42mg | Fiber: 3g | Carbohydrates: 31g | Sugar: 24g

Sauce or Fudge

Once chilled in the refrigerator, this sauce becomes rich and very fudgy. For a sauce that can be drizzled or poured, reheat in the microwave for 10–15 seconds.

Peanut Butter Sauce

Consider trying this recipe in place of chocolate syrup on ice cream or to write a beautiful message on a birthday cake. Guests will assume it's a butterscotch syrup and will be pleasantly surprised by the rich peanut flavor. It's also great over brownies, pancakes, waffles, or fruit.

INGREDIENTS | MAKES ⅔ CUP

⅓ cup unsalted butter
¼ cup coconut sugar
⅓ cup natural peanut butter
⅓ cup unsweetened almond milk

1. In a saucepan over medium heat, melt butter and coconut sugar together. Add the peanut butter and stir until melted. While stirring, add almond milk and stir until smooth and completely incorporated.

2. Store leftovers in an airtight container in the refrigerator.

PER SERVING (2 tablespoons) Calories: 257 | Fat: 21g | Protein: 5g | Sodium: 89mg | Fiber: 1g | Carbohydrates: 14g | Sugar: 12g

Vanilla Cream Filling

When the need for a thick cream filling arises, this is the perfect recipe. For cookie sandwiches, brownie layers, or a simple graham cracker sandwich, this filling does the job!

INGREDIENTS | MAKES 1⅓ CUPS

⅓ cup coconut butter
¾ cup butter, softened
2 teaspoons vanilla extract
1 cup powdered xylitol
⅓ cup spelt flour
3 tablespoons unsweetened almond milk

1. In a small bowl, mix coconut butter, butter, vanilla, xylitol, and flour with a hand-held mixer until smooth.

2. Slowly add the almond milk until desired consistency is reached.

3. Use immediately or refrigerate in an airtight container.

PER SERVING (2 tablespoons) Calories: 117 | Fat: 9g | Protein: 0g | Sodium: 35mg | Fiber: 0g | Carbohydrates: 11g | Sugar: 0g

Homemade Whipped Cream

Homemade whipped cream is so much more delicious than store-bought and so simple to make! Four ingredients is all it takes to make this versatile cream topping at home.

INGREDIENTS | MAKES 3 CUPS

1½ cups heavy whipping cream

2 teaspoons vanilla extract

⅛ teaspoon sea salt

½ teaspoon liquid stevia

Soft or Hard?

Whipped cream can be prepared as a soft cream or as a firm cream that holds its shape. Beat until soft peaks form for a softer, light cream or beat until firm peaks form and cream begins to stiffen for piping.

1. In the bowl of an electric mixer fitted with the whisk attachment, pour in the heavy cream. Begin whipping on medium-low speed until the cream's volume rises.

2. Add the vanilla, salt, and stevia and increase speed to high until the cream is thick and soft peaks begin to form. Store leftovers in an airtight container in the refrigerator.

PER SERVING (¼ cup) Calories: 105 | Fat: 11g | Protein: 0g | Sodium: 35mg | Fiber: 0g | Carbohydrates: 1g | Sugar: 0g

Pumpkin Spice Whipped Cream

This sweet, faintly spiced cream is perfect for fall goodies. Pumpkin pie, granola, and apple cider are well complemented with clouds of this stevia-sweetened cream.

INGREDIENTS | MAKES 1½ CUPS

8 ounces heavy whipping cream, chilled

1½ teaspoons vanilla extract

3 drops liquid stevia

⅛ teaspoon pumpkin pie spice

⅛ teaspoon cinnamon

1. Pour whipped cream in a large mixing bowl and beat until soft peaks appear. Add the vanilla, stevia, pumpkin pie spice, and cinnamon and mix on high speed to fully incorporate all the ingredients.

2. Continue beating until whipped cream is whipped to desired stiffness. Refrigerate for 30 minutes before serving.

PER SERVING (¼ cup) Calories: 140 | Fat: 14g | Protein: 1g | Sodium: 15mg | Fiber: 0g | Carbohydrates: 1.5g | Sugar: 0.5g

Dairy-Free Whipped Cream

Using some creativity with full-fat coconut milk can yield similar results to regular whipped cream. A big bonus is that coconut milk is naturally sweeter and full of healthier fats.

INGREDIENTS | MAKES 1 CUP

1 (14-ounce) can full-fat coconut milk
3 tablespoons white spelt flour
1 teaspoon vanilla extract
½ teaspoon liquid stevia

The Better Part

Only the white firm portion of the coconut milk will whip up similar to heavy cream. If the can does not yield this white portion after chilling, it is a bad can or is not full-fat. The result will still be delicious, but it won't be as thick, and won't whip up like whipped cream.

1. Pour coconut milk in container without a lid and place in the refrigerator for at least 3 hours to chill and harden.

2. In an electric stand mixer, pour in the thickest, whitest part of the milk (the cream, yielding about ¾ cups). Add the flour, vanilla extract, and stevia and mix on high speed to fully incorporate all the ingredients.

3. Continue beating for a couple of minutes, until light and creamy. Serve immediately or refrigerate until ready to serve.

PER SERVING (¼ cup) Calories: 220 | Fat: 21g | Protein: 3g | Sodium: 13mg | Fiber: 1g | Carbohydrates: 8g | Sugar: 0g

Coconut Pecan Frosting

Creamy, crunchy, sweet! This frosting is a unique blend of delicious ingredients that yields a tasty frosting perfect for oatmeal cake, vanilla cake, or even muffins.

INGREDIENTS | MAKES 2½ CUPS

½ cup dates
3 large egg yolks
1 cup coconut milk
½ cup maple syrup
1 teaspoon vanilla extract
½ cup salted butter
1½ cups shredded unsweetened coconut
1 cup pecans, chopped

Whole Milk

Coconut milk creates a super rich frosting that is full of flavor. Whole milk can also be used to create a rich flavor and consistency.

1. In a food processor, process dates until a date paste forms. Set aside.

2. In a medium bowl, whip egg yolks and stir in coconut milk, maple syrup, and vanilla extract.

3. Melt the butter in a medium saucepan over medium heat. Stir in egg and milk mixture and date paste.

4. Cook over medium heat, stirring occasionally, until mixture thickens. Remove from heat and stir in coconut and pecans. Spread on baked goods while warm.

PER SERVING (⅛ cup) Calories: 220 | Fat: 19g | Protein: 2g | Sodium: 40mg | Fiber: 3g | Carbohydrates: 13g | Sugar: 9g

CHAPTER 13

Frozen Treats

Classic Vanilla Ice Cream

Big scoops of vanilla ice cream are perfect for sundaes, in root beer floats, or served with pie. This recipe uses an ice cream machine to get perfectly churned, parlor ice cream at home.

INGREDIENTS | SERVES 6

2 cups half-and-half, chilled
½ cup 2% milk, chilled
1 cup heavy cream, chilled
⅔ cup xylitol
½ cup powdered honey
2 teaspoons vanilla extract
⅛ teaspoon sea salt

1. In a large bowl, whisk together the half-and-half, milk, and heavy cream. Add xylitol, powdered honey, vanilla extract, and salt. Turn on your ice cream maker and pour mixture inside.

2. Mix according to your ice cream maker's directions, about 20–40 minutes. Store ice cream in the airtight container in the freezer for up to 2 weeks.

PER SERVING Calories: 347 | Fat: 24g | Protein: 4g | Sodium: 107mg | Fiber: 0g | Carbohydrates: 37g | Sugar: 11g

Chilling Out

For a soft-serve style ice cream, enjoy immediately after processing in the ice cream maker. For an extra firm ice cream, chill for at least one hour in the freezer.

Soda Lime Slushies

A refreshingly frothy and sweet carbonated drink that is sugar-free and stevia-sweetened. No one will ever guess it's a calorie-free beverage!

INGREDIENTS | SERVES 4

2 cans Zevia Cola
2½ cups ice
1 lime

1. In a blender, combine the Zevia soda and ice. Pulse until the mixture is a slushy consistency. The slushy will be extra frothy and foamy!

2. Cut the lime in half. Squeeze about 1 teaspoon of lime juice into each drink and stir. Slice the remaining half of lime into thin slices for garnish. Serve in chilled glasses and enjoy immediately.

PER SERVING Calories: 0g | Fat: 0g | Protein: 0g | Sodium: 10mg | Fiber: 0g | Carbohydrates: 2g | Sugar: 0g

Zevia

Zevia brand sodas are all-natural sodas sweetened with stevia; they have no carbohydrates or calories and don't raise blood sugar levels. They also contain the same fizzy carbonation other sodas have without the unhealthy colorings and sugars.

Brownie Ice Cream Sandwiches

Frozen chewy chocolate brownies with a creamy vanilla ice cream middle! These must be frozen for an additional hour before serving for best appearance, but this allows these bars to be made days in advance.

INGREDIENTS | SERVES 30

½ cup coconut oil, melted

2 cups coconut sugar

2 large eggs, at room temperature

¼ cup water, at room temperature

1 teaspoon vanilla extract

½ cup cocoa powder

½ teaspoon sea salt

½ teaspoon baking powder

1 tablespoon cornstarch

1½ cups spelt flour

2 (16-ounce) cartons dairy-free, naturally sweetened ice cream, slightly softened

¾ cup chopped chocolate, melted

Garnish Options

Top the chocolate-coated brownies with crushed nuts, sprinkles, cherries, or shredded coconut for extra crunch.

1. Preheat oven to 350°F. Line a muffin pan with liners and lightly spray liners with cooking spray.

2. In a large bowl, mix together the coconut oil, coconut sugar, eggs, water, and vanilla until well combined. Mix in the cocoa powder, salt, baking powder, cornstarch, and flour. Pour 1 heaping tablespoon of batter at the bottom of each muffin liner.

3. Bake this brownie layer for 10 minutes. Remove baked brownies from pan. Repeat this step until all the batter is cooked. Let all the brownies cool.

4. Once cool, unwrap half of the brownies from their muffin liners and set aside.

5. Scoop 3 tablespoons of slightly softened ice cream on top of the remaining brownies which are still in their muffin liners. Gently top each with an unwrapped brownie.

6. Pour about 1 tablespoon of melted chocolate over the brownie sandwiches. Immediately freeze for at least 1 hour or until ready to serve.

PER SERVING Calories: 200 | Fat: 9g | Protein: 3g | Sodium: 77mg | Fiber: 2g | Carbohydrates: 30g | Sugar: 22g

Banana Boat Milkshake

Inspired by the campfire recipe consisting of roasted bananas over a fire mixed with chocolate chips, graham crackers, and marshmallows! This recipe uses healthy ingredients to create a similar frozen version.

INGREDIENTS | SERVES 2

3 frozen bananas

⅓ cup coconut milk

1 teaspoon vanilla extract

¼ cup crushed sugar-free graham crackers

⅓ cup sugar-free chocolate chips

In a high-speed blender, blend the bananas, coconut milk, and vanilla until smooth. Stir in the graham crackers and chocolate chips and serve!

PER SERVING Calories: 315 | Fat: 16g | Protein: 4g | Sodium: 55g | Fiber: 6.5g | Carbohydrates: 65g | Sugar: 21g

Melty Boats

This recipe can be chilled for an additional 1 hour for a firmer, less soft milkshake.

Easy Banana Truffles

Three simple ingredients combine for delectable truffles! Let the natural sweetness of frozen bananas shine in these just-like-ice-cream chocolate-covered bites!

INGREDIENTS | SERVES 4

2 bananas, peeled

½ cup sugar-free chocolate chips or chunks, melted

3 tablespoons crushed peanuts

1. Slice bananas into ¼" slices. Line a baking sheet with wax paper.

2. With forks or tongs, dip banana slices into melted chocolate.

3. Lay dipped slices on wax paper and sprinkle with chopped peanuts. Freeze for 3 hours until firm.

PER SERVING Calories: 148 | Fat: 10g | Protein: 3g | Sodium: 4mg | Fiber: 3g | Carbohydrates: 28g | Sugar: 8g

Blended Milkshakes

Be adventurous with these truffles by adding them to 4 cups of vanilla ice cream in a blender for easy flavorful milkshakes.

Frozen S'mores

There's no need to wait for a warm summer night to enjoy a s'more. Bring the outdoors inside with a "marshmallow" cream and melted chocolate center in these frozen bars.

INGREDIENTS | SERVES 20

40 sugar-free graham cracker squares

1 (14-ounce) can full-fat coconut milk, chilled

3 tablespoons rice flour

⅓ cup powdered xylitol

2 teaspoons vanilla extract

¼ teaspoon liquid stevia

¾ cup sugar-free chocolate, melted

Chocolate Options

Milk, dark, or specialty flavored chocolate are all delicious in these frozen bars.

1. Turn oven on to broil. Line a cookie sheet with parchment paper and place graham cracker squares in rows. Place in oven to broil for about 45 seconds, until crackers have become slightly golden and browned.

2. In an electric mixer, combine the whitest, thickest part of the coconut milk (about ¾ cup), with flour, xylitol, vanilla, and stevia and beat until fluffy. Pour 1 tablespoon of warm chocolate on a graham cracker and top with coconut cream mixture.

3. Cover fillings with a second graham cracker and place in a large baking dish. Continue assembling the s'mores until all are assembled.

4. Place in the freezer for 30 minutes to 1 hour, or until all the s'mores are chilled and firm. Keep stored, covered, in the freezer.

PER SERVING Calories: 85 | Fat: 6g | Protein: 1g | Sodium: 30mg | Fiber: 0.5g | Carbohydrates: 12g | Sugar: 0g

Healthy Orange Slushies

These citrus slushies combine several delicious flavors of the tropics! They are so satisfying, they are sure to become a summertime favorite.

INGREDIENTS | SERVES 4

2 small bananas, frozen

6 large oranges, peeled

⅔ cup coconut milk

4 cups ice

2 teaspoons vanilla extract

In a high-powered blender, add the bananas, oranges, coconut milk, ice, and vanilla. Blend until creamy. Serve immediately.

PER SERVING Calories: 263 | Fat: 9g | Protein: 4g | Sodium: 6mg | Fiber: 8g | Carbohydrates: 47g | Sugar: 33g

Orange These Tasty

These slushies can also be made with any oranges on hand—clementines, mandarins, or blood oranges add a nice flavor twist! Double the quantity of oranges if using small ones like clementines.

Healthy Peanut Butter Milkshakes

Sneak extra protein and potassium into dessert with this power milkshake. Bananas create a creamy ice cream–like base while a healthy helping of peanut butter and vanilla contribute to the delicious taste.

INGREDIENTS | SERVES 2

3 large frozen bananas

3 tablespoons natural creamy peanut butter

2 tablespoons honey

2 tablespoons unsweetened almond milk

½ teaspoon vanilla extract

In a blender, layer bananas, peanut butter, honey, almond milk, and vanilla. Blend until smooth and creamy and enjoy.

PER SERVING Calories: 375 | Fat: 13g | Protein: 9g | Sodium: 120mg | Fiber: 6g | Carbohydrates: 64g | Sugar: 42g

Potassium Spike

A large banana can contain over 420mg of potassium! One serving of this milkshake provides enough potassium to reach the daily recommendation.

Mexican Chocolate Ice Cream

This delicious ice cream has a subtle surprising heat, flavored with cinnamon and a pinch of cayenne pepper.

INGREDIENTS | SERVES 8

2½ cups whole milk

1½ cups heavy cream

1 teaspoon cinnamon

⅛ teaspoon cayenne pepper

5 large egg yolks

⅛ teaspoon sea salt

⅔ cup honey

1 teaspoon vanilla extract

3 ounces dark chocolate, chopped

Double Up

If you don't have a double broiler, an easy substitute is a pot with simmering water and a heat-safe glass bowl on top.

1. In a double broiler, add whole milk, heavy cream, cinnamon, cayenne pepper, egg yolks, sea salt, honey, and vanilla. Stir constantly on medium heat until mixture thickens and coats the back of the spoon. Pour through a mesh strainer to remove any lumps.

2. Stir in the chocolate pieces. Allow ice cream to cool, cover, and place in freezer for 1 hour or until completely cold.

3. Freeze in an ice cream maker, following manufacturer's instructions.

4. Serve immediately for soft-serve consistency, or place in freezer for another hour for firmer ice cream. Store leftovers in an airtight container in the freezer for up to 2 weeks.

PER SERVING Calories: 374 | Fat: 25g | Protein: 6g | Sodium: 94mg | Fiber: 1g | Carbohydrates: 36g | Sugar: 33g

Orange Mousse

Fresh oranges with the white pith still intact over the orange blend into a creamy, foamy mousse pudding! Enjoy this treat's natural dose of vitamin C, bioflavonoids, and antioxidants.

INGREDIENTS | SERVES 2

2 large oranges
2 tablespoons cold water
2 tablespoons xylitol
½ teaspoon vanilla extract

Chilly

Use chilled oranges and very cold water so this pudding stays cool after blending. This mousse can also be frozen for an icy treat.

1. Using a sharp knife, carefully cut off only the oranges' skin, leaving the white pith intact. Quarter the oranges, removing seeds and tough center membranes.

2. In a high-speed blender, add oranges, water, xylitol, and vanilla and blend until recipe doubles in volume and is frothy.

3. Pour into dessert bowls and enjoy immediately.

PER SERVING Calories: 95 | Fat: 0g | Protein: 1g | Sodium: 0mg | Fiber: 3g | Carbohydrates: 27g | Sugar: 12g

Healthy Mint Shakes

Instead of heavy cream, this recipe uses thick, creamy coconut milk for a fantastic flavor in these mint shakes. Garnish with a fresh mint leaf for a pretty presentation.

INGREDIENTS | SERVES 2

1 (14-ounce) can full-fat coconut milk, chilled in freezer for 1 hour
⅔ cup xylitol
½ cup powdered honey
¾ teaspoon peppermint extract
½ teaspoon vanilla extract
⅛ teaspoon xanthan gum
⅛ teaspoon sea salt

1. Pour chilled coconut milk into a medium bowl. Whisk in the xylitol, powdered honey, extracts, xanthan gum, and salt.

2. Pour into an ice cream maker, and let freeze according to your ice cream maker's directions, about 30 minutes.

3. Enjoy immediately as a soft, drink-style milkshake or place in the freezer for an additional hour to enjoy as a thick custard-like shake.

PER SERVING Calories: 670 | Fat: 42g | Protein: 4g | Sodium: 175mg | Fiber: 0g | Carbohydrates: 100g | Sugar: 29g

Vegan Vanilla Bean Ice Cream

*Extra creamy and smooth, this ice cream uses both vanilla beans
and vanilla extract to create a spectacular flavor.*

INGREDIENTS | SERVES 8

3 cups full-fat coconut cream, chilled

1½ cups xylitol

3 tablespoons white spelt flour

Seeds of 2 vanilla beans

½ teaspoon vanilla extract

¼ teaspoon sea salt

Taste the Difference

Different brands of coconut milk have different strengths of coconut flavor. If you prefer a mild coconut milk, the brand Thai Kitchen is a good choice.

1. In a mixing bowl, whisk together the coconut cream, xylitol, spelt flour, vanilla beans, vanilla extract, and sea salt.

2. Pour into an ice cream maker and churn according to your ice cream maker's directions, about 30 minutes.

3. Enjoy immediately for super soft-serve ice cream, or pour into an airtight container and freeze for another 2–3 hours until firm.

PER SERVING Calories: 500 | Fat: 18g | Protein: 2g | Sodium: 110mg | Fiber: 1g | Carbohydrates: 98g | Sugar: 57g

Chocolate Icies

Chocolate milkshakes are so easy to make with the help of unsweetened chocolate almond milk. The almond milk creates fantastic flavor and an unbeatable creamy, frosty texture!

INGREDIENTS | SERVES 4

1¼ cups heavy cream

½ cup half-and-half

1 cup unsweetened chocolate almond milk

½ cup cocoa

1 teaspoon vanilla extract

1 cup xylitol

6 drops liquid stevia

⅛ teaspoon sea salt

Unsweetened Chocolate Milk

Chocolate almond milk can come sweetened and unsweetened. Make sure to use unsweetened to avoid the extra added sugar.

1. In a medium bowl, whisk together the cream, half-and-half, almond milk, and cocoa and mix well. Add the vanilla, xylitol, stevia, and salt and whisk well to incorporate.

2. Pour the ingredients into an ice cream maker and freeze according to ice cream maker's directions, about 30–45 minutes. Enjoy immediately, or place in the freezer for another 30 minutes to freeze more.

PER SERVING Calories: 789 | Fat: 67g | Protein: 8g | Sodium: 180mg | Fiber: 4g | Carbohydrates: 64g | Sugar: 3g

Watermelon Lime Slushies

This slushie is the perfect use for leftover watermelon. A summer treat that replenishes vitamins and minerals in the body, this will leave you energized and refreshed.

INGREDIENTS | SERVES 3

2 cups watermelon, peeled, deseeded, and cut into large cubes, frozen
⅔ cup ice
Juice of 1 large lime
8 drops liquid stevia

In a high-powered blender, add watermelon, ice, lime juice, and stevia. Blend until smooth. Serve immediately.

PER SERVING Calories: 32 | Fat: 0g | Protein: 1g | Sodium: 3mg | Fiber: 0g | Carbohydrates: 8g | Sugar: 6g

Seeds

If you miss deseeding some of the small white seeds in the watermelon, don't worry! They blend up seamlessly, so just make sure to get rid of the big black ones!

Strawberry Rhubarb Sorbet

Fruity ice cream is a dreamy refreshment during any warm summer day. Strawberries and rhubarb pair well in this uniquely flavored sorbet.

INGREDIENTS | SERVES 4

2 cups rhubarb, sliced into ¼" pieces
½ cup water
⅛ teaspoon orange zest
3 cups strawberries, fresh or frozen
¼ cup maple syrup
⅛ teaspoon sea salt

1. Simmer the rhubarb, water, and orange zest in a small saucepan for 5 minutes and remove from heat.

2. Purée strawberries in a blender. Add rhubarb mixture, maple syrup, and salt to the blender and blend till smooth.

3. Pour mixture into a container and chill for 15 minutes. Then pour mixture in an ice cream maker and mix according to ice cream maker's instructions.

PER SERVING Calories: 100 | Fat: 0g | Protein: 1g | Sodium: 80mg | Fiber: 3g | Carbohydrates: 25g | Sugar: 18g

Sour Patch

Rhubarb can be extremely sour when eaten raw and usually needs quite a bit of sugar to sweeten it. Make sure to simmer the rhubarb for the proper time with the orange zest. This step prepares the rhubarb to blend flawlessly with the maple syrup and strawberries for a delightfully sweet sorbet.

CHAPTER 14

Pies and Pastries

Spelt Flour Pie Crust

This basic pie crust is flaky, buttery, and sweetened with powdered honey, which contributes to its fantastic texture. Maple sugar can also be used in this recipe in place of honey.

INGREDIENTS | MAKES 1 (10") PIE CRUST

1½ cups spelt flour
1 tablespoon powdered honey
½ teaspoon sea salt
1¼ cups unsalted butter, diced
2 tablespoons ice cold water

Make It a Double

This basic pie crust recipe is perfect for one-crust sweet or savory pies. For pies such as apple or chicken pot pie, double this recipe to create a top crust, decorative lattice, or cookie cutout design.

1. Preheat oven to 400°F. In a food processor, pour the flour, powdered honey, and salt. Mix together.

2. Add the diced butter and pulse until mixture starts forming into pea-size crumbs.

3. Add the ice cold water while pulsing the mixture until the dough comes together. Add enough water so the dough isn't crumbly, but do not exceed 3 tablespoons or the dough will be sticky.

4. Roll dough out on a lightly floured surface to be used in any pie or tart recipe. Bake for 30 minutes covered with tin foil, remove foil and bake for an additional 10–15 minutes until crust is golden or fill and bake as suggested in the pie or tart recipe being used.

PER SERVING (⅛ recipe) Calories: 333 | Fat: 29g | Protein: 3g | Sodium: 150mg | Fiber: 2g | Carbohydrates: 17g | Sugar: 1g

Pumpkin Pie

Silky pumpkin pie is loaded with sweet spices and coconut sugar. Coconut sugar blends flawlessly into the filling for a smooth rich pie that doesn't taste sugar-free in the slightest. Try it with whipped cream.

INGREDIENTS | SERVES 8

Spelt Flour Pie Crust dough (see recipe in this chapter)

2 cups puréed pumpkin

8 ounces cream cheese, softened

1 cup coconut sugar

¼ teaspoon sea salt

2 large eggs

⅓ cup unsweetened almond milk

1½ teaspoons vanilla extract

1 teaspoon cinnamon

⅛ teaspoon pumpkin pie spice mix

Pumpkin Spice Whipped Cream (see recipe in Chapter 12)

Cream Cheese Substitute

For a dairy-free pie filling, replace the cream cheese in this recipe with a vegan cream cheese.

1. Preheat oven to 350°F. Press pie crust dough into a 9" pie plate.

2. In a large mixing bowl, beat together pumpkin and cream cheese with an electric mixer. Beat until well combined and smooth. Add the coconut sugar, salt, eggs, almond milk, vanilla, cinnamon, and pumpkin pie spice and beat until well incorporated.

3. Pour filling into prepared crust and bake for 50–60 minutes or until pie is set. Cover with foil halfway through baking if it begins browning too quickly. The middle may be a little wiggly when done, but it will firm as it cools. Top with Pumpkin Spice Whipped Cream, if desired.

PER SERVING Calories: 697 | Fat: 50g | Protein: 8g | Sodium: 350mg | Fiber: 5g | Carbohydrates: 55g | Sugar: 30g

Rustic Pear Tart

This handmade pie tart with perfect flaky crust boasts a sweet pear filling that intensifies with flavors of cinnamon and almond.

INGREDIENTS | SERVES 6

½ tablespoon lemon juice

2 medium Bartlett pears, peeled, cored, and thinly sliced

1 tablespoon spelt flour

¼ cup powdered honey

½ teaspoon cinnamon

⅛ teaspoon nutmeg

¼ teaspoon sea salt

½ teaspoon almond extract

Spelt Flour Pie Crust dough (see recipe in this chapter)

Pears

Bartlett pears give fantastic flavor to this tart, but any ripe seasonal pear will work as well.

1. In a medium bowl, drizzle lemon juice over pear slices. Add flour, powdered honey, cinnamon, nutmeg, salt, and almond extract to the pears and mix. Set aside.

2. Preheat oven to 375°F. Line a baking sheet with parchment paper.

3. On a floured surface, roll out pie crust dough to ¼" thick circle. Place the dough circle on the parchment-lined baking sheet.

4. Spoon the pear mixture into the middle of the dough, leaving a 1½" border. Fan out pears to create a decorative star-like shape. Pour any remaining juices over the pears.

5. Gently fold the sides of the dough over the pear mixture, creating a 1" border of dough. Crimp edges to keep the tart in a circular shape. Bake the tart for 30 minutes or until the tart is lightly browned and bubbling. Cool on a wire rack 10 minutes before cutting.

PER SERVING Calories: 550 | Fat: 39g | Protein: 3g | Sodium: 104mg | Fiber: 3g | Carbohydrates: 49g | Sugar: 12g

Chocolate Silk Pie

The healthy, butter-free crust is a snap to whip up and perfect for its creamy chocolate filling.

INGREDIENTS | SERVES 6

2 cups gluten-free oat flour, divided
½ cup white rice flour
½ teaspoon sea salt, divided
2 tablespoons grapeseed oil
⅓ cup plus 1 tablespoon honey
½ teaspoon natural butter extract
2 tablespoons water
1¾ cups coconut sugar
¾ cup xylitol
½ cup ripe avocado
2 teaspoons vanilla extract
½ cup cocoa powder
1¼ cups full-fat cold coconut milk, chilled

Oat Flour

Grind your own gluten-free oats to make the flour for this pie. A gluten-free flour mix could also be used in place of the oat and rice flour.

1. Preheat oven to 350°F. Lightly grease a 10" pie pan.

2. In a medium mixing bowl, combine 1½ cups oat flour, rice flour, and ¼ teaspoon salt. Add the oil, honey, butter extract, and water, and mix until smooth. The dough should be pliable, and not sticky. Add an extra 1–2 tablespoons of water if needed.

3. Smooth dough into pie pan, creating a crust that is about ¼" thick, and bake for 15 minutes. Allow the crust to cool completely.

4. In a food processor, add the coconut sugar and xylitol. Process until smooth and powdery. Add avocado, vanilla, ¼ teaspoon salt, cocoa powder, and 4 tablespoons of oat flour and mix until smooth and creamy.

5. In a separate bowl, beat the thick white part of the full-fat coconut milk with remaining oat flour until it is thick, smooth, and fluffy. Add the chocolate mixture to the cream and beat on high.

6. Pour mixture into cooled pie crust. Place in the refrigerator for at least 1 hour. Garnish with coconut whipped cream and chocolate shavings if desired.

PER SERVING Calories: 650 | Fat: 19g | Protein: 6g | Sodium: 210mg | Fiber: 5g | Carbohydrates: 130g | Sugar: 77g

Individual Raw Chocolate Pies

These pies are almost nutritious enough to serve for breakfast—they contain a serving of fruit, a hidden vegetable, and healthy raw nuts. Indulge in this unexpectedly delicious chocolate treat.

INGREDIENTS | SERVES 4

1 large ripe avocado, peeled and pitted
⅓ cup pumpkin
1⅓ cups unsweetened cocoa, divided
1½ teaspoons vanilla extract, divided
¾ cup maple syrup
1/16 teaspoon sea salt
⅔ cup pitted Medjool dates
½ cup walnuts
⅓ cup unsweetened shredded coconut

1. In a blender or food processor, mix together the avocado and pumpkin. Add 1 cup cocoa, 1 teaspoon vanilla, maple syrup, and salt. Mix until well combined. Set aside.

2. In a food processor, pulse dates until crumbly. Add walnuts and coconut and pulse until well combined. Add the remaining cocoa and vanilla to this mixture and pulse until combined.

3. Divide date mixture between 4 (4-ounce) ramekins. Press the mixture to coat the bottom and sides of the ramekins. Pour prepared chocolate filling in the middle of the crusts and smooth with a spatula. Refrigerate until set, about 1 hour.

PER SERVING Calories: 517 | Fat: 23g | Protein: 10g | Sodium: 55mg | Fiber: 17g | Carbohydrates: 88g | Sugar: 57g

Fresh Fruit Tart

A classic tart with a creamy yogurt cream spread is loaded with piles of fresh fruit. When possible, use local, seasonal fresh fruit and berries in this gorgeous pastry.

INGREDIENTS | YIELDS 10" TART, SERVES 10

1½ cups plus 1 tablespoon white spelt flour

¼ cup powdered honey

½ teaspoon vanilla extract

1¼ cup cold salted butter, cut into ¼" cubes

1 large egg

3 tablespoons ice cold water

Yogurt Fruit Dip (see recipe in Chapter 6)

2½ cups assorted fresh sliced fruit

1. Generously butter the bottoms and sides of a 10" tart pan.

2. In a food processor, mix together flour and honey. Pulse until well combined. Add the vanilla and ice cold butter chunks.

3. Add the egg to the mixture, and slowly add the cold water while pulsing to combine the egg and water into the mixture.

4. Mix until the dough comes together. Slowly add an extra 1 or 2 teaspoons of water if dough is still a little crumbly and not smooth.

5. Using plastic wrap and your fingers, mash the dough into the tart pan and distribute evenly. Cover with plastic wrap and place in freezer for 5 minutes.

6. Preheat oven to 400°F. Remove dough from the freezer.

7. Gently poke the bottom of the tart dough with a fork to prevent rising. Bake covered for 14–16 minutes until golden brown. Cool completely on a wire rack.

8. Spread Yogurt Fruit Dip evenly over cooled crust. Arrange fruit in groups or rows, or as desired. Serve immediately or chill in the refrigerator until ready to serve.

PER SERVING Calories: 612 | Fat: 29g | Protein: 11g | Sodium: 24mg | Fiber: 2g | Carbohydrates: 77g | Sugar: 6g

Mini Pecan Tarts

Sweet and slightly chewy pecan filling is wrapped into buttery soft tart crusts. Cream cheese keeps the tart dough irresistibly tender, and provides the perfect flavorful base for the caramelized pecan centers.

INGREDIENTS | YIELDS 24 MINI TARTS

⅓ cup cream cheese, softened
⅔ cup butter, softened
1⅓ cups spelt flour
1 large egg
½ cup coconut sugar
½ cup honey
1 tablespoon butter, melted
1 teaspoon vanilla extract
¼ teaspoon sea salt
⅛ teaspoon cinnamon
½ cup chopped pecans

1. Preheat oven to 350°F. Grease a mini muffin tin and set aside.

2. In a medium mixing bowl, mix the cream cheese, softened butter, and flour until well combined and mixture forms a soft dough. Roll dough into small balls, about ¾" to 1" in diameter.

3. Place balls in mini muffin pan. Use your index finger to gently press the center of the ball to form a cup. Press the edges up and around the sides of the muffin pan to make room for pecan filling. Place pan in the refrigerator to chill for 10 minutes.

4. In a large bowl, add egg, coconut sugar, and honey and beat until well combined. Add melted butter, vanilla, salt, and cinnamon and mix well.

5. Remove crust from the refrigerator. Fill tarts ⅓ full with chopped pecans. Pour about ½ teaspoon of the filling over the pecans, so they are covered and tarts are about ¾ of the way full. Top the tarts with more pecans.

6. Bake for 18–20 minutes, or until golden brown. Serve hot, warm, or cold.

PER SERVING (1 tart) Calories: 205 | Fat: 9g | Protein: 2g | Sodium: 39mg | Fiber: 1g | Carbohydrates: 30g | Sugar: 10g

Individual Banana Peanut Butter Pies

This banana cream filling is loaded with peanut butter and vanilla. Coupled with a deep-dish chewy cookie dough crust, this is truly a rich indulgence.

INGREDIENTS | SERVES 4

2 cups rolled oats

¾ cup plus 2 tablespoons natural creamy peanut butter, divided

½ cup honey, divided

1½ tablespoons vanilla extract, divided

⅛ teaspoon sea salt, divided

½ teaspoon molasses

2 large ripe bananas, peeled

1. In a food processor or blender, pulse the oats to form a coarse flour. Add 6 tablespoons peanut butter, ¼ cup honey, 1 tablespoon vanilla, and 1/16 teaspoon salt. Mix until just combined. Scoop out dough and press into four (4") ramekins. Set aside.

2. In the bowl of the food processor, add molasses, bananas, and the remaining peanut butter, honey, vanilla, and salt. Process until smooth and creamy.

3. Spoon the filling into the crusts. Cover with plastic wrap and freeze for 20 minutes, until the crust is firm.

PER SERVING Calories: 720 | Fat: 31g | Protein: 20g | Sodium: 340mg | Fiber: 9g | Carbohydrates: 90g | Sugar: 50g

Easy Chocolate Phyllo Cups

Simple pre-cooked pastry cups are warmed up with a chocolate center and finished with a large dollop of whipped cream. These little bite-size treats are the perfect finger food for any gathering.

INGREDIENTS | SERVES 12

12 baked phyllo cups

2 (3.5-ounce) bars sugar-free chocolate

Homemade Whipped Cream (see recipe in Chapter 12)

1. Preheat oven to 300°F. Place ½ ounce chocolate in each phyllo cup. Put cups on a baking tray and place in oven to warm for about 5 minutes, or until chocolate is melted.

2. Let cool for a few minutes. Pipe with whipped cream and serve.

PER SERVING Calories: 152 | Fat: 16g | Protein: 1g | Sodium: 45mg | Fiber: 1g | Carbohydrates: 12g | Sugar: 0g

Raw Chocolate Mint Tart

Packed with mint flavor in each chocolaty bite, this tart is rich, creamy, and refreshing. Avocado adds an extra dimension of creaminess and helps give this tart a healthy dose of nutrients.

INGREDIENTS | SERVES 8

2½ cups whole walnuts

¾ cup unsweetened shredded coconut, divided

¾ cup maple syrup, divided

2 tablespoons ground flaxseed

1 cup plus 3 tablespoons cocoa, divided

1 teaspoon vanilla extract

7 drops liquid stevia, divided

2 large ripe avocados

3 tablespoons grapeseed oil

1 tablespoon peppermint extract

1. Spray a 10" tart pan with cooking spray.

2. In a food processor, combine the walnuts and ¼ cup shredded coconut until they are rough crumbs. Add ½ cup maple syrup and pulse to combine. Add flaxseed, ⅓ cup plus 1 tablespoon cocoa, vanilla, and 4 drops liquid stevia. Press mixture into the tart pan.

3. In food processor, blend remaining ½ cup shredded coconut to create a smooth coconut butter. Scrape inside of the bowl periodically, and keep mixing until it becomes smooth. Add avocados, oil, peppermint extract, and 3 drops of stevia and mix until smooth and creamy. The mixture should look like green frosting. Add the remaining ⅔ cup plus 2 tablespoons cocoa and ¼ cup maple syrup to this mixture and pulse until completely incorporated.

4. Spread the mint filling evenly over the crust. Refrigerate for 1 hour before slicing.

PER SERVING Calories: 509 | Fat: 41g | Protein: 10g | Sodium: 11mg | Fiber: 11g | Carbohydrates: 38g | Sugar: 20g

Sugar-Free Apple Crisp

This grain-free, fruit-sweetened crisp is just as delicious as any sugar-filled one. Natural juice, apples, and spices combine for a truly warm and satisfying treat.

INGREDIENTS | SERVES 2

1 large sweet apple, diced
2 tablespoons 100% natural grape juice
½ teaspoon lemon juice
¾ teaspoon cinnamon, divided
4 Medjool dates
½ tablespoon almond butter
2 tablespoons almond meal

Almond Meal

Almond meal has a great crumb texture that is perfect for grain-free diets. In addition to being a great source of protein and healthy fats, it is very versatile. It creates great toppings for crisps or streusels and is a healthy substitution for bread crumbs to create breading on meats.

1. Preheat the oven to 350°F.

2. In a small bowl, mix together the diced apple with grape and lemon juices and ½ teaspoon cinnamon.

3. Fill small ramekins with the apple mixture. Place ramekins on a baking sheet on the middle rack of the oven and bake for 20 minutes, until the apples are softened but not totally tender.

4. Meanwhile, in a food processor, combine dates, ¼ teaspoon cinnamon, and almond butter. Process until combined. Add almond meal and process until just mixed.

5. Remove the apples from the oven, sprinkle the crisp topping over the tops, and return to the oven for another 4–5 minutes. Alternatively, broil for 15–30 seconds to achieve an even crispier top. Cool slightly before serving.

PER SERVING Calories: 161 | Fat: 6g | Protein: 3g | Sodium: 20mg | Fiber: 4g | Carbohydrates: 28g | Sugar: 21g

Vegan Pumpkin Pie

This vegan version of a holiday favorite is creamy and delicious and complete with a "buttery" vegan crust.

INGREDIENTS | SERVES 8

2 cups spelt flour

1 teaspoon sea salt, divided

2 tablespoons maple sugar

1¼ cups frozen Earth Balance Buttery Baking Sticks, cubed

2 tablespoons ice water

2 cups pumpkin purée

5 tablespoons coconut butter, softened

¾ cup maple syrup

2 tablespoons cornstarch

2 teaspoons vanilla extract

1 teaspoon cinnamon

½ teaspoon pumpkin pie spice

1. In a food processor or blender, combine the flour, ½ teaspoon salt, and maple sugar. Add the frozen Earth Balance Buttery Baking Sticks and water. Pulse until the mixture is coarse and crumbly.

2. Transfer dough to a 9" or 10" pie pan and gently press to the bottom of pan. Shape the edges as desired. Cover and place in the freezer for 1 hour. Remove crust 20 minutes prior to baking.

3. Preheat oven to 350°F.

4. In a large bowl, beat pumpkin, coconut butter, maple syrup, cornstarch, vanilla, ½ teaspoon salt, cinnamon, and pumpkin pie spice. Pour into the prepared crust and cover edges with foil.

5. Bake 45–50 minutes, removing foil for the last 10 minutes. Cool completely before serving. Store covered in the refrigerator for up to 1 week.

PER SERVING Calories: 888 | Fat: 70g | Protein: 4g | Sodium: 1,110mg | Fiber: 3g | Carbohydrates: 62g | Sugar: 23g

Key Lime Cheesecake Pie

Sweet dates and tangy fresh key limes pair so well in this refreshing summertime treat. Sweet and sassy, this pie is sure to liven up any summer meal.

INGREDIENTS | SERVES 10

2 cups walnut halves and pieces

14 pitted Medjool dates, divided

1½ tablespoons cinnamon

¼ teaspoon sea salt

1½ cup cashews, soaked in water for 6–8 hours and drained

½ cup key lime juice

1 cup coconut cream

¼ cup melted coconut oil

1 tablespoon lime zest

Key Lime Juice

Key limes have a distinct aroma and flavor that make them wonderful in cooking and baking. They are fruitier and slightly more tart than regular limes.

1. In a food processor, chop walnuts, 8 dates, cinnamon, and salt for about 30 seconds until it has a grainy consistency. Press mixture into 8" pie pan and place in the refrigerator to firm.

2. In high speed blender, combine soaked cashews with lime juice and blend until smooth and creamy. Add coconut cream, coconut oil, 6 dates, and lime zest and blend until smooth.

3. Pour filling into cooled pie crust and allow to set in the refrigerator for 2 hours.

PER SERVING Calories: 505 | Fat: 38g | Protein: 15g | Sodium: 77mg | Fiber: 5g | Carbohydrates: 40g | Sugar: 25g

Apple Fritters

When apples are abundant in the fall, fritters are a fun way to use them. Drizzle the tops with Easy Vanilla Glaze (see recipe in Chapter 12) to replicate a gourmet bakery fritter or serve warm with a cup of cocoa.

INGREDIENTS | SERVES 4

1 cup white spelt flour
½ cup coconut sugar
1 teaspoon baking powder
⅛ teaspoon sea salt
1½ teaspoons cinnamon
⅛ teaspoon nutmeg
1 large egg, at room temperature
¾ teaspoon vanilla extract
⅓ cup unsweetened almond milk
¾ cup chopped apple
1½ cups grapeseed oil

Sour Apple

To ensure that these are not overly sweet, use a sour apple or a combination of sweet and sour apples to create a perfect balance of flavors.

1. In a small mixing bowl, mix together the flour, coconut sugar, baking powder, salt, cinnamon, and nutmeg. Add egg, vanilla, and almond milk and mix until well combined. Gently fold in the apple pieces.

2. In a skillet or frying pan, pour enough oil to create a 1" layer. Heat oil to between 275°F and 290°F. Line a plate with 2 paper towels.

3. Take 1 tablespoon of dough for each fritter and place in oil. Cook one side of the fritter until golden and then gently flip to cook the other sides. The outside should be crisp and the middle should be light and soft. Be careful not to overcrowd in the oil.

4. When fritters are done, transfer to the paper towel–lined plate. Serve warm or cool.

PER SERVING Calories: 300 | Fat: 7g | Protein: 5g | Sodium: 224mg | Fiber: 3g | Carbohydrates: 55g | Sugar: 20g

Almond Baklava

*Thin phyllo pastry sheets are rolled into delicious almond nuggets full of
a sweet caramelized filling. Enjoy freshly baked or cooled.*

INGREDIENTS | SERVES 8

1 cup ground almonds
1 tablespoon coconut sugar
1 tablespoon xylitol
¾ teaspoon cinnamon, divided
1/16 teaspoon sea salt
½ pound package phyllo dough
½ cup unsalted butter
¾ cup water
¾ cup honey
1 teaspoon lemon juice

Wet Blanket

Lay a damp paper towel over the phyllo
dough that you are not currently working
with to keep it moist and pliable.

1. Preheat oven to 350°F. Butter a 9" square baking dish.

2. In a medium bowl, combine the ground almonds,
   coconut sugar, xylitol, ½ teaspoon cinnamon, and salt.

3. Take 3 sheets of pastry dough and lay neatly stacked on
   top of each other on a clean work surface. Lay a 2" diameter rolling pin or rod on top of the 3 sheets and fold a
   1" section of dough over the rod. Sprinkle about 3 tablespoons of almond mixture over the top dough sheet,
   leaving a 1" edge on the opposite end of folded rod side.

4. Cut thin slices of butter with a cheese slicer or knife
   and lay butter sheets over almond mixture. Use 1–2
   tablespoons of butter for each baklava roll and distribute evenly over the almond mixture, but this time leaving 3" border from the bottom edge. This butter-free
   edge makes it so the butter doesn't melt out the ends
   of the baklava during baking.

5. Roll up the pastry sheets from the rod end to the
   almond/butter-free edge. Scrunch the middle and the
   ends of the rolled baklava gently to make it wrinkly.
   Then gently pull baklava roll off the rod and place in
   buttered baking dish. Repeat until all dough is used.
   Butter tops of assembled rolls with leftover butter and
   sprinkle with remaining almond mixture. Bake for
   50–60 minutes.

6. In a small saucepan over medium-high heat, combine
   water, honey, ¼ teaspoon cinnamon, and lemon juice.
   Bring to a boil, reduce heat to low, and simmer for
   15–20 minutes. Remove from heat and cool slightly.
   Drizzle immediately over hot baklava when out of oven.
   Let cool 10 minutes, then cut into 1–2" rolls and serve.

PER SERVING Calories: 360 | Fat: 19g
| Protein: 5g | Sodium: 157mg | Fiber: 2g
| Carbohydrates: 47g | Sugar: 28g

Granola Berry Crisp

This healthy crisp is packed with delicious berries, and uses granola instead of a typical crumb topping. Using granola cuts preparation time and creates a fantastic crunch. Serve this crisp warm, topped with vanilla ice cream or yogurt.

INGREDIENTS | SERVES 8

4 cups mixed frozen berries
1 tablespoon lemon juice
½ cup powdered honey
1 teaspoon vanilla extract
¼ cup spelt flour
⅛ teaspoon sea salt
1½ cups granola
1 tablespoon coconut oil, melted
2 tablespoons xylitol

1. Preheat oven to 350°F. Spray a 9" round or square baking dish with cooking spray.

2. In a large bowl, combine the mixed berries, lemon juice, powdered honey, and vanilla. Add the flour and salt and mix until well coated. Pour mixture into prepared dish.

3. In a separate small dish, combine the granola, oil, and xylitol. Top the fruit mixture with the granola mixture. Bake covered for 20 minutes. Remove cover and bake for an additional 8 minutes.

PER SERVING Calories: 261 | Fat: 7g | Protein: 4g | Sodium: 45mg | Fiber: 4g | Carbohydrates: 47g | Sugar: 29g

Chocolate Éclairs

This classic French pastry is made naturally sweet and is filled with a decadent chocolate mousse. The pastry dough is easy to whip up, but the presentation makes these look as though they took hours to create.

INGREDIENTS | SERVES 12

½ cup butter

1 cup water

1 cup white spelt flour

4 large eggs, beaten well

¼ cup cocoa

¼ cup coconut oil, softened

1 cup maple syrup

½ teaspoon vanilla extract

¹⁄₁₆ teaspoon sea salt

8-ounce carton whipping cream, whipped to stiff peaks

½ cup melted chocolate, optional

Clear Out the Cobwebs

This recipe creates hollow pastries that are perfect for filling with mousse or pudding. When putting a small hole in the top of the éclair, wiggle a finger inside to remove any "cobweb" like dough that still remain inside. This will help the mousse fill the éclair evenly.

1. Preheat oven to 425°F. Line a baking sheet with parchment paper.

2. In a small saucepan, bring butter and water to a boil on the stove. Remove from heat and add the flour, stirring into a ball. Let this cool slightly. With a hand mixer, mix beaten eggs into the mixture until smooth.

3. Using a pastry bag with no tip attachment, or a plastic food storage bag with a ½" hole cut out of one corner, pipe the dough onto a baking sheet, creating about 3" logs placed 2" apart. Bake for 10 minutes at 425°F, then reduce heat to 350°F and bake for another 35 minutes. Éclairs should be golden brown when done. Allow to cool slightly before making a small finger hole through the top or at the side of cooled pastries for an access point for the filling.

4. In a small bowl, whip the cocoa, coconut oil, maple syrup, vanilla, and salt until smooth. Add the whipped cream and whip until completely combined.

5. Fill a pastry bag, or a plastic bag with a hole cut out of one corner, with mousse filling and gently pipe the mousse into each éclair. Drizzle with chocolate or top with Chocolate Buttercream Frosting (see recipe in Chapter 12). Refrigerate in a covered dish for 1 hour to set before serving.

PER SERVING Calories: 309 | Fat: 20g | Protein: 4g | Sodium: 45mg | Fiber: 1g | Carbohydrates: 30g | Sugar: 16g

Chocolate Pumpkin Éclairs

Create a beautiful fall pastry with a subtly spiced pumpkin filling instead of the traditional éclair. Finish with piped Chocolate Buttercream Frosting and a drizzle of sugar-free white chocolate.

INGREDIENTS | SERVES 12

6 large eggs, divided

¾ cup unsalted butter, divided

1 cup water

1 cup plus 2 tablespoons spelt flour, divided

2 cups almond milk

1 cup pumpkin purée

1 teaspoon pumpkin pie spice

½ teaspoon cinnamon

⅔ cup coconut sugar

2 teaspoons vanilla extract

Chocolate Buttercream Frosting (see recipe in Chapter 12)

Surprise Filling

The charm of these éclairs is in the surprise pumpkin center! Experiment with other frostings to cover these éclairs to create more fun holiday flavors.

1. Preheat oven to 425°F. Line a baking sheet with parchment paper. Beat 4 eggs in a small bowl. Set aside.

2. In a small saucepan, bring ½ cup butter and water to a boil over high heat. Remove from heat and add 1 cup flour, stirring until the mixture forms a ball. Let dough cool slightly. With a hand mixer, mix beaten eggs into the mixture until smooth.

3. Using a pastry bag with no tip attachment, or a plastic food storage bag with a ½" hole cut out of one corner, pipe the dough onto a baking sheet, creating 3" logs, 2" apart. Bake for 10 minutes, then reduce heat to 350°F and bake for another 35–40 minutes. Éclairs should feel firm when done. Set aside to cool.

4. In a medium mixing bowl, whisk together almond milk, 2 eggs, 2 tablespoons flour, pumpkin, pumpkin pie spice, and cinnamon. Mix well and set aside.

5. In a saucepan, melt the remaining butter over medium heat and add the coconut sugar. Cook until sugar dissolves, stirring often. Allow to cool for 5 minutes.

6. Add the sugar mixture to the pumpkin mixture. Add the vanilla and mix until smoothly combined. Fill a pastry bag, or a plastic bag with a hole cut out of one corner, with filling and gently pipe the filling into each éclair. Top éclairs with Chocolate Buttercream Frosting.

PER SERVING Calories: 319 | Fat: 21g | Protein: 6g | Sodium: 78mg | Fiber: 3g | Carbohydrates: 31g | Sugar: 19g

Chocolate Puff Pastries

In this recipe, rich melted chocolate is enveloped by a sweet flaky pastry blanket.
Choose good quality dark chocolate for the most professional results.

INGREDIENTS | SERVES 9

1 sheet puff pastry, thawed
1 (3.5-ounce) sugar-free dark chocolate bar, cut into 9 squares

Sugar-Free Puff Pastry

Some store-bought puff pastry has sugar added, so make sure to choose unsweetened sheets when possible.

1. Preheat oven to 400°F. Line a baking sheet with parchment paper.

2. Lay the puff pastry out on a clean work surface. Cut into 9 even squares.

3. Place 1 square of chocolate in the center of each dough square.

4. Fold the corners into the center, covering the chocolate. Press gently so corners stick together and will hold together while baking.

5. Place pastries on baking sheet 2" apart. Bake for 12–14 minutes. Remove from pan and cool slightly on a wire rack. Serve warm.

PER SERVING Calories: 285 | Fat: 21g | Protein: 4g | Sodium: 115mg | Fiber: 1g | Carbohydrates: 28g | Sugar: 1g

Lemon Cream Cheese Pastries

Delight the senses with a flaky pastry bursting with a citrus cheese filling. Enjoy as breakfast or dessert.

INGREDIENTS | YIELDS 9 PASTRIES

½ cup cream cheese

⅓ cup xylitol

1½ tablespoons fresh lemon juice

1 teaspoon lemon zest

½ teaspoon vanilla extract

1 teaspoon white wheat flour

1 puff pastry sheet, thawed

1. Preheat oven to 400°F. Line a baking sheet with parchment paper.

2. In a small mixing bowl, combine the cream cheese, xylitol, lemon juice, zest, vanilla, and flour and beat until smooth and creamy.

3. Cut the cold, but thawed, pastry sheet into 9 squares. Spoon about 1 tablespoon of lemon cream in the center of each square. Gently fold all the dough corners into the middle, covering the cream. Gently press the centers so they hold together.

4. Place pastries on baking sheet 2" apart and bake for 7–8 minutes. If any corners of the pastries puff up and detach from the centers while baking, gently reshape while still warm. Allow to cool for 5 minutes before enjoying.

PER SERVING Calories: 325 | Fat: 22g | Protein: 4g | Sodium: 160mg | Fiber: 1g | Carbohydrates: 30g | Sugar: 1g

CHAPTER 15

Sweet and Salty Snacks

Silky Chocolate Cups

If clouds were made of chocolate, they would taste like these silky smooth mousse cups. The mousse is creamy and dense, creating the ultimate texture combination in this rich chocolate dessert.

INGREDIENTS | SERVES 12

½ cup full-fat coconut milk

½ cup maple syrup

1 cup walnut halves and pieces

4 soft, pitted Medjool dates

½ teaspoon cinnamon

⅛ teaspoon sea salt

1¾ cups cashews, soaked in water for 6–8 hours and drained

⅓ cup melted coconut oil

1½ ounces unsweetened chocolate, melted

Healthy Sweetened Condensed Milk

Regular sweetened condensed milk is loaded with unhealthy sugar. Using full-fat coconut milk with pure maple syrup creates a healthy replica of this baking staple! Try using this thick, sweet cream as a topping for all your favorite desserts.

1. Place 12 muffin liners in a muffin tin and set aside.

2. In a small saucepan, combine coconut milk with maple syrup over medium-high heat and bring to a boil. Reduce heat to medium-low and simmer for 30 minutes. Pour the condensed coconut milk mixture into a small bowl and refrigerate for 30–60 minutes.

3. Place walnuts, dates, cinnamon, and salt in a food processor and pulse for about 30 seconds or until the mixture is combined and grainy. Divide the mixture among the 12 liners and press into a flat layer on the bottom of the liners. Refrigerate for 30 minutes.

4. In high-speed blender, combine soaked cashews with cooled condensed coconut milk mixture, coconut oil, and chocolate. Blend until smooth.

5. Scoop chocolate cashew mixture into the 12 cups on top of the cooled walnut crust (about 3–4 tablespoons) and refrigerate for at least 1 hour before serving.

PER SERVING Calories: 286 | Fat: 23g | Protein: 5g | Sodium: 30mg | Fiber: 2g | Carbohydrates: 18g | Sugar: 11g

Cinnamon Almond Energy Balls

Get a big burst of energy with these delicious energy balls, packed with protein and a tasty sweet cinnamon maple flavor.

INGREDIENTS | SERVES 5

¾ cup almond butter
½ cup maple syrup
1 tablespoon ground flaxseed
1½ teaspoons vanilla extract
½ teaspoon cinnamon
⅛ teaspoon sea salt
2½ tablespoons vanilla protein powder
⅓ cup oats

1. In a medium bowl, combine the almond butter and maple syrup and stir until smooth. Add the flaxseed, vanilla, cinnamon, and salt. Mix to combine.

2. Add protein powder, and fully incorporate. If "dough" is too oily, add another teaspoon of protein powder. Add the oats and mix well. Roll into small balls. Enjoy immediately or store covered in the refrigerator. Balls will firm up slightly when chilled.

PER SERVING Calories: 374 | Fat: 20g | Protein: 15g | Sodium: 248mg | Fiber: 3g | Carbohydrates: 34g | Sugar: 24g

On the Go

These energy balls are perfect for an on-the-go snack. However, their soft texture makes them easy to smash, so keep them chilled and store in a sturdy container.

Gooey Almond Cereal Party Mix

*Ooey, gooey with a touch of crunch, this party mix is a crowd pleaser. Keep chilled
for easy serving and munching, or serve at room temperature on a warm night
for the sweet caramel sauce to soften and create a even gooier treat.*

INGREDIENTS | MAKES 7 CUPS

6 cups natural shredded oat cereal

1 cup unsweetened shredded coconut

1¼ cups slivered almonds

¾ cup coconut sugar

¼ cup coconut oil

¾ cup honey

½ teaspoon cornstarch

¼ teaspoon sea salt

1 teaspoon vanilla extract

Natural Cereal

Make sure to use a stiff, sturdy natural cereal like Barbara's Morning Oat Crunch. Thin, delicate cereals such as corn flakes won't hold up well when mixed in the caramel sauce, and part of the charm is the cereal's crunch in every bite.

1. Line a baking sheet with parchment or wax paper. Spray a large bowl with cooking spray.

2. To the prepared bowl add the cereal, coconut, and almonds and mix to combine.

3. In a medium saucepan over high heat, stir together the coconut sugar, coconut oil, honey, cornstarch, and salt. Bring to a boil, while stirring occasionally. Reduce heat to medium high and allow to simmer for about 2–3 minutes, stirring constantly.

4. Remove the pan from the heat and add in the vanilla extract. Pour the warm mixture over the cereal mixture and mix to coat evenly. Spread the mixture on the lined baking sheet.

5. Place in the refrigerator to cool for 30 minutes.

PER SERVING (½ cup) Calories: 391 | Fat: 17g | Protein: 9g | Sodium: 45mg | Fiber: 6g | Carbohydrates: 54g | Sugar: 27g

Almond Cinnamon Popcorn

Crunchy, salty popcorn is brought to the next level with a dash of cinnamon.
Enjoy the diverse array of flavors and textures in each bite.

INGREDIENTS | MAKES 16 CUPS

½ cup organic corn kernels
⅔ cup natural creamy almond butter
2 tablespoons coconut oil
½ teaspoon sea salt
¼ teaspoon cinnamon
1 teaspoon vanilla extract

1. Pop the corn kernels in an air popper or other popcorn maker.

2. In a medium bowl, warm the almond butter and oil in the microwave for 20 seconds, and stir to combine. Stir in salt, cinnamon, and vanilla.

3. Pour the popped popcorn into a large bowl and make sure to remove any unpopped kernels. Pour the almond butter mixture over all the popcorn. Gently stir to evenly coat all the popcorn.

4. Enjoy immediately for a bit of a sticky treat, or spread out on a baking sheet and chill in the refrigerator for 15–20 minutes to let set.

PER SERVING (2 cups) Calories: 219 | Fat: 15g | Protein: 7g | Sodium: 247mg | Fiber: 4g | Carbohydrates: 17g | Sugar: 2g

Peanut Butter Chocolate Popcorn

Rich and chocolaty, this popcorn is more sweet than salty. Use all-natural peanut butter to control the sugar in this recipe and substitute coconut oil for butter for a dairy-free treat.

INGREDIENTS | MAKES 16 CUPS

½ cup organic corn kernels

1¼ cups semisweet sugar-free chocolate chips

½ cup natural peanut butter

3 tablespoons butter

½ teaspoon sea salt

1 teaspoon vanilla extract

1. Pop the corn kernels in an air popper or other popcorn maker.

2. In a medium bowl, melt the chocolate, peanut butter, and butter in the microwave and stir to combine. Stir in the salt and vanilla.

3. Pour the popcorn into a large bowl, removing any unpopped or burnt kernels. Pour the chocolate mixture over all the popcorn. Gently stir to evenly coat.

4. Spread out on a cookie sheet and refrigerate to set the chocolate. Cover and store leftovers in a cool place.

PER SERVING (2 cups) Calories: 460 | Fat: 30g | Protein: 8g | Sodium: 229mg | Fiber: 7g | Carbohydrates: 52g | Sugar: 3g

Peanut Butter Truffles

These simple rich truffles have a subtle nutty flavor with a chewy date base to hold them together and provide a nutrient-dense sweetness.

INGREDIENTS | SERVES 10

16 Medjool dates
2 tablespoons peanut butter
2 tablespoons coconut oil
1 teaspoon cinnamon
¾ cup almond flour

1. In a food processor or high-powered blender, process dates until coarsely chopped. Add the peanut butter, coconut oil, cinnamon, and flour and blend until smooth.

2. Form the dough into 1" balls and roll until smooth. Store covered in the refrigerator until ready to serve.

PER SERVING Calories: 129 | Fat: 8g | Protein: 3g | Sodium: 15mg | Fiber: 2g | Carbohydrates: 13g | Sugar: 9g

Raw Applesauce

Supremely flavorful, and totally naturally sweetened, this raw treat is a snap to whip up.

INGREDIENTS | SERVES 6

4 medium apples, peeled and cored
4 teaspoons fresh squeezed lemon juice
4 teaspoons maple syrup
1 teaspoon cinnamon

Chop apples finely in a food processor. Stir in remaining ingredients. Serve immediately or store in refrigerator for up to 2 days.

PER SERVING Calories: 65 | Fat: 0g | Protein: 0g | Sodium: 0mg | Fiber: 1.5g | Carbohydrates: 17g | Sugar: 14g

Apple Pie Chips

For a unique apple pie fix, try these warmly spiced chips. A dehydrator is used in this recipe to keep the nutrients of the apple intact while preserving the chips so they will last for several months.

INGREDIENTS | SERVES 8

4 medium sweet apples
Juice of ½ medium lemon
3 tablespoons maple syrup
2 teaspoons cinnamon
½ teaspoon nutmeg

1. Core apples with an apple corer or by taking a knife to the center of the apple and cutting out the middle core and seeds without breaking the outer portion of the apples.

2. Lay apple down horizontally and begin slicing thin slices (about 1/16") from the base of the apple up to the top. You could also use an apple swirl peeler that de-cores at the same time.

3. Drizzle and rub lemon juice all over the slices, on both sides. Drizzle with maple syrup, cinnamon, and nutmeg and rub with fingers to coat apple slices evenly.

4. Lay the apple slices on dehydrator trays, careful not to overcrowd. Turn the dehydrator on to 135°F and allow the apples to dry for 8–10 hours. Store in airtight bags or glass containers at room temperature.

PER SERVING Calories: 60 | Fat: 0g | Protein: 0g | Sodium: 0mg | Fiber: 1g | Carbohydrates: 16g | Sugar: 13g

Baked Sweet Potato Fries

Even though these potato wedges are baked in the oven and contain less fat than traditional fries, they're just as crispy and flavorful and have a sweet cinnamon coating.

INGREDIENTS | SERVES 3

2 large sweet potatoes
3 tablespoons grapeseed oil
½ teaspoon sea salt
1½ teaspoons cinnamon
2 tablespoons coconut sugar

1. Preheat oven to 425°F. Line a baking sheet with parchment paper.

2. Wash, peel, and slice potatoes and lay them on the baking sheet. Drizzle with oil and sprinkle the salt, cinnamon, and coconut sugar over the fries. Toss fries gently to fully coat and cover all the potatoes, spreading them out evenly on the baking sheet.

3. Bake for 35–40 minutes, flipping fries every 10 minutes to ensure they all bake evenly. Enjoy when warm!

PER SERVING Calories: 237 | Fat: 14g | Protein: 1.5g | Sodium: 440mg | Fiber: 5g | Carbohydrates: 29g | Sugar: 12g

Cinnamon Banana Chips

Turn beautiful ripe bananas into sweet, caramelized bites that are absolutely addicting with a sprinkle of cinnamon.

INGREDIENTS | SERVES 6

3 large ripe bananas
Juice of ½ large lemon
1 teaspoon cinnamon

1. Slice bananas into ¼" slices. Drizzle slices with lemon juice. Sprinkle cinnamon evenly over banana slices.

2. Lightly spray dehydrator sheets with a thin coating of coconut oil or natural olive oil spray.

3. Lay banana pieces on tray. Dehydrate at 135°F for 15 hours for softer banana chips or 18 hours for firmer, crunchier chips. Store chips in an airtight container at room temperature.

PER SERVING Calories: 62 | Fat: 0g | Protein: 1g | Sodium: 1mg | Fiber: 2g | Carbohydrates: 16g | Sugar: 8g

Cinnamon Honey Popcorn

With simple flavors and charmingly sticky, this honey-sweet popcorn is the perfect quick sugar fix.

INGREDIENTS | SERVES 6

¼ cup honey

½ teaspoon sea salt

½ cup organic corn kernels

½ teaspoon cinnamon

Organic Corn

Organic corn, free of genetic modification, has been known to help control diabetes, help with hypertension, and prevent heart ailments, and is rich in vitamins A, B, and E. Antioxidants found in corn can also help ward off cancer and Alzheimer's disease. It can help with digestion, anemia, and reduce the signs of aging.

1. Mix the honey and salt together in a small bowl and set aside.

2. Pop the corn kernels in an air popper or other popcorn maker.

3. Combine honey mixture and cinnamon over popped popcorn and toss until coated.

PER SERVING (2 cups) Calories: 94 | Fat: 0g | Protein: 2g | Sodium: 148mg | Fiber: 2.5g | Carbohydrates: 21g | Sugar: 9g

Cinnamon Flaxseed Applesauce

Brighten the afternoon with a naturally sweetened applesauce treat. Increase the flavor and spice of plain applesauce with raw honey and a pinch of flaxseed. This dish is full of vitamins, minerals, and even protein.

INGREDIENTS | SERVES 2

1 cup unsweetened applesauce

2 teaspoons cinnamon

⅛ teaspoon sea salt

2 tablespoons honey

2 tablespoons ground flaxseed

In a small mixing bowl, mix the applesauce with the cinnamon, salt, and honey. Mix until honey is fully incorporated. Add flaxseed, mix and enjoy.

PER SERVING Calories: 155 | Fat: 3g | Protein: 2g | Sodium: 150mg | Fiber: 5g | Carbohydrates: 35g | Sugar: 29g

Cinnamon Kale Chips

Bitter kale leaves are transformed into a sweet cinnamon treat, fit for the pickiest of eaters. The cinnamon and sugar caramelize this veggie into a healthy green treat that tastes almost like candy.

INGREDIENTS | SERVES 2

2 cups washed and chopped kale leaves
3 tablespoons grapeseed oil
2 tablespoons cinnamon
2 tablespoons coconut sugar
⅛ teaspoon salt

1. Preheat oven to 400°F. Line a baking sheet with parchment paper.

2. Spread the kale leaves on the baking sheet. Drizzle with oil and sprinkle cinnamon, coconut sugar, and salt evenly over the kale leaves. Lightly mix with your hands to evenly cover the chips.

3. Roast the kale leaves for 10–15 minutes, stirring halfway through baking time to evenly bake chips. Allow to cool slightly and enjoy!

PER SERVING Calories: 279 | Fat: 21g | Protein: 2g | Sodium: 177mg | Fiber: 5g | Carbohydrates: 25g | Sugar: 13g

Pretzel Pecan Clusters

Salty pretzel and pecan bundles drowned in melted chocolate create the ultimate professional-looking candy. The best part is that this very addicting candy is extremely simple to make.

INGREDIENTS | MAKES 1¼ CUPS

⅔ cup roughly chopped pretzel sticks
½ cup pecans, roughly chopped
1 cup sugar-free chocolate, melted

1. In a medium bowl, mix the pretzels and pecans with melted chocolate. Pour mixture onto a wax-paper-lined baking dish.

2. Refrigerate for 30 minutes or until no longer shiny. Remove from the refrigerator and break into smaller bite-size clusters. Serve and enjoy!

PER SERVING (¼ cup) Calories: 205 | Fat: 18g | Protein: 3g | Sodium: 155mg | Fiber: 3g | Carbohydrates: 32g | Sugar: 1g

Cinnamon Sweet Potato Chips

The trick to super crispy potato chips is to slice the potatoes as thin as possible. Use a mandolin slicer if possible, to achieve uniform, thin slices that yield perfect chips every time.

INGREDIENTS | SERVES 2

1 large sweet potato
2 tablespoons coconut oil, melted
½ teaspoon sea salt
1 teaspoon cinnamon

Don't Overbake!

These chips can burn easily during the last half hour of baking, which is why the oven is turned off for the last 20 minutes. If chips are sliced on the thicker side, they will not be as crisp as thinner chips. Using a mandolin will ensure that potato slices are uniform and bake evenly.

1. Preheat oven to 250°F. Line a baking sheet with parchment paper.

2. Wash potato; slice as thinly as possible and lay slices on baking sheet. Drizzle coconut oil evenly, then sprinkle with salt and cinnamon. Gently toss to evenly coat.

3. Place on middle rack in oven and bake for 1 hour. Stir chips and rotate pan; bake another 1 hour and avoid opening the oven door until after the chips are done baking. Check on the chips by turning on the oven light and peeking through the window to make sure they are not burning.

4. After the second hour, turn off oven and allow chips to sit in hot oven for an extra 20–25 minutes.

PER SERVING Calories: 179 | Fat: 14g | Protein: 1g | Sodium: 625mg | Fiber: 3g | Carbohydrates: 14g | Sugar: 3g

Healthy Caramel Popcorn

Fairs and amusement parks are notorious for selling monstrous bags of deliciously flavored popcorn. Create this easy popcorn recipe at home for a treat that is just as satisfying and a whole lot healthier.

INGREDIENTS | MAKES 16 CUPS

½ cup corn kernels
½ cup unsalted butter
¼ cup honey
1 cup coconut sugar
½ teaspoon sea salt
½ teaspoon baking soda
1 teaspoon vanilla extract

1. Preheat oven to 250°F.

2. Pop the corn kernels in an air popper or other popcorn maker.

3. In a small saucepan over medium heat, melt butter and stir in honey, coconut sugar, and salt. Bring to a boil, stirring constantly. Boil for 5 minutes on medium/low heat.

4. Remove from heat. Stir in baking soda and vanilla. Pour mixture over popcorn. Place in large baking dish and bake for 45 minutes.

5. Stir popcorn every 15 minutes. Remove from oven and stir popcorn until cool, or let it cool without stirring for popcorn to clump.

PER SERVING (2 cups) Calories: 295 | Fat: 12g | Protein: 2g | Sodium: 230mg | Fiber: 2g | Carbohydrates: 46g | Sugar: 34g

Rosemary Wheat Crisps

*Homemade crackers are delectable with dried herbs and sea salt. They make
a wonderful pairing with all your favorite cheeses and fruits.*

**INGREDIENTS | YIELDS 30 (1½")
SQUARE CRACKERS**

1½ cups whole-wheat flour
½ cup water
¼ cup olive oil
1 tablespoon honey
1 teaspoon rosemary, crushed or ground
1 teaspoon sea salt, divided

1. Preheat oven to 425°F.

2. Mix flour, water, oil, honey, rosemary, and ½ teaspoon salt in a medium bowl with electric beaters until just blended.

3. Knead the dough slightly to form a ball. Roll out as thin as possible (about ⅛") with a rolling pin. Shape dough into a 10" × 14" rectangle.

4. Sprinkle dough with additional ½ teaspoon salt. Using the rolling pin, roll gently over dough to press in the salt. Prick dough all over with a fork.

5. Cut dough into 1½" squares. Place on cookie sheet. Bake for 12 minutes.

6. Remove from oven and separate crackers. Return any crackers not browned to the oven for an additional 2 minutes. Crackers require darkening to be crispy. Store crackers in an airtight container for up to 3 days.

PER SERVING (3 crackers) Calories: 278 | Fat: 6g | Protein: 9g | Sodium: 240mg | Fiber: 8g | Carbohydrates: 50g | Sugar: 2g

Honey Graham Crackers

These graham crackers are better than any store-bought versions and are completely free of unnatural preservatives. They are perfect in s'mores, to dip in chocolate milk, or to crush into a pie crust.

INGREDIENTS | YIELDS 18 CRACKERS

2½ cups whole-wheat flour

½ cup grapeseed oil

½ cup plus 1 tablespoon honey

1 tablespoon molasses

2 teaspoons vanilla extract

½ teaspoon baking soda

1⁄16 teaspoon cinnamon

1⁄16 teaspoon sea salt

Sweeten the Pot

Honey gives great flavor to these homemade crackers. For an even sweeter cinnamon-sugar version, sprinkle crackers with 2 tablespoons coconut sugar and 1 teaspoon cinnamon before baking.

1. Preheat oven to 350°F. Line a baking sheet with parchment paper.

2. In a large mixing bowl, mix together the flour, grapeseed oil, honey, molasses, vanilla extract, baking soda, cinnamon, and salt with an electric mixer.

3. Dump the dough onto a clean work surface. Roll dough about ¼" thick into a rectangle. Cut the dough into 3" rectangles and place on baking sheet about 1 inch apart.

4. Bake for 14–16 minutes for a slightly soft graham cracker or 17 minutes for an extra crispy cracker. Remove from oven and let cool 5 minutes.

PER SERVING (2 squares) Calories: 293 | Fat: 13g | Protein: 5g | Sodium: 90mg | Fiber: 4g | Carbohydrates: 44g | Sugar: 19g

Everything But the Kitchen Sink Popcorn

This incredible popcorn has several sweet and savory flavor combinations that make it the perfect movie treat or party snack. Use gluten-free pretzels for a gluten-free treat or sunflower seed butter in case of peanut allergy.

INGREDIENTS | MAKES 10 CUPS

⅓ cup popcorn kernels

¾ cup natural peanut butter

3 tablespoons grapeseed oil

4 tablespoons raw honey

⅛ teaspoon sea salt

½ teaspoon vanilla extract

½ cup chopped sugar-free dark chocolate

½ cup roughly chopped pretzels

1. Pop the corn kernels in an air popper or other popcorn maker.

2. In a medium saucepan over medium heat, heat the peanut butter, oil, and honey. Stir until smooth. Stir in salt.

3. Turn off heat and stir in vanilla until combined. Pour the warm mixture over the popcorn and stir until all the popcorn is coated. Add the chopped chocolate and pretzels and stir again to combine.

4. Serve immediately or at room temperature.

PER SERVING (2 cups) Calories: 515 | Fat: 33g | Protein: 14g | Sodium: 390mg | Fiber: 7g | Carbohydrates: 56g | Sugar: 18g

Sweet and Salty Peanuts

Honey-sweet glazed nuts get a perfect touch of salt to make this treat perfectly addicting. Maple syrup can also be used in place of the honey.

INGREDIENTS | YIELDS ⅔ CUP PEANUTS

2 tablespoons honey

2 teaspoons unsulphured molasses

⅔ cup unsalted roasted peanuts

¾ teaspoon sea salt

1. Preheat oven to 250°F. Line a baking sheet with parchment paper.

2. Heat honey and molasses in a small skillet over medium heat. Add peanuts and stir for 1 minute.

3. Remove the skillet from the heat, spread the peanuts on the baking sheet, sprinkle with salt and place in the oven for 50 minutes. Remove from the oven and stir peanuts as they cool. Enjoy warm or cool.

PER SERVING (1 ounce) Calories: 220 | Fat: 14g | Protein: 7g | Sodium: 815mg | Fiber: 2g | Carbohydrates: 21g | Sugar: 15g

Appendix A: Additional Resources

Amazon.com

Amazon.com sells a wide variety of natural sugar-free products and alternative ingredients. Find coconut sugar, sugar-free chocolates, agave inulin, and many other items.

www.amazon.com

Arrowhead Mills

Arrowhead Mills sells a great selection of natural flours such as spelt, barley, and wheat.

www.arrowheadmills.com

Beekeepers

Find local beekeepers in your area for raw local honey, often for bulk pricing.

www.localharvest.org/organic-honey.jsp

Coombs Family Farms

Pure, organic maple products such as maple syrup and maple sugar are available year-round from Coombs Family Farms.

www.coombsfamilyfarms.com

Costco

Buy coconut oil, coconut sugar, and spices in bulk. Costco also carries organic eggs, natural snacks, and chia seeds.

www.costco.com

Enjoy Life Foods

Enjoy Life Foods products are a great natural alternative for allergy-free baking, as they are free of gluten, dairy, and soy, and many products are naturally sweetened.

www.enjoylifefoods.com

King Arthur Flour

All-natural flours can be found at King Arthur. From whole wheat to white wheat, King Arthur sells a great natural product. Look for them at any grocery or health food store.

www.kingarthurflour.com

Lucienne's Chocolate

Lucienne's features sugar-free chocolate sweetened with stevia, xylitol, or erythritol. These bars come in a variety of flavors and are great for baking chips or for chocolate coatings.

www.luciennes.com

Nature's Way

Here you will find a great selection of health products and supplements such as protein powders, coconut oil, and herbs.

www.naturesway.com

NOW Foods

Natural, pure food products are sold through NOW Foods, online or at most natural health food stores. NOW Foods sells a variety of sweeteners such as date sugar, molasses, and xylitol as well as other natural foods, such as flaxseed and chia seeds.

www.nowfoods.com

Trader Joe's

Store hours, locations, events, and news are listed on their website. Food items like maple sugar, white whole-wheat flour, dried fruit, and nuts can be found at Trader Joe's for affordable prices. They also carry a few specialty jams and cookies that are naturally sweetened as well as affordable organic produce.

www.traderjoes.com

Vitacost

From herbs and supplements to coconut oil and raw honey, this site is a great source for getting natural food products at a great price.

www.vitacost.com

VitaSpelt

Excellent source for white spelt and whole spelt products, ranging from flours to crackers. Look for their products at natural food stores or order online.

www.natureslegacyforlife.com

Whole Foods Market

For organic, natural, and pure food ingredients, Whole Foods Market has a plethora of options. It's a great source for finding naturally sweetened chocolates, canned coconut milk, and natural flours. Store locations and hours are listed on their website.

www.wholefoodsmarket.com

Wholesome Sweeteners

Enjoy pure, organic sweeteners—such as coconut sugar, xylitol, and molasses—from Wholesome Sweeteners.

www.wholesomesweeteners.com

Appendix B: Recipe Index

Mexican Quinoa **GF, EF, DF, NF, R, V**

Orange Quinoa Mint Salad **GF, EF, DF, NF, V**

Chicken Lettuce Wraps **EF, DF, NF**

Pumpkin Pecan Pasta **EF, V**

Vegan Black Bean Burritos **EF, DF, NF, V**

Vegetarian Cobb Salad **NF**

Vegetable Ranch Pizza **EF, NF**

Spicy Shrimp **EF, DF, NF**

Chapter 6: Sauces, Dressings, and Spreads

Basil-Rich Marinara Sauce **GF, EF, DF, NF, V**

Avocado Basil Spread **GF, EF, DF, NF, R, V**

Creamy Chocolate Pudding **GF, EF, DF, R, V**

Chocolate Peanut Butter Pudding **GF, EF, DF, R, V**

Chocolate Chip Cookie Dough Dip **EF, R**

Dairy-Free Cinnamon Honey Butter **GF, EF, DF, NF, R**

Easy Chocolate Mousse **GF, EF, DF, NF, R, V**

Yogurt Fruit Dip **GF, EF, NF, R**

Gluten-Free Cinnamon Chips **GF, EF, DF, NF, V**

Chocolate Hazelnut Spread **GF, EF, DF** (if using dairy-free chocolate), **V**

Homemade Coconut Butter **GF, EF, DF, NF, R, V**

Honey Mustard Dressing **GF, NF, R**

Walnut Fig Dressing **GF, EF, DF, R, V**

Raspberry Vinaigrette **GF, EF, DF, NF, R**

Dairy-Free Mayonnaise **GF, EF, DF, R, V**

Raw Strawberry Jam **GF, EF, DF, NF, R**

Orange Vinaigrette **GF, EF, DF, NF, R, V**

Raw Caramel Sauce **GF, EF, NF, R, V**

Sweet Poppy Seed Dressing **GF, EF, DF, NF, R**

Strawberry Sauce **GF, EF, DF, R, V**

Pumpkin Pie Dip

Chapter 7: Drinks

Cucumber Green Drink **GF, EF, DF, NF, R, V**

Easy Apple Cider **GF, EF, DF, NF, V**

Green Guzzler **GF, EF, DF, R, V**

Lucky Green Smoothie **GF, EF, DF, NF, R, V**

Holiday Eggnog **GF, NF**

Sparkling Grape Juice **GF, EF, DF, NF, R, V**

Sparkling Pomegranate Lime Juice **GF, EF, DF, NF, R, V**

Sweet Green Juice **GF, EF, DF, NF, R, V**

Pumpkin Juice **GF, EF, DF, NF**

Strawberry Peach Smoothie **GF, EF, NF**

Raspberry Peach Water **GF, EF, DF, NF, R, V**

Raspberry Mint Smoothie **GF, EF, DF, NF, R, V**

Strawberry Lemonade **GF, EF, DF, NF, R, V**

Mint Lemonade **GF, EF, DF, NF, R, V**

Beet It Smoothie **GF, EF, DF, NF, R, V**

Carrot Mango Smoothie

"I Can't Believe It's a Green Smoothie" Smoothie

Chapter 8: Cakes and Cupcakes

Cake Pop Kabobs **NF**

Carrot Cake

Chocolate Cake Waffles **NF**

Vegan Chocolate Cupcakes **EF, DF, V**

Berry Spring Crepe Cake

Coffee Cake

Classic Chocolate Cupcakes

Gluten-Free Chocolate Cupcakes **GF, NF**

Lemon Mint Yogurt Cake **EF, NF**

Oatmeal Cake **DF, NF**

Peach Berry Shortcakes **NF**

Pumpkin Chocolate Chip Cake **NF**

Chocolate Raspberry Cake Roll **NF**

Rich Chocolate Cake **EF, NF**

Single Serving Chocolate Cake **GF, EF, DF** (if using dairy-free chocolate), **V**

Strawberry Shortcake

Vanilla Pound Cake **EF, NF**

Vegan Lemon Cupcakes **EF, DF**

Chocolate Chip Cookie Cupcakes

Walnut Chocolate Chip Cake

Flourless Devil's Food Pudding Cake **GF, EF, DF, V**

Chapter 9: Candy

Easy Banana Bites **GF, EF, DF, R, V**

Honey Cinnamon Almonds **GF, EF, DF**

Almond Butter Cups **GF, EF, DF, R**

Almond Coconut Chocolate Candies **GF, DF** (if using dairy-free chocolate), **V**

Buckeyes **GF, EF, DF** (if using dairy-free chocolate), **R, V**

Candied Pecans **GF**

Chocolate Nut Truffles **GF, EF, DF** (if using dairy-free chocolate), **R, V**

Chocolate-Covered Raisin Fudge **GF, EF, NF, R, V**

Shortbread Bars **EF**

Blondie Bars **NF**

Strawberry Oat Bars **EF, DF, V**

Vegan Lemon Bars **EF, DF, NF, V**

Buckeye Brownies **GF, DF** (if using dairy-free chocolate)

No-Bake Pumpkin Cheesecake Bars **GF, EF, DF, R**

Chapter 12: Frostings, Glazes, and Toppings

Classic Cream Cheese Frosting **GF, NF**

German Chocolate Frosting **GF**

Easy Vanilla Glaze **GF, EF**

Chocolate Buttercream Frosting **GF, EF, NF**

Vegan Chocolate Buttercream **GF, EF, DF, NF, V**

Peanut Butter Fudge Frosting **EF, DF, V**

Dairy-Free Cream Cheese Frosting **EF, DF, V**

Dreamy Chocolate Fudge Frosting **GF, EF, DF, R, V**

Dark Chocolate Fudge Sauce **GF, EF, DF, NF, R, V**

Peanut Butter Sauce **GF, EF**

Vanilla Cream Filling **EF**

Homemade Whipped Cream **GF, EF, NF**

Pumpkin Spice Whipped Cream **GF, EF, NF**

Dairy-Free Whipped Cream **EF, DF, NF, V**

Coconut Pecan Frosting **GF**

Chapter 13: Frozen Treats

Classic Vanilla Ice Cream **GF, EF, NF**

Soda Lime Slushies **GF, EF, DF, NF, V**

Brownie Ice Cream Sandwiches **DF, NF**

Banana Boat Milkshake **EF, DF** (if using dairy-free chocolate), **NF**

Easy Banana Truffles **EF**

Frozen S'mores **EF, NF**

Healthy Orange Slushies **GF, EF, DF, NF, V**

Healthy Peanut Butter Milkshakes **GF, EF, DF**

Mexican Chocolate Ice Cream **GF, NF**

Orange Mousse **GF, EF, DF, NF, V**

Healthy Mint Shakes **GF, EF, DF, NF**

Vegan Vanilla Bean Ice Cream **EF, DF, NF, V**

Chocolate Icies **GF, EF**

Watermelon Lime Slushies **GF, EF, DF, NF, V**

Strawberry Rhubarb Sorbet **GF, EF, DF, NF, V**

Chapter 14: Pies and Pastries

Spelt Flour Pie Crust **EF, NF**

Pumpkin Pie

Rustic Pear Tart **EF, DF**

Chocolate Silk Pie **EF, DF, NF**

Individual Raw Chocolate Pies **GF, EF, DF, R, V**

Fresh Fruit Tart, **NF**

Mini Pecan Tarts

Individual Banana Peanut Butter Pies **EF, DF, R**

Easy Chocolate Phyllo Cups **NF**

Raw Chocolate Mint Tart **GF, EF, DF, R, V**

Sugar-Free Apple Crisp **GF, EF, DF, V**

Vegan Pumpkin Pie **EF, DF, NF, V**

Key Lime Cheesecake Pie **GF, EF, DF, R, V**

Apple Fritters **DF**

Almond Baklava

Granola Berry Crisp **EF, DF, NF**

Chocolate Éclairs **NF**

Chocolate Pumpkin Éclairs

Chocolate Puff Pastries **NF**

Lemon Cream Cheese Pastries **NF**

Chapter 15: Sweet and Salty Snacks

Silky Chocolate Cups **GF, EF, DF** (if using dairy-free chocolate), **R**

Cinnamon Almond Energy Balls **EF**

Gooey Almond Cereal Party Mix **EF, DF, R**

Almond Cinnamon Popcorn **GF, EF, DF, V**

Peanut Butter Chocolate Popcorn **EF**

Peanut Butter Truffles **GF, EF, DF, R, V**

Raw Applesauce **GF, EF, DF, NF, R, V**

Apple Pie Chips **R, V, EF, GF, DF**

Baked Sweet Potato Fries **GF, EF, DF, NF, V**

Cinnamon Banana Chips **GF, EF, DF, NF, R, V**

Cinnamon Honey Popcorn **GF, EF, DF, NF**

Cinnamon Flaxseed Applesauce **GF, EF, DF, NF**

Cinnamon Kale Chips **GF, EF, DF, NF, V**

Pretzel Pecan Clusters **EF**

Cinnamon Sweet Potato Chips **GF, EF, DF, NF, V**

Healthy Caramel Popcorn **GF, EF, NF**

Rosemary Wheat Crisps **EF, DF, NF**

Honey Graham Crackers **EF, DF, NF**

Everything But the Kitchen Sink Popcorn **EF**

Sweet and Salty Peanuts **GF, EF, DF**

Standard U.S./Metric Measurement Conversions

VOLUME CONVERSIONS

U.S. Volume Measure	Metric Equivalent
⅛ teaspoon	0.5 milliliter
¼ teaspoon	1 milliliter
½ teaspoon	2 milliliters
1 teaspoon	5 milliliters
½ tablespoon	7 milliliters
1 tablespoon (3 teaspoons)	15 milliliters
2 tablespoons (1 fluid ounce)	30 milliliters
¼ cup (4 tablespoons)	60 milliliters
⅓ cup	80 milliliters
½ cup (4 fluid ounces)	125 milliliters
⅔ cup	160 milliliters
¾ cup (6 fluid ounces)	180 milliliters
1 cup (16 tablespoons)	250 milliliters
1 pint (2 cups)	500 milliliters
1 quart (4 cups)	1 liter (about)

WEIGHT CONVERSIONS

U.S. Weight Measure	Metric Equivalent
½ ounce	15 grams
1 ounce	30 grams
2 ounces	60 grams
3 ounces	85 grams
¼ pound (4 ounces)	115 grams
½ pound (8 ounces)	225 grams
¾ pound (12 ounces)	340 grams
1 pound (16 ounces)	454 grams

OVEN TEMPERATURE CONVERSIONS

Degrees Fahrenheit	Degrees Celsius
200 degrees F	95 degrees C
250 degrees F	120 degrees C
275 degrees F	135 degrees C
300 degrees F	150 degrees C
325 degrees F	160 degrees C
350 degrees F	180 degrees C
375 degrees F	190 degrees C
400 degrees F	205 degrees C
425 degrees F	220 degrees C
450 degrees F	230 degrees C

BAKING PAN SIZES

U.S.	Metric
8 × 1½ inch round baking pan	20 × 4 cm cake tin
9 × 1½ inch round baking pan	23 × 3.5 cm cake tin
11 × 7 × 1½ inch baking pan	28 × 18 × 4 cm baking tin
13 × 9 × 2 inch baking pan	30 × 20 × 5 cm baking tin
2 quart rectangular baking dish	30 × 20 × 3 cm baking tin
15 × 10 × 2 inch baking pan	38 × 25 × 5 cm baking tin (Swiss roll tin)
9 inch pie plate	22 × 4 or 23 × 4 cm pie plate
7 or 8 inch springform pan	18 or 20 cm springform or loose-bottom cake tin
9 × 5 × 3 inch loaf pan	23 × 13 × 7 cm or 2 lb narrow loaf or pâté tin
1½ quart casserole	1.5 liter casserole
2 quart casserole	2 liter casserole

Index

Note: Page numbers in **bold** indicate recipe category lists.